New York Undercover

HISTORICAL STUDIES OF URBAN AMERICA
Edited by Timothy J. Gilfoyle, James R. Grossman, and Becky M. Nicolaides

ALSO IN THE SERIES

New York Undercover

Private Surveillance in the Progressive Era

JENNIFER FRONC

The University of Chicago Press
Chicago and London

Jennifer Fronc is assistant professor of history at the University of
Massachusetts, Amherst.

The University of Chicago Press, Chicago 60637
The University of Chicago Press, Ltd., London
© 2009 by The University of Chicago
All rights reserved. Published 2009
Printed in the United States of America

18 17 16 15 14 13 12 11 10 09   1 2 3 4 5

ISBN-13: 978-0-226-26609-1 (cloth)
ISBN-10: 0-226-26609-5 (cloth)

Library of Congress Cataloging-in-Publication Data

Fronc, Jennifer, 1974–
    New York undercover : private surveillance in the Progressive Era / Jennifer
Fronc.
        p. cm.
    Includes bibliographical references and index.
    ISBN-13: 978-0-226-26609-1 (cloth : alk. paper)
    ISBN-10: 0-226-26609-5 (cloth : alk. paper)   1. Undercover operations—
New York (State)—New York—History. 2. Social problems—New York
(State)—New York—History. 3. Social action—New York (State)—New
York—History. 4. New York (N.Y.)—Social conditions—History. 5. New
York (N.Y.)—History—1898–1951.   I. Title.
    HN80.N5F764 2009
    303.48'4097471—dc22
2009023518

The final, definitive version of chapter 4 was published in the *Journal of Urban
History* as "The Horns of the Dilemma: Race Mixing and the Enforcement of
Jim Crow in New York City," 33, no. 1 (November 2006) by SAGE Publications Ltd. The online version can be found at http://juh.sagepub.com/cgi/
content/abstract/33/1/3.

♾ The paper used in this publication meets the minimum requirements of the
American National Standard for Information Sciences—Permanence of Paper
for Printed Library Materials, ANSI Z39.48-1992.

CONTENTS

ACKNOWLEDGMENTS

I am pleased to finally be able to acknowledge and thank in writing all of the amazing people who have helped me with this project. Betsy Blackmar has been involved with this undertaking since the earliest stages, and her brilliance and creativity have inspired and motivated me. Alice Kessler-Harris has been an incredibly patient and supportive mentor. Sam Roberts, Ann Fabian, and Ariela Dubler provided invaluable feedback and insight that helped me revise the book manuscript. I also thank Professors Arthur Goren, Dan Czitrom, and Allen Steinberg, who shared materials and expertise.

While attending graduate school in New York City, I had the opportunity to learn with a brilliant and engaged cohort beyond Columbia University. In part, this unique experience was the result of working for Big Onion Walking Tours, which introduced me to every nook in lower Manhattan and allowed me to befriend graduate students from outside my program. So much of this project was forged in conversations on long subway rides back to Brooklyn after a seminar, or on leisurely Saturday strolls through the Lower East Side and Chinatown, or during spirited conversations over pitchers of beer in the East Village after a tour. For this, and so much more, I thank Shannan Clark, Jim Downs, Megan Elias, Kathy Feeley, Beverly Gage, Libby Garland, Jacob Kramer, Nina Kushner, Cindy Lobel, Annie Polland, Matthew Raffety, Jeffrey Trask, and Theresa Ventura. Special thanks go to Theresa Ventura for being excellent company and comic relief during one particularly grueling research trip to the National Archives. In addition, I thank all of my friends from my union, Graduate Student Employees United/UAW, with whom I had wide-ranging and edifying conversations on the picket line, especially Shannan Clark.

In Richmond, Virginia, Yücel Yanikdağ, and John Herman have been good friends and supportive colleagues. Brent Spencer deserves special mention for taking this expatriate New Yorker under his wing. Deepest and most heartfelt thanks to Kristy King for her company, kindness, and empathy during the final stages of this project.

I could not have produced this book without the help of the librarians and archivists at the New York Public Library, especially Valerie Wingfield. I also thank the staff of the Rare Books and Manuscript Library at Butler Library at Columbia University, and at the National Archives in College Park, Maryland. In addition, the College of Humanities and Sciences at Virginia Commonwealth University granted me a semester of scholarly leave and a Career Enhancement Award, which permitted me to complete the book.

Robert Devens, my editor at the University of Chicago Press, has been enthusiastic, eternally patient, and supportive. Tim Gilfoyle went beyond his obligation as series editor by providing extensive feedback and meticulous editing of the manuscript. His exhaustive knowledge and expertise, along with that of the two anonymous readers, have made this an immeasurably better book. Of course, any errors that may remain are my own.

I dedicate this book to the memory of my grandfather, Henry J. Fronc.

Natalie Sonnichsen did not have high hopes for her evening out at the Strand Roof Garden, as it did not have a reputation as a fashionable or posh place. After all, female philanthropists had opened the Strand as "a sort of settlement idea" and alternative to the numerous commercial dance halls that catered to working-class girls.[1] As soon as Sonnichsen walked through the door, however, she was impressed with the pleasant atmosphere. Couples expertly performed the latest dances, while others enjoyed a meal in the peaceful setting high above the busy Manhattan streets. Although this establishment catered to a decidedly working-class population, the smartly dressed young men and women and the live music all exceeded her (admittedly low) expectations.

Sonnichsen was still absorbing the scene when a young man approached and asked her to dance. After a couple of spins around the dance floor, she was ready to leave, and her new friend escorted her to the subway station. As they strolled down Lexington Avenue, the young man said he had a confession to make but that he feared it might change her initial impression of him. He was a pimp. Rather than recoil in horror, Sonnichsen became more intrigued. She wanted to know more but was savvy enough not to bombard the young man with questions, which might drive him away. Instead, she "led him on, making him believe that [she] was of the underworld." He concluded that since she "knew the game," she would be able to "hustle" for him. With his "familiarity with every nook on Broadway" and her charm, he thought they could successfully ply their trade while, as he explained, "minimizing the efforts of the reform movement."[2] Sonnichsen and the young man then parted ways with plans for a date.

Sonnichsen never contacted the young man for that date. Instead, she recorded his words and his story in an elaborate narrative report. She was not "of the underworld," and when they parted company, she resumed her place as a middle-class, professional woman, one who worked as an undercover investigator for the Committee of Fourteen, one of New York City's most influential private, Progressive organizations that sought to expose "vice" in the city and lobby for more stringent regulation of urban life and leisure.

Did the young man know that Sonnichsen was not "of the underworld"? Possibly. Her performance could have been pitifully transparent, and he might have known that she was not an underpaid shop girl out for a thrill. Surely there were clues: her stockings probably had no runs; the heels of her shoes were not worn down. Her grammar, diction, or accent could have identified her with a particular neighborhood or class background. The young man may have been amusing himself by giving her what she had come out for—an experience with the "other half," a personal encounter complete with danger and pleasure. Telling Sonnichsen he worked as a pimp might even have given the young man the opportunity to step outside of his own ordinary, boring life for a few hours. Maybe he thought that the only way to keep her interest was to invent this pimp persona. Then again, maybe Sonnichsen was the duplicitous one; maybe she saw through him and knew he did not work as a pimp, but her devotion to her employers' goals may have led her to faithfully represent his misrepresentation in her report.

Even as Sonnichsen and the young man skirted the truth, in the end, the possibility that he may have lied to her never mattered. By asserting the veracity of his story in her report to her employers, Sonnichsen created the truth. As the narrator of her experience discovering pimps even in this "settlement type" dance hall, she had the power to propel the Committee of Fourteen to take action against a leisure establishment—action that varied from near-constant surveillance to recommendations to revoke liquor licenses to smear campaigns against the proprietor. Sonnichsen was but one participant in a complex process in which undercover investigators, employed by private social reform organizations, interacted with working-class, immigrant, and African American New Yorkers in establishments that these organizations deemed in need of improvement, and then reported their impressions back to their employers.

New York Undercover: Private Surveillance in the Progressive Era examines the efforts of five of New York City's most influential private organizations of social activists during the Progressive Era: the Committee of Fifteen, the Committee of Fourteen, the Colored Auxiliary of the Committee of Fourteen, the People's Institute, and the National Civic Federation. All of these organizations were composed of a balanced mixture of clerics, academics, businessmen, labor leaders, settlement house workers, and practitioners of the new social sciences. In addition, they regularly collaborated with advocates for improved housing conditions, good government, parks and playgrounds, and social hygiene. Between 1897 and 1920, each of these five organizations pursued its own agenda for a more efficient city with less criminality, immorality, and graft; oftentimes their visions overlapped, but sometimes they competed. Despite their differences, all of these organizations relied on undercover investigation to further their goals, a method that distinguished them from their predecessors as well as some of their contemporaries. Their pioneering use of undercover investigations yielded new types of knowledge about urban neighborhoods and their residents, which enabled them to intervene and attempt to reconstruct social conditions in New York City and beyond.

The organizations considered in this book enforced their own moral codes, through both formal and informal relationships with businesses, other groups based in an older tradition of reform (such as purity reformers, church-affiliated organizations, and temperance advocates), or the municipal, state, and federal governments. For these organizations, the problems they perceived, such as prostitution, gambling, race mixing, juvenile delinquency, and radical political movements, represented the failure of government both to police behavior and to provide adequate social services to the city's working-class, immigrant, and African American populations. Because of the essential role of undercover investigations in creating social knowledge and constituting political authority, this book explicates the history of investigation and the reporting of perceived social ills as well as the formal qualities of undercover performance and observation. It also traces the eventual appropriation by federal, state, and municipal agencies of the investigative methods that these private organizations had developed. By analyzing how private citizens and groups without official sanction defined and regulated morality, appropriate behavior, and illegality in a democracy, *New York Undercover* challenges notions of "reform," politics, and the process of state formation in America in the period preceding and during the First World War.

When Sonnichsen's new friend, the pimp, bragged about the knowledge that permitted him to "minimize the efforts of the reform movement," she knew exactly to what he was referring. The meanings of "reform" and "reformers" are quite complicated, however, and require further consideration, particularly in light of the diversity of Progressive Era activism intended to transform social conditions in the factories, on the streets, in barrooms, and in bedrooms.[3] The terms "reform" and "reformers" have become convenient shorthand for historians and now often conjure up images of persons concerned chiefly with social control as an end unto itself and who were motivated to suppress the poor as a result of their own needs, fears, and anxieties. This vantage point focuses too much on the reformers themselves and obscures the point of view of the objects of reform; the undercover investigators' reports are imperfect representations of the voices and opinions of the workers, immigrants, and African Americans who were the targets of the reformers, but they open a window into the New York City that Natalie Sonnichsen's alter ego inhabited. During the Progressive Era, a panoply of persons and organizations sought to reconstruct American society along more orderly lines. But they did not share the same social vision, and the umbrella term "reformer" obfuscates their reality.

"Reformers" can refer to a multiplicity of publicly minded individuals: philanthropists, club women, black business owners, social scientists, suffragists, temperance activists, settlement house workers, socialists, members of organized labor, those affiliated with religious organizations (be they churches, synagogues, or various women's auxiliaries), good government reformers, eugenicists, anti-obscenity activists, and free speech advocates. Although many of these people pursued divergent social and political agendas and seemingly had little in common with each other, during the Progressive Era they sometimes forged temporary coalitions to achieve specific goals.[4] Through these kinds of arrangements, for example, white, upper-middle-class Protestant clergymen came to work with Booker T. Washington's cohort in Harlem to encourage black-owned, single-race leisure establishments; the New York City Department of Education turned to a left-leaning organization that mainly trained community workers for immersion in poor neighborhoods to create an education program for recent immigrants; and men from the chamber of commerce relied on their connections to settlement house women with socialist leanings. An instrumentalist pragmatism, in which the ends justified the means, informed many of these social programs and initiatives. It is in this regard that the Progressives were quite different from their predecessors; they attempted with varying degrees of success to put aside petty squabbles, turf wars, and internecine battles to achieve particular goals.

In place of the terms "reform" and "reformers," I use the term "social activists" to describe the proponents of a wide range of programs and policies for social improvement during the first two decades of the twentieth century. This term emphasizes both the activists' concern with problems that they perceived as social in nature, and not simply as the consequence of individual deficiency or moral failing, and the fact that they actively participated in organizations, movements, and campaigns to vigorously push for remedies. As former settlement house resident and People's Institute director Frederic C. Howe argued (and then rejected) about the nature of reform and reformers, "We are not on the level in our moral crusades; worse still, of their hidden effects we are crudely ignorant. Possibly this is another by-product of the evangelical-mindedness that seeks a moralistic explanation of social problems and a religious solution for most of them."[5] Although the term "activist" is now frequently invoked to signify a person of left-leaning or liberal proclivities, in the specific historical context of this book it refers to anyone who was publicly fighting for social change, regardless of his or her ideological or political stance. In this way, I can more accurately and adequately represent the diversity of persons and issues that populate this narrative.

By dispensing with an oversimplified notion of "reform" that generations of historians have used in their desire to impose organizational synthesis on the contingency and chaos of a nation in the midst of unprecedented industrial development and urban growth, *New York Undercover* moves beyond earlier interpretations of early twentieth-century American history. Instead of concealing the conflicting motivations and objectives of social activists under the rubric of "reform," this book explicates the complexity and instability of the coalitions formed to pursue particular issues and explains how erstwhile adversaries could sometimes quite suddenly become allies. Lumping the subjects and objects of reform together hides that reality and tells us little about local conditions in the neighborhoods and the city, including the politics of class and status. In fact, the terminology of "reform" and "reformers" not only obscures the politics and identities of the advocates for social improvement, but it robs the poor, the working class, the recent immigrants, and the tenement dwellers of their agency.

One evening in 1915, an undercover investigator from the Committee of Fourteen was drinking at the Chatham Inn and chatting with its proprietor. The Committee of Fourteen was keeping the Chatham Inn under surveillance because the proprietor allegedly permitted ex-convicts and loose women to frequent his establishment, which was technically a violation of the section of the penal code related to "disorderliness." The undercover investigator convinced the proprietor that he was just an ordinary, regular patron, one who was interested in the general goings-on of the bar and the neighborhood. Forging a more personalized relationship with this proprietor proved useful to the investigator, as the proprietor verbally "abuse[d] the police and reformers . . . cursing them roundly and complaining of the fact that 'a guy can't do no business or get nuthin nowadays with these s— of b— after him all de time.'"[6] Undercover investigation served as a means for social activists concerned with a wide range of issues to confirm their suspicions and subsequently guide their agenda. Open surveillance, by contrast, failed to afford social activists access to a similarly wide range of information and locales. In social milieus that ranged from dance halls to immigrant neighborhoods to anarchist camps, investigators with no particular training produced new forms of social knowledge that became powerful tools for judging and then regulating the behavior of others.

Early twentieth-century social activists perceived a number of problems plaguing New York City, which they believed required entirely new approaches to reform. These "problems" included gambling, prostitution and sexual immorality, "race mixing" and miscegenation, juvenile delinquency, and the radical political activities of immigrants. As this book shows, social activists themselves defined these problems and in many ways created them when they sent investigators to generate conditions in certain neighborhoods and situations. This entire process was teleological; the predominantly middle-class social activists set the parameters of the investigations, had their concerns confirmed by their investigators' findings and reports, and then moved to solve the problems their employees uncovered (or caused).

Investigators' reports, such as the one concerning conditions at the Chatham Inn, illuminate the interactions that took place during those investigations in the service of social change. First, this investigator took the concerns of his employers (about "loose women," criminals, and other unsavory types hanging out in "public houses," where regular people might come into contact with them and become corrupted) into the Chatham Inn and found exactly what they feared—an undisciplined and angry proprietor who had no regard for the constituted authorities. Moreover, this proprietor was just trying to make money and did not care how he had to do it—if that meant catering to criminals, so be it. Second, an untrained and possibly inexperienced undercover investigator who was "passing" in a location to which he would not ordinarily have access produced this report. He managed to collect his information by forging a relationship with the proprietor, and the techniques that different investigators used to accomplish this varied greatly—from telling lies about their own ethnicity or experiences in similar leisure establishments in the city to pretending to be a member of a dangerous, radical political organization. Finally, because this investigator was literate enough to produce a narrative of his experiences, his report became the data that informed the actions of the private organization that had dispatched him. The Committee of Fourteen sent an investigator to the Chatham Inn because it suspected that the proprietor ignored various city ordinances and state liquor laws. Investigations of leisure establishments were often triggered in this way; the Committee received tips from neighbors, or during investigations of other establishments, or from reconnaissance walks through the neighborhoods about offending establishments. These private organizations, however, technically lacked the legal authority to respond to such violations. Social activists formed organizations like the Committee of Fourteen partly in response to the negligence of municipal, state, and federal law enforcement agencies; working outside the mechanisms of state power and policing, they formed temporary coalitions with interested businesses and other parties to address "problems."

New York Undercover explores the individual tensions that emerged among the private organizations' native-born, middle-class leaders; the undercover investigators they employed (who came from an array of class backgrounds); and those who were the subjects of their concerns and investigations—working-class, immigrant, female, and black New Yorkers. The reformers hired investigators based on who or what they wanted investigated or where they needed investigations conducted. These untrained investigators were then sent out equipped with a set of assumptions and expectations, which their investigations tended to confirm. The consequences of the undercover method ranged from the introduction of new forms of de facto racial segregation in public accommodations (such as restaurants, hotels, and theaters) to the unexpected complicity of undercover agents in planning criminal activities, such as bombings and assassination plots, to the eventual normalization (if not tacit acceptance) of government surveillance in the lives of ordinary Americans.

Historians have paid little attention to the significance of private and public undercover agents as catalysts for social change during the first decades of the twentieth century.[7] Yet undercover investigation was central to the constitution of political authority and the extension of state power during the Progressive Era and beyond. *New York Undercover* examines several facets of the history of undercover investigation. It considers the rise of undercover investigation as used by private interests to collect data on (and then control) the behavior of individuals. By examining the enormous amount of material accumulated by these organizations, and focusing in particular on the detailed undercover investigators' reports, *New York Undercover* demonstrates how social activists produced the knowledge necessary to alter conditions.

The undercover investigators' reports are the raw material on which the majority of this study is based. The investigators produced boxes upon boxes of reports—literally thousands of pages—some handwritten, some typed, some on official forms, some on personal stationery. The reports range from pat and boring to florid and lurid, replete with narrative flourishes, fascinating details, drawings, and ephemera (business cards, beer mats, flyers) collected during an evening's work. Working with these kinds of sources has required me to interrogate the investigators' narratives by reading between the lines of the reports, by reading their silences, and by comparing an individual investigator's reports across situations as well as different investigators' reports of the same events.[8] Whether reports were mediated or rewritten by supervisors, or represent the raw and unedited recollection of the investigator, they raise the same fundamental questions about the process by which undercover investigation and surveillance created knowledge.

In all, the reports are compelling, and their most revealing moments are those in which the persons under investigation—much like the young man at the Strand Roof Garden or the proprietor of the Chatham Inn—indicated an awareness that the reformers' agents were prowling the city's dives and iniquitous resorts. Through the undercover agents' reports, it becomes evident that even though many New Yorkers were critical of these private organizations and their tactics, they also realized that they would be at a disadvantage in their relationship to power if they were to attempt to stop these organizations. As one female proprietor alleged (in earshot of an undercover investigator), Committee of Fourteen executive secretary Frederick Whitin had "a yacht and takes new girls on it for 3 or 4 days then ships them back but forms committees for the poor people." She continued, "There ain't a man can touch Whitin with money no matter how much he's got. . . . as Henry Beecher once said do as I say but don't do as I do."[9] The private organizations aspired to create conditions in which members of society learned, embraced, and then enacted self-policing disciplines. They succeeded.

Ordinary New Yorkers, once they became aware of the reach, the power, and the impunity of these private organizations, absorbed and then redeployed the ideas and strictures of the social activists by policing the gambling, sexual morality, and interracial sexual partnering among themselves, their friends, their neighbors, and, in the case of saloon keepers, their patrons. One bartender, for instance, confided to an undercover investigator (whom he believed to be an ordinary patron) that he could not admit un-accompanied women to the back room of his saloon. He complained that "between the police, the Excise Department, and the Committee of Four-teen," saloon proprietors have "to be cautious." Despite "whatever you can do with the police," he discovered that "it [was] absolutely impossible to 'handle' the Committee of 14."[10] In their bitter complaining, all of these proprietors and bartenders identified the key to the reform organizations' success: municipal police, who often existed in a symbiotic relationship with the entrepreneurs of the underground economy, were easily bribed. The investigators for the private organizations did not occupy the same po-sition as the police and were not held to the same standards of account-ability as public employees (for example, investigators were not expected to take the witness stand). They might not have taken bribes, but they still benefited personally and professionally by encouraging behavior to become more debauched in the places they investigated.

People's Institute director Edward F. Sanderson argued that, in the realm of social activism, "there are two kinds of non-official enterprise." The first was "designed to criticize and accelerate government" and the second aimed "to do the things government does not yet do or should not do."[11] The cooperation among each of the five organizations considered in this book and the municipal, state, and federal governments satisfied both sides of Sanderson's assertion: by criticizing the government, social activists conse-quently prodded it to attend to the issues that it had been ignoring or failing to address.

The members of the Committee of Fifteen, the Committee of Fourteen, the Colored Auxiliary of the Committee of Fourteen, the People's Institute, and the National Civic Federation challenged the government (at local, state, and federal levels) for its negligence and corruption. Ironically, their criticism pushed them into unique collaborations with the government. This style of collaboration was familiar to these social activists, but working within the government was a novel experience and gave the activists a new place of power and authority. By the period of World War I, much of that power and authority passed out of the hands of the private organizations to agencies of the government, with consequences that many of the activists may have neither anticipated nor supported. The government's co-optation of the private organizations during World War I emerged out of a process of evolution in the New York city, state, and federal governments.

In nearly all of the alliances between social activists and the munici-pal and federal governments during World War I, the private organizations believed that they had been tapped and sanctioned to assist the government and pursue their own particular agenda because of their expertise. In some cases, this was true. The government did not have the personnel or proficiency to pursue what it came to recognize as serious problems, such as un-Americanized immigrants and streetwalking prostitutes, and it sought out the assistance of private organizations to take up this work as part of the state. Some of the private organizations (the Committee of Fourteen and the People's Institute) were granted semiofficial status and worked with the staff of municipal and federal government agencies, whereas the National Civic Federation (NCF) occupied a liminal and vigilante status. It continued to work on behalf of its own aims, which it imagined the government shared, and sent its information to the government; although the NCF was kept in the shadows and never credentialed or acknowledged, its investigators' zeal and willingness to tamper with civil liberties, cross lines, and perform tasks that would have been illegal for the legally constituted authorities to do made them extremely useful to the growing national security state during (and after) World War I.[12]

New York Undercover follows the exploits and discoveries of social activists, investigators, and the investigated alike as they wind their way through the alleys of Chinatown in search of gambling parlors, and as they cross the East River to explore the delights of Coney Island and the cabarets of Rockaway Beach. It watches them as they react to the "black and tans" of Greenwich Village and Harlem. It listens in on conversations with gang members and meetings with anarchists. By focusing on these private organizations and their undercover investigators, *New York Undercover* demonstrates how they were central to the creation of a stronger federal state during the Progressive Era and World War I, one that became increasingly repressive in the interests of a national security agenda. Moreover, these collaborative efforts between private organizations and agencies of the state also signaled the normalization of the presence of undercover investigators and surveillance in American life; by the 1920s, Americans were not surprised to learn that they were watched, followed, and listened to by persons who worked for the government. Ultimately, this book uncovers an aspect of America's history that has heretofore lurked in the shadows.

ONE

A Genealogy of Undercover Investigation

Undercover investigation in the United States has an unusual genealogy. Progressive social activists did not invent undercover investigation; rather, they adapted existing techniques to their unique goals and needs. Nor did well-intentioned, objective social scientists or righteous law-enforcement officials create modern methods of detection. In the United States, undercover investigation began in the mid-nineteenth century with the emergence of private detective agencies, which developed to fill (and profit from) the void in the system of public policing. Although U.S. historians widely regard cities as having sophisticated law enforcement systems by the middle of the nineteenth century, these systems were not highly developed. As late as the 1850s, city police departments still functioned on a constable or night-watch system and only gradually claimed larger powers of arrest as the cities' physical territories expanded. Private detectives made common law arrests, as any other private citizen could, and governments initially found private detectives useful for discovering and monitoring criminal behavior because then they could be used as complainants and courtroom witnesses.[1] Through this connection, private detective agencies developed close working relationships with official police forces. For the police, one of the main benefits of collaborating with private detective agencies was that the legal constraints limiting their own activities did not restrict private detectives.

In the postbellum period of industrial and railroad expansion, personal ties between employers and employees slowly but steadily eroded. Employers relied on private detective agencies to evaluate employees' attitudes and behaviors. The Pinkerton National Detective Agency, founded in 1850 by Allan Pinkerton, was the first and best known in the United States.[2] The post office in Chicago granted Pinkerton "special agent" status, and in the early years of the agency his responsibilities were threefold: he was to decrease the number of mail robberies, to issue regular reports on the local post offices to Washington, D.C., and to monitor workers' honesty. In this context, Pinkerton honed the skills that became the showpiece of his agency's arsenal—spying on employees.[3] By the 1890s, the Pinkerton National Detective Agency expanded its services in the labor control arena by opening more branch offices and providing "strike services" to employers, such as strikebreakers and armed guards. Pinkerton adeptly responded to the needs of his clients; as they became increasingly nervous about the radicalism among the predominantly immigrant labor force, Pinkerton offered new and improved services intended to head off possible uprisings, strikes, or rebellions.[4]

From the founding of his agency, Allan Pinkerton relied on "shadows"—agents who followed suspects and gathered evidence. During the solving of a major embezzlement case between 1858 and 1860, Pinkerton realized the importance of undercover agents to his agency's mission and continued success. The Adams Company, an express line for the railroads, had been robbed of $40,000, most likely by an employee. After two years of detective work, the Pinkerton investigation zeroed in on Nathan Maroney, an office manager for the company. Pinkerton, who believed that criminals were constitutionally incapable of keeping secrets, placed one of his agents in the jail cell with Maroney, who eventually relieved his guilty conscience by telling the agent everything. Using the testimony of his agent, Pinkerton secured Maroney's conviction in 1860.[5]

Although the Pinkerton Agency is best known for services to employers, it (and other private detective agencies) also played a role in the national conversation about the future of policing in the United States. Private detectives functioned in a netherworld between no law enforcement and limited urban police forces. They were deployed to make up for the deficits in the nation's city, state, and federal law enforcement systems. This increased reliance on private detectives, however, also depended in part on their acceptance by the public. And detectives fascinated the American public, who thrilled to reading scintillating tales of their successes and exploits. By the 1870s, the pulp literature genre was well established, and the *National Police Gazette* was one of its most popular iterations. The reading public of the 1860s and 1870s especially enjoyed dime novels about crime and criminals. In 1875, Allan Pinkerton stepped into the fray with his first book, *The Expressman and the Detective*. He wrote several more books before his death in 1884, and many of the stories came directly from his agency's crime files.[6] By the late nineteenth century, however, readers' allegiances had shifted, and they began to sympathize with the pursued rather than the pursuer.

At roughly the same time, female journalists started to use an undercover technique to produce exposés for newspaper audiences. These journalists, however, employed undercover techniques differently than the Pinkertons had; for the "girl stunt reporters," undercover served as a means to expose scandals, entertain readers, and boost the circulation of the newspapers for which they worked. Girl stunt reporters took on the role of those about whom they wrote: starving sweatshop wretch; poor, downtrodden, insane asylum inmate; overworked, harassed waitress; and other sentimental roles with which the public could easily sympathize.

For women attempting to break into journalism in the late nineteenth century, "stunt reporting" was an avenue to professional success. These women refashioned their gender from professional liability to professional asset and, in the process, created a new way of producing social knowledge. By becoming the objects of their study—however temporarily—they could claim special purchase on their subjects. Participating in the wage-labor force or the world of an insane asylum, for example, allowed a girl stunt reporter to speak with authority. This position of authority, however, was short-lived, as the stunt-reporting phenomenon disappeared from the features pages of the nation's newspapers by the early twentieth century.

Nellie Bly is widely acknowledged as "the first and the best" in the genre.[7] In 1887, Bly, under commission from the *New York World*, feigned a descent into madness and, in her own words, "became one of the city's insane wards." During her ten-day stay in the New York State Women's Lunatic Asylum on Blackwell's Island, she "experienced much, and saw and heard more of the treatment accorded to this helpless class of our population." Fortunately for Bly, when she "had seen and heard enough" of life in the asylum, her bosses at the *World* "promptly secured" her release.[8] The published exposé that resulted from this stunt, "Ten Days in a Mad-House," was the first of its kind; it not only created more work for Bly but also inspired legions of impersonators.[9] This style of reporting enjoyed cultural sanction; the exposés were enormously popular among the reading public, and newspaper editors rushed to have their own version of Nellie Bly fill their pages.

Despite the decline of stunt reporting in the early twentieth century, the undercover technique remained useful for an emerging educated middle-class population increasingly concerned with social issues. Starting in the late nineteenth century and continuing through the 1920s, "down-and-outers" adopted the sartorial style of tramps, waitresses, and factory operatives to investigate and subsequently educate the reading public about the burgeoning underclass. The best known of the genre are works by Stephen

Crane, Hutchins Hapgood, and Jack London.[10] Although also concerned with social issues, the male down-and-outers produced work that was primarily literary and voyeuristic in nature.

Female down-and-outers approached their topics from a slightly different perspective. These women were largely college educated and involved in political activities, such as suffrage or unionization campaigns. Taken as a whole, they constituted what became known as the Chicago Women's School of Sociology, a loose network of women whose work linked "social theory, sociological research, and social reform."[11] Investigation had been a useful technique for female labor activists and social scientists in the early twentieth century. Some, such as Alice Hamilton and Mary Van Kleeck, had conducted aboveboard investigations of factories and industries, inspecting conditions and interviewing employees. Investigators in this category were empowered by state labor bureaus or the federal government, and the information they gathered was used to implement safety and health standards or labor legislation.[12] Undercover investigators or down-and-outers, though, were not imbued with official powers, and had different goals and audiences in mind. For example, female down-and-outers such as Bessie Van Vorst and Maud Younger decided that the only way to truly assess the mentality of the woman worker was by becoming a worker, not just watching workers. Bessie Van Vorst described herself as acting as a "mouthpiece for the woman labourer."[13]

Similar to the girl stunt reporters, female down-and-outers (such as psychologist Amy Tanner, union activist Maud Younger, and sociologist Annie Marion MacLean) aspired to break into male-dominated professions that systematically excluded them—in most cases, the professoriate or academia. Their goal, however, was not exclusively personal, professional gain; rather, the undercover technique allowed them to do the work for which they were trained in graduate school. Even though these women were not welcomed as full-time faculty at universities, they succeeded in authoring and publishing important articles that appeared in leading professional journals, and they preceded what is known as the Chicago School of Sociology by a decade.[14]

Annie Marion MacLean, for example, earned a Ph.D. in sociology from the University of Chicago in 1900. Upon completion of the degree, she taught in the Extension Division at the University of Chicago because the male students refused to be taught by a woman. Still, she maintained an active research agenda and published prolifically until her death in 1934.[15] MacLean also worked for the New York State Tenement House Commission, the National Consumer's League, and the YMCA.[16]

MacLean wrote extensively about women's work and wages throughout her professional career. Her article "Two Weeks in Department Stores" was published in the *American Journal of Sociology* in 1899 and is considered one of the first examples of participant-observer research; it was conducted in part for the National Consumer's League.[17] For this piece, MacLean secured a position as a shopgirl in a well-known department store in Chicago during the Christmas rush. In the article she illuminates some of the difficulties employees faced, such as the unexpected rudeness of customers and the discomfort in not being able to sit down all day. The first morning on the job, the question " 'Can I possibly stand up all day?' was . . . the thought uppermost in [her] mind." She quickly discovered that "abusive language was the share of the one who was found sitting down" when she witnessed a manager berating a co-worker, yelling "Get up out of that, you lazy huzzy, I don't pay you to sit around all day!"[18] From unexpected firings to changing wages to unacceptable facilities for employees to physical abuse at the hands of co-workers, MacLean detailed the many indignities that women in these positions suffered. The goal of her article was to raise consumers' awareness of the employment conditions in places where they spent their money; as MacLean noted, "employers are always ready to tell the best conditions that exist; it remains to others to find the worst."[19]

In 1903, MacLean continued in this same vein with "The Sweat Shop in Summer." In this piece, she began by noting that the number of stories and articles by those who "belong outside of the manual laboring class" had become so widespread that she felt obliged "to apologize to the long-suffering public for thrusting upon it still another 'experience.' " Moreover, she was critical of those who had, "in a dilettante fashion," secured jobs and spent time "with the so-called dregs of society long enough to focus a figurative kodak on little groups of workers here and there, for the purpose of ekeing out 'copy.' " MacLean argued that for those who were serious about social change, these pieces were "valueless." The general audience might have exhibited "a morbid sort of interest," but "to the toiler it is an insult."[20] Although she made a distinction between her work and that of dilettantes, she could not have arrived at her conclusions and written her piece without "enduring" the same hardships.

Amy E. Tanner was another female academic engaged in participant-observer research. She held a Ph.D. in psychology and worked with G. Stanley Hall at Clark University. In 1907, she and a friend, a fellow teacher "with a commingled yearning for adventure and philanthropy," decided to "submerge [them]selves still further into the masses." Tanner and her friend secured positions as waitresses in a hotel café "frequented by army and navy officers," for which they were paid $15 a month including room and board, and excluding laundry. Even though they were fed as part of their compensation, these waitresses did not eat well; they only received bread and butter for lunch and leftovers for dinner. Tanner listed the other indignities she and her co-workers suffered—exhaustion, bruises, and a lack of time or energy to bathe or maintain their uniforms properly. Tanner also discovered that, when the working day was over, she was too tired to do anything. She wrote, "The effect upon me, and I think it was much the same with the rest, was that my mind became more and more engrossed in the present." During the working day, Tanner found that any "thoughts of my outside interests, my friends, my books, even my family . . . became far away and uninteresting. They lost their tang." She had become, like her co-workers, "a creature ruled chiefly by sensations."[21]

Tanner believed she had achieved a special understanding of the plight of working girls by sharing their experiences; she felt able to speak for them and to vouch for the fact that work sapped one's mental energy and made anything other than material concerns and pleasures seem insignificant. She turned this experience into an article for the *American Journal of Sociology* in which she offered insight and drew conclusions about why unionization campaigns and other efforts to "uplift" working-class women had failed. "This same inertia" that she experienced made it "wellnigh impossible for such girls to organize themselves so as to command an eight-hour day and better wages." Any organizer who attempted to reach these women would, according to Tanner, "need strong personal qualities, to draw these tired girls out to anything so stupid as a meeting."[22] Tanner absolved these women for not organizing themselves (they were too tired) and insisted that women like herself would need to remain involved in reform projects to "save" these girls. Tanner thus marshaled her education, her experience as a "waitress," and her sympathy toward working-class women to fashion herself as an expert voice on an important social matter.

Although published the same year as Tanner's piece, Maud Younger's article for *McClure's*, "The Diary of an Amateur Waitress: An Industrial Problem from the Worker's Point of View," was written in an engaging narrative style and for a very different audience. Younger was not an academic, and she was not speaking to an academic or activist audience. Born to a wealthy San Francisco family, she began a career as an activist in 1901, when she came to New York City to spend a week in College Settlement House and ended up staying five years. Her experience in the settlement house movement translated into deep personal involvement in the issues of trade unionism, women's suffrage, and protective labor legislation. In 1904, she joined the Women's Trade Union League, signed with the Waitresses Union in 1907 (during her stint for the *McClure's* piece), and returned to San Francisco in 1908 to assist in the founding of its Waitresses Union.[23]

Younger's narrative of her experience as a waitress, unlike Tanner's, charted a complete transformation—from wealthy society lady to deadened, overworked waitress, to enlightened, lively, pro-union waitress working at Childs, the best house in the city. She noted early in the article that "it was a great surprise to me to find out how hard it is to 'get a job.' I always supposed that any one who was willing and able to work could get one. We have so many ideas about things we have never tried." She was finally hired on a trial basis for her first waitressing job, and she realized, much to her chagrin, that she would have to start immediately, even though she had a dinner engagement for that evening. She thought longingly of the brand-new dress that had been delivered to her home before she left for her odyssey.

After working at a few different restaurants, Younger demonstrated her transformation by slipping restaurant lingo into her article, relating tales of male co-workers who found her charming, telling stories about the tribulations of her female co-workers, and reporting on friendships she cultivated with fellow waitresses—one in particular named Katie, who advocated and believed passionately in the unionization of waitresses. Unlike Tanner, Younger was writing for a popular and largely nonacademic audience, so she expressed the necessity for unionization and protective legislation for female workers through the words of her friend and co-worker Katie.[24] Like Tanner, Younger fashioned herself as both an expert voice and a unique spokesperson for the workingwoman, because only a woman could delve into this particular culture.

The articles by MacLean, Tanner, Younger, and others of their cohort raise issues of truth, experience, and the uses of social knowledge. MacLean hoped that her piece could be a "rational ground for constructive action"; Tanner openly admitted a desire for adventure and philanthropy. Both of these claims rest on the quintessentially Progressive notion that "the Truth" could only emerge out of experience, data, and facts.[25] Ultimately, the down-and-outers believed that the link between social investigation and social transformation had to be forged through the collection and dissemination of knowledge.

The concept of social investigation was not new to the early twentieth century, but the use of undercover agents by private reform groups was innovative.[26] By the postbellum period, moral reform had passed from the hands of women—as members of benevolent societies or church auxiliary associations—into those of well-placed men. These men, who were often in business, academia, or a religious institution, created organizations known as preventive societies. The first preventive society in the United States was the American Society for the Prevention of Cruelty to Animals (ASPCA), founded in 1866. The Society for the Prevention of Cruelty to Children (SPCC, or Gerry Society) emerged from the ASPCA's work and became an organization unto itself in 1872. Anthony Comstock established the Society for the Suppression of Vice (SSV) at roughly the same time that the SPCC was established, and the Society for the Prevention of Crime (SPC, also known as the Parkhurst Society) was organized in 1878.[27]

In New York City, the municipal government began extending limited law enforcement powers to the preventive societies, which meant that they held public and governmental power. For instance, the American Society for the Prevention of Cruelty to Animals became the first preventive society empowered to issue arrest warrants. Anthony Comstock, under the auspices of the Society for the Suppression of Vice, became a special agent of the United States Post Office in 1873; in this position, he possessed the legal authority to make arrests. In 1876, New York State's attorney general and the New York City district attorney appointed the Society for the Prevention of Cruelty to Children as the city and state's exclusive representative in all cases pertaining to the abuse of children. Both the private organizations and the government benefited from these symbiotic relationships: in their attempts to solve social problems and protect the innocent and vulnerable, the private organizations compensated for the lack of social services provided by the municipal government, and the arrangement relieved the city of the burden of providing those services.[28]

In late nineteenth-century New York, the municipal government had not developed sufficiently to meet the needs of the rapidly growing and changing urban population. Responsibility for the care of the poor and the vulnerable and the disciplining of the criminal and immoral were gladly taken up by private organizations like the preventive societies.[29] As a consequence, during this period a novel situation resulted—one in which government and private actors enjoyed a dialectical relationship with a permeable membrane between them. The situation that brought the private organizations and public agencies together was largely the consequence of neglect, negligence, and corruption rather than an intentional partnership on either's part.

Eschewing the overtly evangelical tone of their predecessors, the preventive societies based their operations on the authority and social position of their members. As a result, they were able to conduct their investigations openly. Instead of focusing on individuals' moral failings as the cause of society's problems, preventive societies blamed corrupt police officers and the selective enforcement of laws regarding liquor, gambling, prostitution, and disorderliness. They construed problems with the police force as the cause of the "moral degeneration" of New York City. Their response was to turn to vigilante and extralegal measures, such as highly publicized raids, to further their goals.[30]

These preventive societies slowly assumed more expansive law enforcement powers, sometimes through relationships with sympathetic, reform-minded mayors and sometimes through informal, personal relationships with government officials. The Society for the Prevention of Crime in particular was motivated by distrust of and disgust with the New York Police Department, and drove its president, the Reverend Charles H. Parkhurst, to use private detectives to prove his point about municipal police corruption.[31] In many ways, the SPC bridged the transition from preventive society to the more scientifically influenced Progressive Era social activist organizations considered in this book. More precisely, it was the SPC's missteps that precipitated the move to undercover investigators, backroom bargains struck with insurance companies and liquor dealers, and end runs around the police and uncooperative municipal authorities on the part of the Progressives.

The Reverend Charles Parkhurst's assumption of the leadership of the Society for the Prevention of Crime in 1891 was a watershed moment in the struggle between the police and the preventive societies. Parkhurst, as the minister of the Madison Square Presbyterian Church, was distressed by the illegal activity in the vicinity of his church. Rather than focusing on individual saloons or brothels or gambling parlors, Parkhurst went to the source, pointing to the system of graft, bribery, and payoffs between proprietors and police that kept illegal and disorderly places running. In February 1892, he delivered a sermon detailing the city's horrors and laying blame at the doorstep of the police department and "its Tammany overlords." Only slightly rattled by these accusations, Tammany and the police department cunningly responded to his allegations by calling for a grand jury investigation, at which Parkhurst would have to testify and present solid evidence. Tammany and the police sat back, confident that Parkhurst could not hold up under the scrutiny of a grand jury.[32] They underestimated Parkhurst's determination, however. Although his first sermon consisted mainly of unsubstantiated allegations and conjecture, this deficiency did not mean he would not be ready for the grand jury. Parkhurst hired a private detective.

In March 1892, Charles Gardner, the detective hired by Parkhurst, took the reverend and his friend and parishioner John L. Erving on several excursions through New York's underworld. Gardner helped the two men select appropriate costumes for their journey so they would not arouse the suspicion of the "natives" of the places they visited. After a brief sojourn in a brothel staffed by "big, fat, greasy, and not very pretty women" on Water Street, Parkhurst exclaimed to Gardner, "I see now that I underrated the situation when I arraigned Tammany Hall and the municipal authorities. The unspeakable horror of that house tells more than I could in a million sermons." Little did Parkhurst know that he was in for far more disturbing experiences.[33]

Gardner arranged to take Parkhurst and Erving through the neighborhood known as the Old Tenderloin (bounded by Fourteenth Street to the north, Sixth Avenue to the west, the Bowery to the east, and Bleecker Street to the south), populated by Italian and French immigrants and African Americans, and infamous for its variety of "circuses" and other bawdy houses. Contemporaries regarded the area as possessing the "worst vices" in all of New York City. Gardner, Parkhurst, and Erving first stopped into the Golden Rule Pleasure Club on West Third Street. Gardner wrote that this club was divided into a number of smaller rooms, each occupied by "a youth, whose face was painted, eye-brows blackened, and whose airs were those of a young girl. Each person talked in a high falsetto voice, and called the others by women's names."[34]

Parkhurst initially did not understand how or why the Golden Rule Pleasure Club was unique or different from any other brothel. Gardner quickly explained that "fairies," young men who dressed as women and worked as prostitutes servicing other men, staffed this particular house. After receiving this information, Gardner noted that Parkhurst "instantly turned on his heel and fled from the house at top speed." The group next stopped into Marie Andrea's house on West Fourth Street. As they approached the house, a "big policeman" was standing right on the corner, nonchalantly swinging his billy club and "apparently not caring whether there was vice about him or not." Once inside, Marie Andrea asked if they had come to see the "French Circus." They replied in the affirmative, and a troupe of girls entered the room. Mme. Andrea told the men to pick out their ladies. The entertainment then commenced. Detective Gardner wrote, "I cannot tell you what happened. . . . And the Doctor never quivered. I must say I admired his nerve." The French Circus was essentially an orgy in which the ladies performed cunnilingus on each other for the titillation of the male audience. Parkhurst confided to Gardner that it was "the most brutal, most horrible exhibition" he had ever witnessed.[35] Parkhurst concluded that "New York was indeed a modern Sodom and Gomorrah."[36]

On March 13, 1892, about a month after his original sermon, Parkhurst returned to the pulpit. This time he was armed with incontrovertible evidence drawn from his experiences. He spoke convincingly about the flagrant violations of excise law, the brothels that ran "wide open," and the pervasiveness of gambling dens. Parkhurst now had details—"names, dates, and addresses, as well as a bundle of sworn affidavits describing his adventures and the findings of his investigators."[37] The Society for the Prevention of Crime argued that Parkhurst intervened in this issue not because he was "a moral reformer" but because he was "a relentless foe of civic corruption." Parkhurst, with his sermon and affidavits, had "demonstrated the corrupt combination of criminals and sworn officers of the law." According to the SPC, Parkhurst warned that "no political organization which fattened upon the ill-gotten gains of commercialized vice, could long endure."[38]

After Parkhurst's second sermon, the police department and Tammany Hall scrambled to cover their tracks. The police superintendent resigned under suspicious circumstances, and Inspector Thomas Byrnes took on the position. Byrnes arranged for his men to conduct a series of raids (entirely for publicity's sake) that resulted in "the closing of 444 houses of ill fame during his first seven months in office."[39] As a consequence of Parkhurst's revelations, New York voters handed control of the state legislature to the Republicans in the 1893 elections. The following year, Republican boss Thomas Platt brought a bill to the floor that would transform the structure of the New York Police Department; most important, it called for the creation of a bipartisan police board. The citizens who had agitated for an overhaul of the police system, however, opposed the plan, arguing that a nonpartisan police force was essential to a clean, noncorrupt New York City, and that Platt's proposed bill would merely allow for a "mutual sharing of the spoils" and not actually solve the problem of corruption. The Republicans and citizens disagreed over how to transform the police department, but they held the same opinion that a far-reaching investigation of the police department was in order—particularly one that probed its relationship to organized crime and Tammany Hall.[40] Nevertheless, the bipartisan board of four police commissioners was appointed: Theodore Roosevelt and Colonel Fred Grant represented the Republicans, Avery Andrews and Andrew Parker the Democrats.[41] At the first meeting of the board, Roosevelt was unanimously elected its president.

Platt and his cronies continued to push for an investigation into the police department, but Democratic governor Roswell Flower vetoed the bill. The state senate overrode the veto and appointed Senator Clarence Lexow to chair the investigative committee. Those concerned with the relationship between the police, municipal government, and the underground economy, however, were dissatisfied with this plan and pushed for a more sweeping investigation. While the Senate bowed to the wishes of the "good-government" activists, the governor vetoed the appropriation necessary for such a far-reaching investigation. Undeterred, the good-government activists and their cohort, under the auspices of the New York Chamber of Commerce, raised the money and funded the investigation anyway.[42]

In February 1894, the Lexow Committee convened and began its investigation, funded by private monies but conducted by state legislators. It was far from a nonpartisan effort, as the investigations and questions focused on Tammany Hall and police department corruption. The committee was supposed to complete its work in a few weeks, but the task ended up stretching until the end of December.[43] The array of witnesses was unprecedented: paraded before the committee were crooked cops, brothel keepers, professional gamblers, and other brands of criminals, all of whom testified to the system of payoffs and bribes to the police and Tammany politicians that kept the underground economy operational and profitable.

In general, during this period no love was lost between the police and social activists. Each group had different ideas about the other's respective duties. Social activists felt the police ignored, if not breached, their responsibilities; the police charged that the activists overstepped their bounds by usurping police authority, engaging in illegal raids of gambling dens and brothels, and pushing the police to assume unpopular tasks. Perhaps more important, the activists and the traction they gained by publicizing the lucrative financial relationship that ordinary policemen and precinct captains enjoyed with criminals—especially keepers of brothels and gambling parlors—threatened the police department's power and reputation in both the legitimate economy and the underworld.[44]

Ultimately, the Lexow investigation revealed to the public that the police managed the vice economy. Cops had their hands in everything—from prostitution to counterfeiting to gambling to supervising (and in some cases fixing) elections—and this state of affairs had been true for decades. Until the late nineteenth century, New York City's propertied classes had not cared what kind of illegal business the police tolerated or participated in, so long as the labor movement, strikers, immigrants, and radicals of all stripes were kept under control. For social activists and the upper classes, however, the driving force behind the Lexow Committee was the fact that the police department was also in charge of the Board of Elections. Although the Lexow Committee had begun as an inquiry into voter and election fraud, it quickly turned into something else as the witnesses had far more ominous stories to tell.

The Lexow disclosures revealed that the government, through the police department, was actively involved in organizing crime. At this point, the reverie of the city's elite was shattered, and they became concerned about the connection between those who were charged with enforcing the law and those who broke it. Perhaps most significantly, the Lexow Committee caused them to question both the methods used by the police and the organization of the police department. The old system gave virtually limitless, autonomous power to individual police officers, sergeants, captains, and on up the ranks, particularly in the way they chose to deal (or not deal) with organized crime. Following the Lexow revelations, though, reorganization of the police department created a more rational, bureaucratized system, one that had built-in oversight mechanisms. Moreover, a panoply of citizens' organizations emerged in the wake of the Lexow investigations, and these groups kept the police and municipal government in their crosshairs.[45]

After consolidation of the five boroughs into the City of New York in 1898, each borough's police force was combined into the larger New York Police Department. The four-man, bipartisan board of commissioners was retained, however, and despite objections, the Board of Elections remained part of the police department.[46] This structure did not change until 1900, when another sweeping investigation, the Mazet Commission, ended. The Mazet Commission made the Lexow investigation look tame. A *New York Times* editorial noted that witnesses were insulting the examiners and their lawyers; the "attitude of Tammany [was] that of a tough old outlaw who sets his dog on the process-server and takes a pot shot at the Sheriff who comes to seize him in his mountain retreat."[47]

The Mazet Commission proved more successful than the Lexow Committee, and convinced the state legislature to adopt a single-commissioner system for the police department in order to disentangle partisan politics and policing. More important, the Board of Elections was moved out of the police department.[48] Taken together, the Lexow and Mazet investigations revealed the police department and Tammany Hall as extremely corrupt and above the law, and the good-government and antivice activists looked like the city's saviors.

Because they could not count on the police department and municipal government to separate policing from the underground economy, the preventive societies of the late nineteenth-century developed their own policing methods, which included hiring and relying on private detectives. In the process, however, the preventive societies, emboldened by the powers granted them by the government, reached beyond their sphere of influence—mainly those living in poverty and abused children—and focused their attention on the sexual, political, and leisure habits of the city's residents. By the late nineteenth century, the preventive societies, encouraged by the positive response from the government and the public, began to pursue not just those issues on which the government sought their assistance but their own goals as well. To this end, they began to rely more heavily on private detectives to gather the information they needed. For instance, Comstock hired detectives from the infamous Pinkerton Detective Agency to carry out raids against some gambling establishments.[49] The Society for the Suppression of Vice refused to publish details of its work because "its activities were sometimes inconsistent with the law."[50]

A broad spectrum of New Yorkers began to react negatively to the excesses of the preventive societies, which seemed to be driven by the megalomaniacal personalities of their leadership. For example, Anthony Comstock overstepped boundaries with a couple of his campaigns, which caused the public to pull back support for his methods, although not necessarily his cause. In 1906 he raided the Art Students' League in New York City because a mother had called his attention to its catalog, which she claimed had corrupted her daughter. He burst into the league's office and requested a copy of the catalog, which featured sketches and other artistic representations of nude figures. He thereupon arrested the young woman who sold him the catalog and declared that the material produced by the Art Students' League was "improper and immoral." The case went to court, and Comstock's arguments convinced the jury; the catalogs featuring the nudes were destroyed. The court of public opinion, however, pilloried Comstock for moving his campaign forward to attack "legitimate art."[51]

Nor did the Society for the Prevention of Crime escape the public's increasing skepticism about its methods. When the police refused to close brothels based on information provided by Parkhurst and his detectives, the SPC took matters into its own hands. Conducting warrantless raids that were often destructive of property, SPC employees, including legal counsel Frank Moss, broke into cafés that violated excise laws and into hidden gambling parlors, using sledgehammers and axes, and firing pistols into the air to intimidate the denizens of these dens.[52] In addition, Charles Gardner, the detective who had guided the Rev. Parkhurst on his midnight jaunts through the city's notorious dives, was arrested for extortion. Released on appeal, Gardner later demonstrated that a syndicate of police, gambling parlor operators, and keepers of disorderly houses had formed an alliance to frame him. As the police realized their sources of income (in the form of protection money) were under attack, they had moved quickly to eliminate Gardner. Gardner later explained in his memoir that it was "impossible to reach" or impugn Parkhurst; the only way to impede the Society for the Prevention of Crime was to stop its head detective.[53]

As a consequence, private detectives came to be seen not only as corrupt but also as corruptible. Although private detectives-for-hire fell out favor with the preventive societies and the public, the undercover technique did not—at least not among Progressive activists, who continued to use undercover operatives to gather knowledge about excise and tenement-house law violations in the name of cleaning up the city's moral conditions.

The preventive society model faded with the dawn of the twentieth century, and a new kind of organization evolved, one that drew on the lessons and successes of its predecessors but adopted slightly different tactics to meet its goals. These new organizations relied less on personal relationships to sympathetic mayors or other public officials and instead conducted their work through backroom bargaining tactics—with businesses and insurance companies, for instance—and local spheres of influence, especially settlement houses and the social work community.[54]

New York City's new, private, activist organizations, including the Committee of Fifteen, the Committee of Fourteen, the People's Institute, and the National Civic Federation, all of which are considered in this book, used undercover investigators to further their agenda. A number of other groups adopted similar tactics: the Kehillah (Jewish Community of New York), the Association of Neighborhood Workers, the Society for the Prevention of Crime, the New York County Medical Society, and the Committee on Amusement Resources of Working Girls.[55] Although these groups used undercover tactics, they did so irregularly and were never as sophisticated as some of their contemporaries.

The Kehillah, founded in 1908 by Dr. Judah L. Magnes, began to direct and conduct investigations of gambling, prostitution, and other forms of criminal behavior among Jews on the Lower East Side after police commissioner Theodore Bingham alleged that 50 percent of the criminals in New York City were Jewish.[56] In response, the Kehillah created and maintained a Committee on Vice and Crime, whose main investigator was Abe Schoenfeld (he later went on to work for the Rockefeller-funded Bureau of Social Hygiene). The Kehillah, as Dr. Magnes explained, was mainly interested in the "neighborhood actually tak[ing] its cleaning into its own hands."[57] This course of action, he imagined, would also prevent the spread of anti-Semitic feelings toward the new Jewish immigrants from eastern Europe.

The Kehillah's practice, with its undercover investigator's reports, was to submit evidence on Lower East Side gambling parlors directly to the police; it also made an arrangement that any information Schoenfeld gathered on "disorderly saloons" would be turned over to the Committee of Fourteen. Most of the reports from the Committee on Vice and Crime were lists of addresses of places that harbored gambling or prostitutes; the reports are not narrative in style. Simply put, the Kehillah was engaged in undercover work, and it collaborated with other, similar organizations, although its organizers never refined the use of such tactics. It was, however, very much a part of this zeitgeist.[58]

During the winter of 1906, the Public Health Committee of the Association of Neighborhood Workers dispatched a trained nurse, F. Elisabeth Crowell, to conduct an undercover investigation of midwives and midwifery practice in New York City. The New York County and Kings County Medical Societies, the Academy of Medicine, the Board of Health, and the New York Obstetrical Society were all greatly concerned with the "usual type of woman who follows the calling of midwife in this country," according to Crowell. She explained that the majority of midwives were "foreigners of a low grade—ignorant, untrained women who find in the natural needs and life-long prejudices of the parturient women of their race a lucrative means of livelihood." Not only were these midwives preying on vulnerable women, according to Crowell's report, but they also lacked training and legal regulation. Crowell visited five hundred midwives, most of whom were located on the Upper and Lower East Sides, neighborhoods that contained significant Italian and Jewish immigrant populations. In most cases, she presented herself as an inspector from the Board of Health, requested that they produce their diplomas, asked questions about their practices, and inspected the contents of their bags. She looked for instruments and herbs that could be considered abortifacients to assess how many midwives performed or aided in abortions, which were illegal in New York State. Crowell never posed as a woman requiring the aid of a midwife, but neither was she an employee of the Board of Health. She followed up on advertisements in foreign-language papers to determine what, precisely, midwives offered their clientele. Ultimately, Crowell and her supervisors lobbied for a state law defining "the province and duties of the midwife and providing ample punishment for any violation of the limitations prescribed by such law, and requiring absolute evidence of her professional fitness as a condition of licensing her practice, would operate as a safeguard against the usurpation of the function of the physician."[59]

The Association of Neighborhood Workers also conducted an investigation of craps shooting and published a report in the same issue of *Charities and the Commons* in which Crowell published her survey of midwives.[60] Ultimately, this organization turned to undercover investigation to gather knowledge, but it did not use the technique in the sustained fashion of other organizations considered herein.

Organizations such as the Kehillah and Association of Neighborhood Workers engaged in surveillance activity, but ultimately their pursuits paled in comparison to those of the Committee of Fifteen, the Committee of Fourteen, the Colored Auxiliary of the Committee of Fourteen, the People's Institute, and the National Civic Federation. Significantly, all five of these groups shared an ideology that valorized the use of undercover investigations as a vehicle for social activism and reform. These new private organizations were the most sophisticated and developed among the many groups that experimented with these methods and strategies of policing. They regarded the connections between Tammany Hall, the police, and the underground economy as archaic, a part of the "old" city, not worthy of the new, modern, integrated metropolitan center. Good-government activists and their allies wanted to replace machine politics and corrupt elections with a rational, routinized bureaucracy based on knowledge, education, and expertise, not on personal relationships (at least not those between Irish "criminals" and their cohort). To this end, social activists endowed themselves with power and authority, rooted in the knowledge collected by their undercover investigators. Their next step was twofold: they sold themselves to the municipal government as the solution to future investigations into police and municipal corruption, and they created widespread fear among the general public of surveillance, economic consequences, and their power to create legal problems or trigger deportation for offenders.

The private organizations began by pursuing their own goals, mostly as an end run around the fact that the city and police department did not share their concern with ephemeral issues that could not necessarily be legislated in democratic society—morality, sexual practices, leisure behavior, and political beliefs. When it became clear that the government would not (or could not) pursue such issues, these private organizations not only intervened but also aggressively pursued these capacious powers. Their efforts ended in collaborations with the government, an arrangement that both increased the traditional reach of government while saving it from having to assume directly this unpopular work. Therefore, private organizations, even though they were not official parts of the government qua government, had made themselves a part of the state by the period of World War I.[61]

Furthermore, for the Committee of Fifteen, the Committee of Fourteen, the Colored Auxiliary of the Committee of Fourteen, the People's Institute, and the National Civic Federation, their belief in "truth" and social science separated them both from their predecessors and from their contemporaries in religious organizations, such as the Salvation Army and the YMCA. When these Progressives spoke of morals, it was not from a religious perspective. Rather, they used the term as a smokescreen for what they perceived as the real problems—immorality among those in immigrant and working-class neighborhoods and the possibility of the moral contamination of other New Yorkers. They sought structural, rather than individual, solutions to social and behavioral problems. They did not believe in the abolition of alcohol, commercialized leisure, or even prostitution; they acknowledged that outlawing prostitution would lead to more serious crimes, such as "seduction" and rape. They sought regulation, not outright bans.

The desire to control and regulate—rather than "save" or "redeem"—differentiated Progressive Era activists from their predecessors and their religious contemporaries, with whom they did occasionally collaborate. In the end, these powerful middle-class activists wanted to ensure that they successfully controlled and regulated the ways in which immigrant and working-class New Yorkers spent their leisure time, how much and when they drank alcohol, and where their political affinities lay. Maintaining and regularly dispatching a stable of undercover operatives allowed them to define conditions and then identify them as needing alteration, which was the key to their copious powers. These organizations relied on undercover investigation because they believed this technique gave them special purchase on the reality of social problems; by masking their authority, investigators could gain access to previously concealed sites and information.

The private organizations, with their faith in knowledge, used that information to confirm their perceptions or define new forms of social danger, particularly in terms of the sexual and political behavior of immigrants (with a focus on the Irish, as well as newer immigrants from China and southern and eastern Europe) and black Americans. Although these Progressive Era social activists eschewed the use of professional private detectives by this point and instead hired persons from a variety of backgrounds and professions—reformed gamblers, residents of the neighborhoods under investigation, reporters, social workers, former employees of the state Department of Excise—to work as undercover investigators, the men and women they hired received little, if any, specialized or formal training. Rather, their employers selected them for other qualities such as race, ethnicity, or gender. To the staff of these private organizations, investigators had to possess the ability to "pass" in certain situations. Jewish men, for example, posed as Greek men; newspaper reporters posed as denizens of downtown gambling parlors.[62] All of the investigators then wrote detailed reports of what they observed, to whom they spoke, where else that person took them, and what they did together.

The private organizations then sold themselves to the city, state, and federal governments as practitioners of innovative methods because of the information their undercover investigators gathered. When the private organizations surveilled immigrant, working-class, and black New Yorkers' private behavior, the mantle of "reformer" protected them from criticism that they were meddling in a sphere in which they did not belong. Moreover, neither the city nor federal government stopped them; during the war years, in fact, local and federal government agencies collaborated with the Committee of Fourteen, the People's Institute, and the National Civic Federation in an effort to consolidate power in ways that did not raise concerns about the government acting beyond its sanction. The federal state did not entirely replace these private organizations; rather, it permitted various organizations to participate by asking them to pursue their own agenda. In the case of the People's Institute, for example, the organization built "Americanization" programs in concert with the municipal and federal governments; the Committee of Fourteen continued to work on ending prostitution as adjunct of the War Department. Or the federal government tolerated the organizations' intervention, as in the case of the National Civic Federation and the policing of immigrant radicalism. By the period of World War I, federal agencies such as the Military Intelligence Division and the Bureau of Investigation gladly received reports by private organizations of their findings and occasionally hired investigators from the organizations or loaned them their own employees.[63] These relationships expanded the involvement of the government in the policing of private behavior. Working with private organizations permitted the government to extend its reach into new fields of power.

Despite the appeal of the undercover technique during the war years, Congress had long been reluctant to create a federal police system. Many members feared such a reform would become a "secret political service," a "spy system," or "system of espionage." As a consequence, up through the nineteenth century government agencies such as the Treasury Department and the Post Office relied on private detectives, rather than government agents, to investigate counterfeiting and mail fraud.[64] After the 1892 Homestead Strike, in which Pinkerton agents opened fire on and killed striking workers, the reputation of private detective agencies was badly damaged in the eyes of the public and the government. In response, Congress prohibited the government from using any detectives "from any source outside the government." Despite the loss of their adjunct police force, Congress remained unwilling to establish a federal police force; in 1908, it denied Attorney General Charles Joseph Bonaparte's request to start his own investigation bureau. Congress also disallowed the use of secret service agents by other government agencies. Ironically, the new restrictions on the use of secret service agents hastened the creation of a federal police system. On July 1, 1908, President Theodore Roosevelt and Bonaparte went ahead and created their own Bureau of Investigation anyway.[65] The Bureau was formalized under the next attorney general, George Wickersham, but was limited to investigating crimes against the federal government, such as violations of antitrust and postal laws and land fraud.

In 1910, Congress appropriated funds for the Department of Justice to conduct investigations under the direction of the attorney general, which subsequently resulted in an expansion of the Bureau's authority.[66] According to a 1909 *New York Times* article, however, the growing public fear that "scores of thousands of women had been imported into this country for immoral purposes" finally pushed Congress to overcome the stigma of a federal police system.[67] This moral panic led to demands for the federal government to act and resulted in the Mann (White-Slave Traffic) Act of 1910.[68] The Mann Act required the extension of the fledgling Bureau, which included expanding the staff and opening regional offices to handle the additional workload. Over the next two years, the Bureau of Investigation's staff of investigators grew to thirty-five; it opened its first field offices outside of Washington, D.C.; and it began an extensive card file system to track the movements of prostitutes, madams, and procurers around the United States. Agents pursued foreign-born pimps and prostitutes with the goal of deporting them before they ripped apart the nation's moral fiber. The Bureau of Investigation soon had over two hundred agents stationed throughout the country, mostly in urban centers, and by 1912, "white slave investigations" constituted the vast majority of the Bureau's work.[69] The fear that immigrants were responsible for the "white slave trade" convinced a reluctant Congress that the growing United States required an organized federal police system. The intertwined fears of sexual danger represented by immigrants and their criminal machinations created the modern Bureau of Investigation and extended its reach into people's personal lives for the first time in U.S. history.[70]

Despite the growth of the Bureau of Investigation, the line between private and public policing remained blurred in the period leading up to and during World War I. Both the Bureau of Investigation and the Military Intelligence Division remained limited in their abilities to investigate domestic political subversion. As a consequence, private organizations deputized themselves to fill in the gaps in the federal police system by conducting undercover investigations of prostitutes, immigrants, "slackers" who had failed to register for the draft, labor radicals, and political subversives. The private organizations then sent their undercover agents' reports to the proper federal authorities, who had the official powers to make arrests and begin deportation hearings (in the case of immigrants) or criminal proceedings. This informal system of cooperation became a useful way for the government to suppress domestic political subversion (particularly among African Americans) and to prosecute and deport "dangerous radicals" in order to head off any possible crimes against the United States. Thus, during the war, a mechanism and partnership developed and was formalized between these private organizations and government agencies that served the interests of an increasingly repressive domestic agenda. Through these temporary wartime coalitions in particular, the federal state expanded its reach without expanding its personnel or its footprint. Undercover investigation was intimately bound up with the development of increasingly sophisticated and far-reaching federal power in the early twentieth century—through the period of World War I and beyond.

TWO

Public Raids, Undercover Investigators, and Native Informants

Late one February evening in 1901, Austen G. Fox, prominent Wall Street lawyer and founding member of the Committee of Fifteen, arrived at the West Thirtieth Street police station in the heart of the infamous Tenderloin district with eight of his Committee colleagues. Dressed in his finest evening clothes and a silk top hat, Fox presented the desk sergeant with arrest warrants for the proprietors of eight different gambling parlors and brothels. The nine committeemen, bedecked in formal wear, each set out with a police officer to oversee the arrest of the offending parties. The arrival of Fox and his colleagues in the Tenderloin, traipsing around in opera clothes accompanied by policemen, drew the attention of the neighborhood's denizens, who followed these strange pairs on their rounds.[1]

The raids Fox engineered were unsuccessful largely because the gambling parlors were not in operation that particular night. These raids were not uneventful, however, as they did attract attention. On the streets and in the *New York Times*, observers commented on the Committee members' hats and apparel, which indicated that upper-middle-class social activists were yet again "trying to purify" the city "with eau de cologne."[2] That accusation was not entirely incorrect in that Fox and other members of the Committee of Fifteen were seen regularly on the city's streets, conducting numerous public raids.

In June 1901, for example, Committee member Robert Grier Monroe, running a bit late for his scheduled raid, broke down the door of the targeted establishment and burst inside. Monroe had made a terrible mistake, however; he had broken down the wrong door. This blunder dawned on him when he found himself on the stage of the Volksgarten Music Hall with two scantily clad female performers in the middle of their routine.

The audience, performers, and Monroe were all equally shocked, and the newspapers made much of this error.[3]

The case of Fox's unsuccessful and relatively innocuous raid, when set against Monroe's embarrassing debut at the Volksgarten, highlights why the Committee of Fifteen, only a year into its work, was forced to seriously reexamine its strategy. In a decision that distanced itself from its predecessors, the Committee adapted undercover investigation to its vision for the future of New York City.

From its founding in 1900, the Committee of Fifteen, by employing techniques such as public raids and undercover investigation, gathered information on conditions in New York City (particularly in the overcrowded immigrant neighborhoods of Chinatown, Little Italy, and the Lower East Side) that its members regarded as "disorderly" and, by extension, morally unpalatable. The surveillance netted the Committee documentation that pregnant women worked as prostitutes, mothers turned tricks while their children slept in the same bed, candy shops concealed brothels, young boys served as cadets and procurers for bawdy houses, and ordinary offices operated simultaneously as gambling parlors. Despite this overwhelming evidence to the contrary, the men who comprised the Committee of Fifteen believed that the Lower East Side was populated by moral, upstanding people who were just trying to earn a living and raise a family but did not have the political power, clout, or cash to put a stop to the gambling and soliciting that plagued their neighborhoods. These innocent New Yorkers were victimized by the "vice syndicate" of corrupt police officers, local politicians, brothel keepers, pimps, prostitutes, gambling parlor operators, and their customers.

The Committee of Fifteen's strategy of conducting public raids of disorderly establishments and gambling parlors aroused derision among the public as well as among its own membership. In June 1901, the Committee held an emergency meeting at which the members decided to abandon the tactic of raiding establishments in favor of something less controversial and, more important, less visible. The only statement that Committee chairman William H. Baldwin, Jr., made to the public regarding the strategy meeting was that "the Committee has no idea of stopping the work, and it will continue along the lines of its original programme."[4] As of July 1, 1901, the Committee announced, it would focus on "ferreting out . . . evil in tenement houses and the banishment . . . of women of bad character from the tenement districts."[5]

Ultimately, the Committee of Fifteen decided that the public raids brought too much unwanted publicity and scrutiny, which made achieving its goals—of a "morally clean" New York, one that was relieved of the weight of Tammany Hall, political patronage, and police corruption—even more difficult. A practical problem with the Committee's public raiding technique was that the police, who benefited financially from the underground economy, taught the gamblers and brothel keepers to recognize the faces of the Committee members and employ lookouts to bar their entry. In addition, many New Yorkers, although frustrated with the relationship of Tammany Hall and city hall to the underground economy, were no happier with the actions of the Committee of Fifteen. They thought that the Committee only reinforced Tammany's strength among "personal liberty" voters, who did not want to be subjected to "the prying and snuffling of Carrie Nationism."[6]

The notoriety the Committee acquired because of its public raids threatened to diminish its members' reputations as New York's leading citizens. As a consequence, the Committee turned to the technique of employing undercover investigators and "native informants" from the tenement districts, which allowed the Committee to continue to gather the information that permitted it to impose its agenda on New York City. The Committee of Fifteen's abandonment of public raids in favor of undercover investigation represented a break from the preventive societies' mode of reform, as exemplified by temperance advocate Carrie Nation and purity crusader Anthony Comstock, and a move toward "scientific" surveillance. This latter version of reform relied on investigators gathering data about violations of particular laws and acting on that information. The Committee began to emphasize the implementation of certain laws as a means to restoring moral order.

Using their connections to the business, religious, and settlement house communities, the founding members of the Committee of Fifteen built their own syndicate for combating "vice." Mobilizing a keen interpretation of the Tenement House Laws (which some of their members had helped to write), they hired undercover investigators to gain access to places that were otherwise inaccessible. They sought to sever the connections that Tammany Hall had cultivated and maintained between its denizens and the police, brothels, and gambling parlors over the preceding three decades. According to the Committee, power in the city should be in the hands of educated professionals, defined and controlled by neutral and well-intentioned laws, and not based on the connections between ethnic groups and favoritism. When residents of Chinatown, however, reached out to the Committee of Fifteen for assistance in eliminating the gambling parlor scourge from their neighborhood, the Committee's finely honed, well-reasoned, and rational techniques collapsed like a house of cards.

At the opening of the twentieth century, New York City's foremost business-men and clergymen, after appraising the rapidly changing demographics and political organization of the city, concluded that the metropolis was seized by disorder. According to the Committee of Fifteen, the "flagrant offences against public morality and common decency" that thrived in "certain districts" startled men and women in business, good-government, and social activist groups.[7] The Committee believed that the city's criminal element was growing exponentially, which forced "respectable residents . . . to fasten their doors and windows . . . so that the sounds and sights of the debaucheries . . . might not reach them." If they dared venture outside, New Yorkers would encounter "naked women danc[ing]" in the streets. "Degenerate men prowled the street and aided in the traffic [in women] with the knowledge and permission of the police. Even little children were trained to decoy men to these dens of vice."[8] This bombastic description highlights developments the Committee's members found distressing—sexual promiscuity, excessive gambling, alleged trafficking in women (orchestrated by immigrant men and women, and victimizing immigrant and native-born women alike)—all supported by corrupt police officers and politicians. Taken together, activists concerned with morality and political corruption imagined that a vast corrupting influence victimized those innocent families and children who had no other choice but to live in poor and run-down sections of the city. But it was also an expression of fear on the part of the Committee of Fifteen that the city's power base had shifted—perhaps permanently.

New York City's social activists had grappled with the problems of poverty and morality for decades, but at the dawn of the twentieth century they decided that these old problems required new strategies. In addition, the realities of the consolidation of the five boroughs into the greater city of New York (the incorporation was achieved on January 1, 1898, and took effect in 1901) complicated matters. Despite the good intentions that motivated consolidation, upper-class Protestant, "good-government" reformers perceived the city of New York to be moving away from its organization as a city dominated by the merchant, business, and clergy class and toward one of working-class immigrants coming into their own political power—official and unofficial, legal and illegal. As the "respectable" classes observed the success enjoyed by the "criminal" elements, they feared the loss of business in and to the city, and they intervened.

Tammany Hall retained its power during and after consolidation by shoring up its base in Manhattan and cooperating with Democrats in the outer boroughs—Brooklyn in particular. Tammany Hall's leaders, however, also realized that good-government activists presented a real threat to their power and that temporarily cleaning up their act might keep a political revolution at bay. So in 1900, Tammany leader Richard Croker appointed a Committee of Five, whose sole purpose was to investigate the city's moral conditions. The clergy and businessmen who worked tirelessly to exterminate vice, corruption, and bribery were appalled; they charged that the very idea of this corrupt political machine cleansing the city (and itself) was ludicrous. In response to this Tammany travesty, the New York Chamber of Commerce hosted a meeting in November 1900, out of which emerged the Committee of Fifteen. The Committee of Fifteen's founding aim was to "carefully watch the actions of the constituted authorities, whether or not they will perform to their full extent the duty imposed upon them *by law* to prevent and eradicate vice in every form."[9]

The Committee of Fifteen's founding members were in a good position to challenge the corruption of Tammany Hall and its allied crime syndicates. The founders were businessmen, academics, and religious leaders influential beyond their own denominations. For instance, William Henry Baldwin, Jr., the first (and only) chairman of the Committee of Fifteen, came from a prominent Massachusetts family and was raised to believe in active intervention on behalf of the less fortunate. His father, a philanthropist, had served as president of the Massachusetts Society for the Prevention of Cruelty to Animals as well as the Children's Mission to the Children of the Destitute. After graduating from Harvard, the son moved to New York City, where he became president of the Long Island Railroad and an active philanthropist. He supported organized labor; to him, "there was no line between classes and masses." Baldwin financially supported black education and was a trustee of the Tuskegee Institute; he counted Booker T. Washington among his personal friends. Locally, Baldwin dedicated his energy to cleaning up the Lower East Side; he believed that "vice was not born there, but dumped there, and the people did not know their own rights, some one must perforce teach their rights to them."[10]

Other founding members of the Committee of Fifteen included Alexander E. Orr, president of the Rapid Transit Commission, and Columbia University literature professor Charles Sprague Smith, who was also the founder and director of the People's Institute. Columbia University economist Edwin R. A. Seligman, who was, among many other things, affiliated with the Educational Alliance, president of the Tenement House Building

Committee, a founder of the American Economics Association with Richard T. Ely, and a founder of the New School for Social Research, crafted many of the Committee's policies. Seligman was the secretary of the Committee and largely responsible for compiling the research that became the Committee's first publication, *The Social Evil: With Special Reference to Conditions Existing in the City of New York*. Dr. Felix Adler, founder of the Ethical Culture Society and the Committee on Public Morality of the Educational Alliance, and philanthropist Jacob Schiff represented the interests of the Jewish community, while W. J. O'Brien, president of the Granite Cutters' Association, and Andrew J. Smith, president of the Central Federated Union, represented organized labor's interests. Joel B. Erhardt, president of the Lawyer's Surety Co. and a former collector of the port of New York, and Austen G. Fox, a Wall Street lawyer, were also original members. Former president of the New York Chamber of Commerce Charles Stewart Smith; banker and director of the Home Insurance Company of New York J. Harsen Rhoades; banker, businessman, and philanthropist John S. Kennedy; banker, businessman, and philanthropist George Foster Peabody (who supported the Hampton and Tuskegee Institutes and after whom the Peabody Awards for Journalism are named); and George Haven Putnam of G. P. Putnam's Sons publishing company were also among the founders.[11] These men believed that their ecumenical group represented a diverse cross-section of New Yorkers and that the inclusion of leaders from the labor and Jewish communities would head off any criticism of their efforts that might emerge from those quarters.

George Wilson Morgan, a graduate of Columbia University Law School, came to the Committee of Fifteen through his work with Felix Adler's Committee on Public Morality and the Educational Alliance; he worked as the Committee's assistant secretary. Colonel Robert Grier Monroe was the Committee's attorney. Ex–chief of police and state superintendent of elections John S. McCullagh was the chief agent for the Committee on Investigation.[12] As head of the Committee of Fifteen's Committee on Investigation, McCullagh maintained a Bureau of Investigation staffed by undercover investigators, who became the Committee's secret weapon. Baldwin emphasized to the city's newspapers that his Committee had undercover "agents at work" all over the city, who were "mostly detectives from upstate who would not be recognized by the gamblers and prostitutes."[13] This announcement was not true, however. Baldwin had designed this statement to strike fear in the hearts of the gamblers and prostitutes, and the syndicates that maintained and profited from them. Although the Committee did employ agents all over the city, they were not from upstate. In reality, many of the investigators lived on the Lower East Side.

The Committee of Fifteen had thus set itself up as an extragovernmental and extralegal organization to police the conditions and relationships that contributed to the perceived moral decay in the immigrant and working-class quarters of New York City. For this newly constituted committee, neither the regulation of prostitution nor the repression of "vice by mere restrictive legislation" would solve the city's problems. Instead, New York City needed "a definite policy," one that was not "based on the delusive hope of radically altering in a single generation the evil propensities of the human heart." In this way, the Committee of Fifteen distanced itself from its reform predecessors (and some contemporaries, such as the Rev. Charles Parkhurst or Anthony Comstock), who took a moral approach to the subject. Rather, the Committee wanted to see "a policy [put in place] that shall be practical with respect to the immediate future, and shall at the same time be in harmony with the ideals which are cherished by the best men and women in this community."[14] The members of the Committee did not want to alienate the rest of their community; they just wanted to lead it.

To realize this ambition, the Committee avoided the evangelical tone of its predecessors in favor of an approach grounded in social and political science and the movement for "good government." The Committee declared its intention to effect change in the battle against vice; to do so, its members pledged to ignore "all political or partisan spirit of every kind whatsoever" in the pursuit of results and to cooperate "with individuals or any body of men . . . without regard to party."[15] Despite these claims, the Committee of Fifteen was an expressly political organization, closely allied with the Fusion political party.[16] According to its published materials, the Committee and its allies orchestrated "the overthrow of the control of the municipal administration by Tammany Hall and the success of the Reform movement in the municipal campaign in 1901 (a campaign in which the information supplied by the Committee of Fifteen constituted a very important factor)."[17] This fact notwithstanding, the Committee wanted to avoid appearing partisan in its efforts. To this end, it focused on particular laws, which its members believed had inadvertently created the "social evil" in New York City, and on others that could be reinterpreted and mobilized to eliminate prostitution and gambling. The Raines Liquor Tax Law of 1896 was the Committee's first target.

The Raines law was designed to shift control of liquor licensing from the municipal to the state level. State senator John Raines, however, had an ulterior motive: he wanted to reduce drinking in the Irish, German, eastern European, and Italian immigrant and working-class districts of New York City. To accomplish this mission, the law outlawed Sunday sales, except under special circumstances. For example, the law distinguished between hotels and saloons.[18] The Raines law required hotels to have at least ten bedrooms "of specified dimensions," as well as "a dining room and a kitchen with accommodations for a specified number of guests." If a hotel met these qualifications, it was permitted to serve alcohol on Sundays so long as it also served meals with the drinks. The class prejudice of the Raines law was obvious—ordinary neighborhood saloons technically could no longer serve alcohol on Sundays, but a "respectable" establishment like the Waldorf Hotel could continue to serve alcohol to its clientele in both the dining rooms and the guest rooms.

The Raines law did not function as its authors and supporters intended, however. Instead, the law produced rampant Sunday sales and created a new symbiotic relationship between saloon keepers and prostitutes in the "disorderly" saloons and neighborhoods the law was designed to clean up. In order to obtain a Sunday license, saloon keepers converted their saloon spaces into "hotels." Some converted upstairs spaces into "hotel rooms"; others simply hung up a curtain in the rear of the bar and put cots behind it. They then made these "rooms" available to prostitutes, who paid a small portion of their earnings to the saloon keeper. This arrangement was an easy way for saloon keepers to increase profits, and it provided prostitutes with safer places to work.

The Raines law hotels posed a unique problem. According to the Committee of Fifteen, they tended to be "ordinary saloons" frequented after work by "the average citizen [who] goes there to drink his glass of beer and to listen to the bad music and worse jokes"—a practice the Committee did not object to in and of itself. These unwitting customers, however, often found themselves "subject to solicitation which has the appearance of a mere flirtation; if he yields, it is with the least possible shock to his moral sensibilities; he may feel that he did not seek vice, but was overcome by circumstances." These were men "who would hesitate to enter a brothel or notorious rendezvous" but who easily fell prey to the prostitutes working in Raines law hotels. "The uncompromising moralist will probably say that it is a matter of small importance what befalls such moral imbeciles. He might, however, change his opinion if he knew how many of them there are."[19]

The Committee of Fifteen considered prostitution to be an unavoidable fact of modern society. It also believed, however, that prostitution should not occur in residential neighborhoods for fear that the sight of it would corrupt the way recent immigrants and children would perceive the moral conditions of the city and encourage them to engage in immoral or criminal behavior. Thus, unlike nineteenth-century moral reformers who prayed in front of brothels, encouraged individual prostitutes to read the Bible, or published the names of men who frequented brothels, the Committee did not seek to transform the prostitutes or their customers.

The Committee believed that, for many women, prostitution was a temporary occupation, borne out of economic necessity. As its study *The Social Evil* explains, "there are in every large city classes of working women whose normal income is sufficient to permit them to live honorable lives, but who are left at times of temporary depression with no means of escaping from starvation except prostitution." Until society can "solve the problem of poverty," there will always be a "class of women, not necessarily congenitally defective, who will choose a life of vice." Regulation was not an option for the Committee's members, however. Their main objection to instituting a European-style system of regulation was that it required an efficient police force experienced in identifying and policing prostitutes and the "social evil," which would take too long to develop in New York. In addition, they argued that the character of women and street life in New York City was drastically different from that of European cities. As *The Social Evil* noted,

> in Paris, [the police] could arrest a young woman who waited for her husband at the door of a shop, "because no decent woman lingered upon the sidewalk." Imagine a New York agent of police acting upon such inferences! It is needless to dwell upon this fact, since anyone can understand that American habits of life make it possible for a discreet prostitute to exercise her vocation much longer without rousing the suspicion of a limited force of police agents than she could possibly do in Paris or Berlin.

In addition, the Committee of Fifteen believed that "the American impatience of authority" would make it exceedingly difficult for the police to regulate prostitution, as they doubted the prostitutes themselves would cooperate with a regulatory authority. Therefore, the Committee chose to focus on separating "vice" from "legitimate pleasures," and it prioritized keeping prostitution out of the tenement houses.[20]

The Committee adopted a modern, "scientific" approach to prostitution. It identified tenement house prostitution as a distinct violation of the Tenement House Law of 1901 and designed instructions to its investigators based on this fact. The Committee regarded tenement house prostitution as one of the most visible signs of the city's degeneration. Half-naked women hung out of tenement house windows at all hours, calling to male pass-ersby. Scantily clad women lounged on the stoops of tenement buildings, advertising their wares in full view of neighborhood children. The Commit-tee labeled these behaviors as violations of the Tenement House Law and proceeded accordingly.

Since the 1860s, housing reformers and advocates for the poor had been acutely aware of the problems engendered by the quality of hous-ing in the immigrant and working-class districts of New York City (and other large and rapidly growing cities). The New York legislature passed the first Tenement House Law in 1867, which was intended to minimize crowding and maximize sanitation and ventilation. Real estate speculators, however, found ways to defy the statute. By the late 1870s, concerns about cholera and the allegedly poor moral conditions encouraged by close, filthy quarters prompted those working with the Association for Improving the Conditions of the Poor and the Charity Organization Society to find new solutions. Many housing reformers saw a connection between the physical condition of the neighborhoods and their moral condition; without access to fresh air, surely people would become stunted both physically and mor-ally. This notion resulted in the Tenement House Law of 1879, which, most notably, required a window in every room in the apartment.[21]

By the 1890s, as the city's housing stock aged and scores of new immi-grants landed at Ellis Island and flooded into Lower East Side tenements, social activists such as Lillian Wald, Jacob Riis, and Committee of Fifteen members Felix Adler and E. R. A. Seligman took a renewed interest in the "tenement house problem." The Charity Organization Society's newly formed Tenement House Committee began open investigations of housing conditions and, in 1900, mounted a public exhibit to raise public aware-ness of this perennial issue, all of which culminated in the Tenement House Law of 1901. In addition to specifying the sizes of individual rooms and the total percentage of the lot a building could occupy, the law also created the New York State Tenement House Department, which employed inspectors responsible for overseeing improvements in the "old law" buildings and supervising construction and maintenance of "new law" buildings.

The Committee regarded the new Tenement House Law as a way to "pre-vent in the tenement houses the overcrowding which is the prolific source of sexual immorality."[22] If the poorly conceived Raines law increased prostitu-tion, the Committee reasoned that a better application and enforcement of the Tenement House Law would curtail prostitution—at least in residential buildings. By pairing specially selected undercover investigators with an expansive interpretation of the Tenement House Law of 1901, the Committee developed a modus operandi that eschewed some of the overt, crusading moralism of its predecessors.

Because undercover investigators were the means by which the Committee gathered its data on violations of the Tenement House Laws, it had to proceed cautiously in hiring investigators. Assistant secretary George Wilson Morgan tapped his networks to encourage cooperation from local social service organizations and settlement houses. The Settlements Association, for example, willingly offered some young men "in the way of patrolling and special investigation."[23] Morgan solicited recommendations from James Bronson Reynolds of the University Settlement Society located on the Lower East Side, the Association of Neighborhood Workers, the Central Federation of Churches and Christian Workers, the Church Association for the Advancement of the Interests of Labor, and the West End Association—all of which assisted the Committee in locating appropriate investigators.[24] Reynolds "recommend[ed] very cordially" William Lustgarten, "a young man here in this house [who] is reliable and ambitious. I think you would find him energetic and thoroughly trustworthy."[25] Lustgarten lived at 97 Orchard Street and worked for Greenberg and Berger, dry goods jobbers at 96 Orchard Street.[26] Settlement house worker Henry Moskowitz recommended his brother Max for undercover work.[27] Lillian Wald of the Nurses/Henry Street Settlement House suggested that the Committee contact the Presbyterian Church of the Sea and the Land, which ran a club for reformed gamblers. Wald surmised that those men "could undoubtedly give information regarding pool rooms and saloons that might be valuable [and] some of the men could be . . . valuable reporters of conditions."[28]

In addition to preferring investigators who possessed a familiarity with the neighborhood and recommendations from trustworthy allies, the Committee prized investigators who spoke languages other than English. Investigator Jacob Kreiswirth, who lived at 102 Allen Street, spoke German in addition to English.[29] Another investigator, L. L. Rosenbaum, spoke Yiddish and described himself as "a linguist capable of speaking and understanding the language of the class of people we would mostly have to deal with."[30] The Committee imagined that these insider investigators had a vested interest, above and beyond material compensation, for taking these positions. All of these men might have been interested in seeing their neighborhoods become "cleaner," or may have seen this job as a way to distance themselves from the "slums" of the East Side. Ultimately, for the Committee, the benefit of using men from the neighborhoods meant that they could stroll the streets of the Lower East Side, recording addresses and observations without arousing suspicions among their neighbors. These investigators would be familiar faces to the people of the neighborhood; ideally, or at the very least, they looked and sounded like they belonged. They were truly undercover.

To guide investigations and ensure that the necessary information was collected, the Committee created forms titled "Disorderly Tenement House in the City of New York." The standard form asked for the following information:

Place of Visit:
Date of Visit: Duration of Visit:
In company with:
Flights up:
Location of Apartment (front or rear: north, south, east, or west)
Solicited by (description)
Solicited from
Amount paid:
Paid to (description)
In presence of
Remarks:
Investigator:
Sworn to before me this ____ day of_____, 1901.

Finally, each completed Disorderly Tenement House form required a notary public's signature. Assistant secretary George Wilson Morgan notarized most of them, after which they became sworn testimony and legal evidence admissible in court.[31]

The forms dictated the procedures to be used by the Committee's undercover investigators; the process and practice of investigating were instantiated in and created by the very forms that were supposed to serve as reflections of what the investigators discovered and observed. The physical layout of these forms constrained how the interactions between the investigators and prostitutes would take place and precluded any out-of-the-ordinary possibilities. As a result, most of the reports followed a formulaic narrative pattern. The first line of the form required the investigator to provide personal information: "[name] residing at [address] being duly sworn, reports as follows."[32] In order to hold up in court, every investigator's story needed to be corroborated, which explains why the Committee dispatched investigators in teams of two or three. The forms, therefore, contained a blank for the name(s) of the coinvestigator(s). The investigators' completed

Disorderly House Report.

5th ___ Police Precinct.

Location No. _8 James St_

Character of Building _House of Prostitution_

Date of Visit _June 5th /01_

Duration of Visit _45 Minutes_

Floor Visited _____ Room _____

Solicited by _Madame_

Solicited from _Street_

Amount paid _____

Paid to _____

REMARKS.

_Mr Wilson, Kreisworth and
myself were solicited by
a stout woman who invited
us in to 8th James St.
She said she is the wife of Chas Kramer_

Name of Operator _Max Moskowitz_

Residence _118 Chrystie St. NY._

Report filed _June 5th_ 1901.

Sworn to before me, this 6th

day of _June_ ___ 1901.

George W Morgan

Notary Public 177, N.Y. Co.
~~Commissioner of Deeds~~

1. Committee of Fifteen investigator Max Moskowitz's report of 8 James Street, which notes another investigator who worked with him and briefly describes how they were solicited. (Max Moskowitz, Disorderly House Report, 8 James Street, 5 June 1901, box 4, folder "Precinct 5: James Slip–84 James Street," Committee of Fifteen records, Manuscripts and Archives Division, The New York Public Library, Astor, Lenox, and Tilden Foundations.)

forms were supposed to reflect their shared experience. For example, the forms required the investigators to pay the prostitutes or the madams in the presence of the investigating partner.

The final section of the form, reserved for "Remarks," is only nine lines long, and most investigators wrote pat, routine comments. In nearly all of the reports about tenement house prostitution, the investigators simply noted that they paid the required amount either to the prostitute or the madam in the presence of their investigating partner. One investigator would make a note of being taken to a private room by the prostitute, who would expose "her person" for "prostitutional" purposes. The investigator would then report declining the offer. His investigative partner's role was to note that he saw his partner head upstairs with a woman. His report recounted his experience downstairs while his partner was upstairs, often noting that other women were taking men upstairs, or that a madam was accepting payments or making change. Once the partners regrouped, they headed out to the next brothel and repeated the routine.

A particularly illuminating example came from Committee of Fifteen investigators E. C. Becherer and J. W. Earl in 1901. While out for a stroll, these two men encountered two French prostitutes, Carmen Gravier and Celia Husson, who solicited them in front of the Metropolitan Opera House. Becherer's report explained that he and Earl accepted the women's invitation to return to their apartment building at 563 Seventh Avenue. According to Becherer's report, the men each paid three dollars to the women in one another's presence. The women disrobed and exposed "their persons" to the investigators. Becherer "made an excuse that [he] was sick and was going to a drug store and Earl said that he would go with me."[33] The two men never returned to the apartment; Earl's report corroborated Becherer's story.

In essence, the investigators' data served as raw material for the staff of the Committee of Fifteen. When Morgan and his colleagues on the Committee found particularly disturbing or egregious cases, such as the one in Becherer's and Earl's reports, they turned the reports into affidavits, which Morgan used to build a legal case against offenders. Morgan translated the raw material of the Disorderly Tenement House forms, employing legal language.

The affidavits that reinterpreted Becherer and Earl's experience offer a different understanding of the evening's events. Once Morgan put the story into starkly legal terms, assigning blame and culpability, the figure of the undercover investigator vanished. In general, all of the affidavits in the Committee of Fifteen's records are nearly identically worded, with specific details, like names and addresses, merely plugged in. For example, Becherer's affidavit, after "being duly sworn," stated that Becherer was twenty-nine years old and lived at 42 W. 129th Street in Manhattan. He gave his occupation as simply "investigator." After stating that the events occurred in the city and county of New York, the affidavit established the commonly accepted definition of a tenement apartment building:

> That a certain structure or building in the City of New York, Borough of Manhattan, known and designated on the map thereof as Number Five Hundred and sixty-three Seventh Avenue, and so numbered, wherein apartments in

suite are rented, leased, let or hired out, to be occupied, and are occupied as the home or residence of three or more families living independently of each other, and doing their cooking upon the premises, and having a common right in the halls and stairways therein, the yard or yards appurtenant there to, and the water closets or privies therein, or some of them, is a tenement house.[34]

This wording established that the building was a tenement house and therefore that the incident in question was a violation of the Tenement House Law, creating the legal basis from which the Committee of Fifteen could file a complaint. By setting the complaints in the context of violations of a particular law, the Committee of Fifteen avoided the moral valences of the issue.

The affidavit explained that Becherer and Earl were "accosted by two women" and then "invited by the said women to, and together with, and under the direction and guidance of the said women, did accompany the said women to and into the above mentioned tenement house." The violation was not simply that the women were soliciting; it was that they were soliciting in a tenement house. The investigators' sworn statements noted that these apartments were used "as a house of ill fame or assignation or a house or place for persons to visit for unlawful sexual intercourse, and for lewd, obscene and indecent purposes, as a bawdy house, a house of prostitution or disorderly house, in contravention of and contrary to the peace, good morals and dignity of the people of the State of New York." The two women, "whom deponent denominates and styles Jane Doe and Harriet Roe," were "lewd, lascivious, obscene and indecent characters, prostitutes, disorderly persons and vagrants, who . . . were plying and did ply their avocation of prostitution in the said suite of apartments." By doing so, Jane Doe and Harriet Roe were guilty of violating "the terms and provisions of Chapter 334, Section 141, Title 3, of the Laws of the State of New York, commonly known and designated as the Tenement House Law."[35]

In the next section, the affidavit detailed the methods of the Committee's investigators: "That deponent and the said Earl thereupon assented to said solicitation by said women respectively, and thereupon, and in the presence and sight of each other, deponent and the said Earl severally paid to the said women respectively said stated price of Three Dollars as a condition precedent to deponent and said Earl severally having sexual intercourse with the said women respectively." It goes on to explain how, after money changed hands, each woman removed her clothes and then "laid herself, in the aforesaid nude or partially nude condition, upon a bed in the last mentioned room in the presence and sight of deponent." Upon exposing their naked bodies, the women "by word of mouth . . . offered her body to, urged and tempted deponent to there and then have sexual intercourse with her, which offer, urging and tempting of and by the said woman deponent thereupon and there declined to accept or accede to."[36] The affidavit stated that, after Earl declined the woman's invitation to engage in sexual congress, the two investigators left the premises. The issue is made clear: the owner permitted "lewd, lascivious, obscene, and indecent characters" to solicit in his building. This process allowed the Committee of Fifteen to appear modern and scientific, not like moralizing meddlers.

What the investigators' Disorderly Tenement House forms sometimes revealed, however, and which the affidavits omitted, was that investigators would get "worked up" by these same "indecent characters." To get the prostitutes to commit violations, Committee of Fifteen undercover investigators had to pay the women. It was not enough for the investigators merely to be solicited; the woman had to take the money and remove her clothes for the exchange to count as a violation. The Committee of Fifteen's methods made their investigators participants in the very violations they were charged with eliminating.[37] For example, investigators Max Moskowitz, Arthur E. Wilson, and Jacob Kreiswirth filed reports of their investigation of 8 James Street. Each of the three investigators reported similar information of the encounter, and together their reports are typical of the information returned to the Committee of Fifteen by their operatives. Moskowitz's report stated

> In company with Mr. A. E. Wilson and J. Kreiswirth, we were solicited by a woman, who seeing us pass called us in. . . . The woman whom solicited us we found to be the madame, and the wife of Mr. Charley Kramer, as she informed us that the said gentleman owned and ran the house. After the first round of treats the madame asked us each to go upstairs with a girl; we told her to wait, and after two more rounds of drinks, in the meantime a new girl having come in, Mr. Wilson and Mr. Kreiswirth each went up with a girl. The madame asked me to go upstairs with the remaining girl, but I declined.[38]

Moskowitz remained downstairs to orchestrate a longer conversation with this Mrs. Kramer. His role in the investigative team was to gather additional information regarding the conditions and administration of the disorderly house. The madam told Moskowitz that the house was not under police protection, which meant that it was subject to police raids. She explained, however, that once Mr. Kramer received "some protection," she expected to get "nice girls in the place."[39] Moskowitz discovered that the police department's system of graft and corruption was in full operation in this neighborhood, and that even those bound to uphold the law could not be trusted to act in that capacity.

While Moskowitz was downstairs chatting about police protection and nice girls, Wilson headed upstairs with one of the prostitutes. He reported that the girl took him to her room and "asked . . . for one dollar." Wilson paid her the money, then "she stripped herself of her clothes, laid on the bed and offered herself to me for prostitutional purposes. She said that she had the monthly but it would be all right for me to stay with her." Wilson wrote that he "told her [he] would call again" another time, and then he "excused" himself "from having sexual intercourse and left her room and went down to the parlor where the madame was."[40] Wilson's role in the investigative team was to ascertain whether the women in this house were actually selling sex, which would indicate that the Kramers violated the Tenement House Law. Despite the fact that the investigator paid the prostitute for intercourse, he forfeited that money when he fabricated his excuse and left before sexual contact occurred. In a small way, the Committee of Fifteen financially supported the commercial sex it intended to eradicate.

Kreiswirth, the third investigator on this team, also went upstairs with a girl. His report corroborated Moskowitz's; the madam told him that she did not have "many girls in the place, but as soon as Mr. Chas. Kramer has police protection she will have more girls."[41] Between these three investigators' reports, the Committee had sufficient information to pursue legal action against Charles Kramer and his house of prostitution for violating the Tenement House Law.

Despite the fact that the Committee designed its forms to standardize and depersonalize its investigators' experiences, some did not always have (and therefore could not report on) an impersonal experience. What about the men whose reports did not state explicitly that they declined the prostitute's offer? For example, on September 25, 1901, L. L. Rosenbaum investigated 90 James Street with Max Moskowitz. He paid one dollar to the Italian girl who solicited him; his report explained that he proceeded down the hallway "to rear apartment. After paying . . . woman she exposed herself to me in adjoining bedroom."[42] In this report, however, written on the Disorderly Tenement House form, Rosenbaum does not state explicitly that he turned down the prostitute's offer, left the room, or anything similar. Did he have contact with her? And what of Max Moskowitz's report of 55 Oliver Street from September 25, 1901, in which he explained that a French woman solicited him, he paid her a dollar, and "she took me to the last bedroom and offered herself for prostitutional purpose"?[43] Moskowitz did not state that he told her he was "sick with the ____ ," as Charles Copeland did on August 22, 1901, or drunk and thus unable to perform; he did not state in his report that he declined her offer and left the room.[44] Albert Conklin also investigated 55 Oliver Street on August 23, 1901, and was solicited by a "Jewish American girl about 24 years of age." His report explained that Mr. Moskowitz "also took a girl to the bedroom, while I took the girl above mentioned."[45] The report ends here—without acknowledgment of a refusal, an excuse, or an exit strategy. In reports like these, silence dominated. Although other investigators remarked in a standardized way that they made up an excuse or found another way to leave the room before sexual contact occurred, these investigators failed to note how and when they left the prostitute behind. These reports, full of silences, raise the question of whether the investigators had sexual contact with these women.

John W. Earl's report of 331 E. 122nd Street represented the most extreme in this category. He explained that, "in company with [fellow investigator] Becherer," he was solicited by a prostitute on the corner of 119th Street and Third Avenue." The three returned to the tenement house where she lived; Earl watched Becherer "give her the money and proceed to the bedroom for intercourse." When this woman returned to the kitchen where Earl was sitting, he noted, "she commenced trying to work me up. I pretended I would have intercourse with her whereupon she took me to the bedroom, played with me and exposed herself, but I refused to have intercourse with her."[46] Whether Becherer had intercourse with the woman is unclear from the reports, but Earl's report suggests that it was at least a possibility. Earl, for his part, had the pleasure of being "worked up," fondled by this young woman, possibly to the point of climax, while on the job as an investigator for an organization dedicated to eliminating the "social evil." What if some of these investigators were in the practice of indulging their desires while on the job? Was this practice a conflict of interest? Did it matter to the Committee of Fifteen, so long as their investigators returned addresses that helped it to crack down on the problem?

Such examples suggested that each evening held the potential for pleasure for each investigator. At the very least, every Committee of Fifteen investigator found himself in a position to see at least one naked woman every evening he was at work, which might have served as an added incentive to perform the work. Yet the form that the Committee designed and required its investigators to fill out did not allow for the possibility that they may have indulged their sexual desires. Part of the Committee of Fifteen's rationale for constructing the form in this way was to control its labor force. And for the investigator, the act of filling out the form may have been a cleansing ritual. Because the form asked the investigators to distill their experiences into a brief narrative, investigators may have felt as if they were both purging and purifying, and may have felt shored up in their innocence, that they had engaged in these acts for the greater good. Others probably felt they were getting away with something; they were getting paid to have sex, and someone else was footing the bill for the elicit encounters.

The methods of the Committee of Fifteen, as enacted by the undercover investigators, then, were not as morally infallible as its board members imagined; the Committee of Fifteen, however, clearly had the strength of legitimacy on its side, supplied by the affidavits, forms, and citations of legal codes. Yet all of this meant little without the "unofficial" powers of the undercover investigators, who were largely "invisible" and kept the Committee out of the newspapers, unlike the more public raiding technique. The employment of investigators permitted the Committee to get inside the neighborhoods and their cultural habits and reveal the "truth" and "authenticity" of these situations. Investigation begged for a certain amount of local knowledge, a sense of the logic by which not only the city but also the neighborhoods functioned—block by block, and building by building. In this sense, Jewish and Italian neighborhoods were easy. Settlement houses were located in and ministered to eastern and southern European immigrant communities; members of the Committee of Fifteen enjoyed professional relationships with settlement house workers, which yielded connections to these ethnic groups. Other neighborhoods, however, defied the Committee of Fifteen's methodology.

When a detailed letter from the Young Men's Chinese Christian Association arrived at the Committee of Fifteen's office, its members were stunned by the explanation of how Chinatown organized its gambling syndicate. According to the letter, "Each table pays $10 per week to Tom Lee, the ex-Mayor of Chinatown, for protection and also an extra $1 each table to the Chinese Yue Mason Society which meets at #16 Pell Street Top floor. The policy shop pays $12 per week and the money is collected every Sunday afternoon or evening by a Chinaman named Lee Won who is related to Tom Lee." The letter's writer concluded: "These games are run openly without any fear of the Police." Attached to this letter was a "complete list of Gambling and Policy Shops of Chinatown," including "the names of the proprietors and number of tables operated."[47]

The Committee found this specialized information in and of itself useful; the list not only revealed some of the hidden secrets of Chinatown's

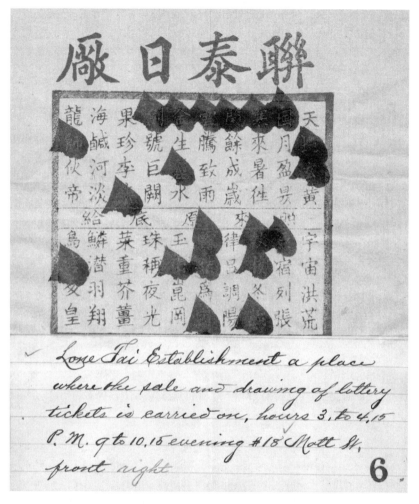

2. Quan Yick Nam conducted reconnaissance walks through Chinatown for the Committee of Fifteen and filed dozens of reports. (Quan Yick Nam, Lone Tai gambling establishment report, box 4, folder "Precinct 6: 12 Chatham Square–52 Mott Street," Committee of Fifteen records, Manuscripts and Archives Division, The New York Public Library, Astor, Lenox, and Tilden Foundations.)

gambling syndicate, but it also hinted at the underground political and economic organization of the neighborhood and the many overlapping circuits of power and politics in immigrant New York. The Chinese Masons, also known as the On Leong tong, was the strongest of the Chinatown gangs, and Tom Lee was the president.[48] By naming names, the Chinese Christian men laid bare the system of protection in Chinatown: in addition to paying the police, gambling parlor operators paid money to gangs. The information provided by the YMCA was later confirmed by Quan Yick Nam, a resident of Chinatown who worked as an informant and interpreter for the police in the Sixth Precinct.[49] Quan Yick Nam also wrote several unsolicited letters to the Committee (and he was eventually brought on officially), informing them of the locations and proprietors of various gambling parlors and other vice resorts, many of them located inside tenement apartment buildings.[50]

Without Quan Yick Nam and the men of the Chinese YMCA, the Committee of Fifteen would not have become involved in Chinatown's problems. These informants provided the Committee of Fifteen with valuable and startling information. The Committee attempted to use their letters to guide investigations in Chinatown but quickly ran up against the problem of access to what was an insular subculture. The Committee's white ethnic investigators could not gain admission to the buildings that housed Chinatown's gambling parlors, opium dens, or brothels to evaluate whether they violated the Tenement House Law. The Committee needed someone to guide their investigators through the neighborhood's lures and snares, someone who would remove suspicion from their white ethnic investigators. Little did the Committee's members know that when they agreed to help in Chinatown, they opened a Pandora's box of long-standing rivalries, violence, and intra-ethnic conflict.

In the late nineteenth century, as New York City's Chinatown grew, so did negative impressions of its residents. One prime example comes from Frank Moss, counsel to the Society for the Prevention of Crime, trustee of the City Vigilance League, and president of the New York Board of Police, who acquired intimate knowledge of Chinatown during his investigations for the Lexow Committee. In his multivolume work *The American Metropolis*, published in 1897, Moss described a Chinatown that likely matched his curious readers' impressions—and confirmed their worst fears. He explained:

> In Chinatown live some eight hundred Chinamen, with a varying number of degraded white women. There are about fifty stores, but how many gambling, lottery and opium dens there are, only the Chinamen and the police who . . . protect . . . them can tell, and you may be sure they will not tell. Here live many Chinamen who have no visible means of support. . . . Dingy Doyer and Pell Streets are filled with throngs quietly chattering, slipping in and out of doorways, and pattering up and down stairs. . . . The doors [are] watched by wary sentinels, and the flaming posters in Chinese characters, are sufficient to inform all, except certain thick-witted, blue clad personages, that the Chinamen are engaged in their national vices, regardless of the law of the land.[51]

This negative impression was fostered, in large part, by the real increase in New York's Chinese population in the wake of federal anti-Chinese legislation. In 1882, the U.S. Congress passed the Chinese Exclusion Act, the first racially based immigration act in U.S. history (which was set to expire ten years later, in 1892). Paradoxically, New York City's Chinese population increased after passage of the Exclusion Act—from 2,000 in 1882 to 7,000 by 1900—when many Chinese men living in California migrated east, to New York, which had a small and established Chinese community and no history of violence against the Chinese.

In addition, Chinese immigrants who arrived before the Exclusion Act were sojourners—men who came for a short period of time with the intention of making money and returning home. As a result, they tended to come alone, leaving their wives and families in China. After passage of the Exclusion Act, Chinese men already in the United States were not permitted to bring their wives and families over to join them, and as a result, Chinatowns throughout the United States developed as "bachelor societies"—communities without wives, children, and extended families. By 1900, there were fewer than two hundred Chinese women in New York City.[52] Chinatowns throughout the United States evolved as insular communities with their own hierarchies and modes of association.

Three principal types of organizations developed in American Chinatowns: surname associations, regional associations, and secret societies. The surname and regional associations functioned as mutual aid societies, with membership in the former restricted to persons with a particular name, and in the latter to those from a particular region. These organizations assisted their members in finding employment or housing, and granted loans or funeral expenses. They also provided legal defense for members. Finally, there were the secret societies, also called Triad lodges or tongs, which did not depend on family or regional ties for membership; they merely required their members to undergo a secret initiation ritual.[53] The men who joined tongs tended to come from weak surname or regional associations. Lower-class Chinese men were not only discriminated against by American economic and social institutions, but they were also excluded by elements of a hierarchical Chinatown community. Therefore, tong membership was aided by these other forms of exclusion.

Membership in tongs and participation in the illegal economies of gambling, opium, or prostitution became important avenues of upward mobility for Chinese men of lower-class standing. Moreover, because these enterprises were not legal, the tongs relied on their secretive connections and exploited the bonds among their members to keep their businesses going. For example, a portion of the tongs' profits went toward paying off Tom Lee, who paid protection money to the police on behalf of those who were running gambling parlors.[54] Ultimately, the tongs provided economic opportunities for some Chinese immigrants. More important, in the context of exclusion that prevailed in early twentieth-century New York City, the tongs appealed to the needs of lonely and marginalized men.[55]

Despite the legitimate psychological needs served by the tongs, these groups were dangerous and unpredictable bands of disenfranchised men who solved problems through abduction, extortion, and, as necessary, murder. Contemporary racist attitudes toward the Chinese aside, New York City's Chinatown was in reality an intermittently dangerous place, and the evidence on the Hip Sing and On Leong tongs attests to the fact that these organizations were sporadically violent and criminal.[56]

Chinatown, however, never appeared on the Committee of Fifteen's radar until the unsolicited letters from the Chinese YMCA began to arrive in spring 1901. How could they—a group of white business- and clergymen affiliated with the chamber of commerce and interested in "good government"—gain access to Chinatown's underground? Chinatown, as a geographic and cultural space, posed several problems for these activists. They could not control it, and as white men of social standing and refined backgrounds, they could not "see" it for themselves. They would not be permitted access to its insular spaces, maintained by and for Chinese gang members. Therefore, the Committee of Fifteen had to use undercover investigators, and those investigators needed to be accompanied by someone with credentials and stature within the Chinatown community.

The Committee quickly realized that it needed the help of Chinese native informants and neighborhood insiders. Some members of the Chinese community wanted to open up Chinatown to the rest of the city, perhaps out of a desire to wrest control of the neighborhood, its businesses, and its other activities from the tongs and other illegal syndicates. Chinese merchants, as they came to rely more on the tourist trade for their economic success, increasingly resisted the power of the local tongs and their extortive practice of collecting "protection" money. Eventually a turning point was reached among residents of Chinatown, and a decision had to be made: Would the neighborhood support a "legitimate" tourist industry that peddled tea and chop suey to white visitors? Or would gambling, prostitution, and opium form the economic backbone of the community? The neighborhood could not physically accommodate both, because the more dangerous aspects of the illegal economy kept away the customer base of the legitimate tourist trade . It was not until 1913 that, collectively, Chinatown's merchants were sufficiently strong to suppress the activities of the tongs.[57] In the interim, there were a few outside efforts—including that conducted by the Committee of Fifteen—to suppress the tongs and their gambling syndicates.

To the Committee of Fifteen, Chinatown's underground economy was especially opaque, not only because of race and language barriers but because of other cultural differences. Local tongs maintained gambling parlors for Chinese men, not white men. Indeed, the gambling parlors employed a lookout whose job was to keep out white men and women, "unless vouched for" by a trusted friend, and to warn of the arrival of the police.[58] Moreover, the games themselves baffled white investigators because they were not "American" games, such as policy or betting on horses. If an investigator managed to get past the doormen and into these Chinese gambling parlors, he could never pass as a denizen because he did not know how to play the popular Chinese games of *pak kop piu* or fan-tan.[59] Even Chinatown resident Quan Yick Nam, who was known throughout Chinatown as a police informant, could only walk the streets on reconnaissance missions and provide lists of addresses that might harbor opium dens or gambling parlors; even he could not solve the problem of access for the Committee.

Here is where the *lobbygow*, or tour guide, became vital to the Committee of Fifteen's efforts in Chinatown.[60] For decades, tour guides had led New York City's middle class through the wretched and rundown tenement districts. Slumming parties first evolved as a way for respectable New Yorkers to experience the titillating and horrifying sights of the Five Points tenement district, but it was not until Charles Dickens visited New York City in 1841 that slumming became a fashionable pastime.[61] Often headed by police escorts, these slumming parties ventured into the immigrant quarters to see how the other half lived.

By the late nineteenth century, slumming had become an acceptable form of entertainment for white visitors to Chinatown. Many slummers preferred to explore Chinatown with a guide who could take them to all of the neighborhood's dives and resorts. In response to this demand, white gangsters, in cooperation with Chinese gang members, developed small tour-guiding outfits. These *lobbygows* promised to escort slummers and tourists through the alleys and winding seventeenth-century streetscape of Chinatown so they could observe the shocking displays of decadence and human depravity.[62] The guides set up fake opium dens, staged fights, identified any white woman on the street as a "slave wife," and pointed out other curiosities to the tourists.[63] As a consequence, the Chinatown New Yorkers thought they knew was actually a lurid spectacle that had been created for their consumption, which in turn fostered the sense that the place was badly in need of being cleaned up.

In addition to leading slumming parties, *lobbygows* occupied an interesting and overlooked position in the realm of social activism. For example, the members of the Chinese YMCA pointed to the fact that there was a gambling problem in Chinatown. The YMCA, however, could not assist the Committee in getting its investigators past the tongs' sentries and into Chinatown vice resorts because they themselves would not have been welcome. So when Wong Aloy and Wong Get, Chinese interpreters and members of an influential organization in Chinatown, contacted the Committee of Fifteen's George Wilson Morgan and offered to "furnish 5 or 8 of [their] best entrusted large and able bodied Chinamen" to accompany the Committee's appointed investigators through the neighborhood, Morgan jumped at the opportunity. This level of access would give his investigators (and, by extension, the Committee) the opportunity to collect the necessary evidence that could be rolled into affidavits; little did Morgan know that he was stepping into a maelstrom.

Morgan selected Arthur E. Wilson to journey through Chinatown's dens of iniquity. In March 1901, Arthur Wilson and another investigator, Mr. Rogers, headed to Chinatown to rendezvous with their new Chinese friend, Wong Aloy. Aloy promised Wilson an exciting evening, complete with visits to gambling parlors, opium dens, and brothels. Wilson and Rogers arrived at Wong Aloy and Wong Get's office on the appointed evening, where Aloy and several of his guards were waiting for them. "These Chinese friends" went ahead of the group to various gambling parlors and other resorts to give the "signal . . . at the places named in this report" so that when Wilson, Rogers, and Aloy arrived, "the Chinese [invited them] into each house." Wilson was relieved that "none of the Chinese inhabitants or residents of Chinatown suspected or surmised anything wrong [with the presence of two white men]" and was pleased that they "were conducted through the gambling houses" with ease.[64]

After doing a little gambling, Wilson and Rogers "saw the way the Chinese visited the [white] girls in these houses, went into the rooms occupied by these girls, were solicited by them." Wilson met Annie Gilroy, a white prostitute and opium addict, who lived and worked in Chinatown. She made Wilson an interesting offer: "If you wanted to go to an opium den where society women from the uptown districts [and] women from families of refinement [spend time], I would be pleased to take you and your friends." Gilroy had only one stipulation: "Wong Aloy [must] be with the party."[65] Arthur Wilson made several important discoveries that evening. Most important, he discovered that alliance with Wong Aloy was a powerful method for battling what his employers considered vice. Because of *lobbygow* Wong Aloy, Wilson was above suspicion and thus gathered the evidence the Committee of Fifteen needed to prosecute a number of offenders.

In addition to accompanying investigators to Chinatown gambling parlors, Wong Aloy and Wong Get regularly sent lists of Chinatown gambling houses to the Committee of Fifteen. In their first letter, they explained that they wished "to destroy the gambling houses and stop [their] countrymen from being robbed by Chinese expert gamblers, also of having police levy tribute and blackmail upon gambling and houses of prostitution." Most of the addresses they provided were Mott Street locations that paid "$10 per week to Tom Lee for police protection." Clearly, Wong Aloy and Wong Get were paragons of virtue, men who shared the Committee of Fifteen's worldview. Or were they?

Although the Committee members welcomed Wong Aloy and Wong Get's information as valuable and congratulated themselves for entering uncharted territory, they remained unaware of the power differentials and prejudices within the Chinatown community. As it happened, Wong Get was the head of the Hip Sing tong, a crime syndicate that operated several opium dens, gambling parlors, and brothels in Chinatown. Moreover, Wong Get held a long-standing grudge against Tom Lee, head of the rival On Leong tong. To Chinatown residents, their enmity was legendary, but the Committee of Fifteen's members were oblivious to the background, politics, and vendettas in Chinatown. Despite their influence and power in their own social and political circles, they were naïve when it came to Chinatown.

Starting in the 1880s, Tom Lee worked to consolidate his power and become recognized as the "mayor of Chinatown"—by insiders and outsiders alike. His reputation stemmed from earlier work outside the neighborhood; as it turned out, Tom Lee was an important Tammany Hall ally and was responsible for rounding up Chinatown's handful of eligible voters on Election Day.[66] In 1880, through his growing connections to "official" political power, Lee was appointed a deputy sheriff of New York County.[67] He wore his sheriff's badge on his chest, strutted around Chinatown, personally raided gambling parlors, and demanded protection payments to keep the police out.[68] That same year, Lee and a small group of friends founded the On Leong tong, or Chinese Freemasons, to promote "friendship, brotherly love and service to the Supreme Being by mutual succor in distress and aid in sickness, poverty, adversity, and affliction."[69] The On Leong tong became New York's largest and strongest tong. And Tom Lee's connections and personality led many prominent white New Yorkers to believe that the On Leong tong was a "meritorious organization" whose membership was comprised of "most of the merchants of Chinatown." Tom Lee had started an effective public relations campaign, one that painted his rivals, the Hip Sings, as criminals, and his organization as one that sought "to encourage and promote good order and . . . respect to the laws of the land and city which gives the Chinamen hospitality and protection."[70]

Chinatown's gambling parlor operators were not going to stand idly by and allow Lee to extort money from them and not provide the promised protection in return, so they filed a complaint against Lee with the district attorney. Lee's subordinates moved quickly, threatening those who had filed affidavits with physical harm, and the case quickly fell apart. Through his connections to city politicians, Tom Lee consolidated his power in the illegitimate and underground gambling economy in Chinatown by being the local force who could keep the police out—or send them in—entirely at his discretion.

In 1894, several years before his relationship with the Committee of Fifteen, Wong Get had opened a fan-tan parlor. Fan-tan was a popular game among the Chinese, but more important, it was lucrative for its operators. In fan-tan, a large pile of coins was placed on a table. The coins were then removed, four at a time, until no more than four remained. Gamblers placed bets on how many coins would be left on the table, and those who guessed correctly won three dollars a round. The fan-tan operators made a 7 percent commission per bet.[71]

Shortly after the opening, Tom Lee approached Wong Get, demanding a $16-a-week payment to keep the police from raiding the establishment, and threatened him with violence if he did not comply. Wong Get paid the fee to Lee for four weeks, but the police raided his establishment anyway. In his testimony before the Lexow Committee, Wong Get alleged that "Detective Farrington broke in the door and destroyed the furniture." Wong Get appealed to Tom Lee for redress and asked why he was paying protection "if he was to suffer in that way from police interference." Tom Lee promised to intervene on Wong Get's behalf, and later that day, Farrington returned to Wong Get's fan-tan parlor "with a screwdriver and himself put the door which he had broken down back on its hinges." Farrington refused, however, to reimburse Wong Get for the table or the fan-tan chips he had destroyed.[72]

Dissatisfied with this resolution, Wong Get decided to challenge Tom Lee's position in Chinatown. To further his cause, Wong Get formed an alliance in 1900 with Mock Duck, a fearsome gangster and master gambler known as the "terror of Chinatown." In 1901, Mock Duck approached Tom Lee and threw down the gauntlet: Lee must pay Mock Duck "half interest in the gambling privileges of Chinatown, or prepare to fight."[73] Although many in Chinatown avoided tangling with Mock Duck (mostly because of his reputation for closing his eyes and firing his gun indiscriminately when he was mad), he was no match for Tom Lee, and the rest of the Chinatown community knew it. The consequence of Mock Duck's attempted power grab was an intense rivalry between the Hip Sing and On Leong tongs that raged intermittently for more than a decade.

Unfortunately for Wong Get and the Hip Sings, neither physical intimidation nor negotiation solved their Tom Lee problem. They therefore decided to enlist the help of prominent white men by assisting them in recognizing that Tom Lee was not as virtuous as he seemed. Here is where the Committee of Fifteen fit into the equation. The extensive list of gambling parlors Wong Get sent to the Committee, most of which were located on Mott Street between Pell and Doyers, were all maintained by Tom Lee or members of his organization, the On Leong tong. Wong Get, by controlling the Committee of Fifteen's access to information, now controlled which gambling houses would be investigated and when, which allowed him to cement his organization's control of gambling interests in Chinatown.

Wong Get's scheme to win the confidence of the Committee of Fifteen by convincing its members that he shared their desire to stamp out vice in Chinatown illuminates both the necessity and danger of using *lobbygows* in the investigation of gambling and prostitution in New York City's immigrant neighborhoods. Wong Get had freely offered his services to Morgan and the Committee; he made them believe that he wanted to assist them in achieving their goals. The fact that he was so willing to escort Wilson through Chinatown—ferrying him between opium dens full of white prostitutes and gambling parlors, teaching him to play fan-tan—caused the Committee's members to reasonably assume that he was honest and sincere. They could not imagine that Wong Get himself had designs for his own vice syndicate. By allying himself with the Committee's efforts, Wong Get ensured that his gambling parlors would continue to run unmolested, without the interference of Tom Lee, the police, or social activists.

The Committee of Fifteen and its undercover investigators failed to recognize Wong Get's hidden motives. Despite the use of native informants and *lobbygows* to gain access to Chinatown gambling parlors, the Committee of Fifteen and its investigators relied on assumptions about the common experience of working-class men in the city, which blinded them to the self-interest of their new Chinese allies. Their myopia was ultimately detrimental to the Committee of Fifteen's project. Without Wong Get, however, its access to the insular Chinatown community would remain limited, if not totally inaccessible.

In 1904, the Hip Sing tong tried again. Mock Duck contacted the Society for the Prevention of Crime and gave Frank Moss, counsel for the Society, addresses of On Leong gambling parlors to be raided and subsequently shut down. Then Mock Duck and Wong Get reopened those parlors under Hip Sing management. When an outraged Tom Lee explained to Moss and the Rev. Parkhurst (president of the SPC) that Mock Duck and Wong Get were taking advantage of them, he was ignored. After all, Tom Lee was a notorious criminal. Furthermore, Tom Lee had not stepped forward and offered to help the SPC clean up Chinatown, as Wong Get and Mock Duck had. This conclusion resulted in all-out warfare between the two tongs on the streets of Chinatown. The Hip Sings and On Leongs battled for control of Chinatown, and only after hundreds of shots had been fired and many killed did each agree to seek peace.

In 1906, F. F. Tong, a Chinese official studying in the United States, asked Judge Warren W. Foster of the Court of General Sessions to mediate the dispute between the Hip Sing and On Leong tongs. The American lawyers for each tong and their respective leaders came together in Foster's chambers at the Criminal Courts building, where each side was persuaded to sign a peace treaty.[74] The treaty required both sides to close their gambling parlors but permitted them to continue to collect dues from their members. Unfortunately, the peace treaty was not successful and ended up formalizing the divisions between the Hip Sings and On Leongs, especially in terms of territorial divisions. It granted Mott Street to the On Leongs and Pell Street to the Hip Sings, and Doyers was to be neutral territory. Any tong member who dared to enter the rival's territory would be "shot on sight."[75]

Neither the Committee of Fifteen nor the SPC ultimately succeeded in Chinatown. Gambling and internecine fighting continued unmolested, even after the peace treaty of 1906. In 1913, a group of Chinatown merchants formed the Chinese Peace Society. These merchants had long opposed the tongs and their tactics but to this point had been too weak to compel the tongs to arbitrate their differences. This shift of power—from the tongs to the merchants—signaled the decline of the tongs' power and the rise of the merchants'. It also signaled the rise of Chinatown as a popular tourist destination, one that offered a commodified version of "traditional" Chinese culture for the consumption of "respectable" New Yorkers.

An examination of the tactics of the Committee of Fifteen—its transition from public raiding to its reliance on undercover investigators, native informants, and *lobbygows* in particular—reveals how tense the relationship between ethnic New Yorkers and social activists was during the opening years of the twentieth century. Much was at stake on both sides. For the men of the Committee of Fifteen, the persistence of ethnic social, political, and economic power deeply threatened the tenuous hold they had on the new New York City. The elites were trying to Americanize (or New York-ize) these ethnic neighborhoods, putting the power to do so in the hands of educated professionals employed in bureaucratic positions, not just rewarding loyalty. For the members of the ethnic communities, though, the question was whether they would be able to retain power within their neighborhoods, or whether they would be cooperating with—or capitulating to—New York City's elite.

The struggle over the distribution of economic and political power and control in New York City took place at many sites, with vice being one of them. Could power and control—no matter how circumscribed—be allowed to accrue to ethnic leaders? And if so, what kind of ethnic leader? The Committee of Fifteen was part of a larger movement that defined and saw ethnic, local activity (particularly activity that occurred in Chinatown) as vice, and as contrary to the public good, even while its own actions reflected no moral purity. That the members of the Committee of Fifteen willingly engaged in the very acts they condemned suggests the extent to which, at heart, their battle against vice was actually a fight for control. The starkly ethnic lines along which such struggles took place point toward a new understanding of the importance of the intersections of local knowledge, ethnic geographies, and the trade-offs made between ethnic and elite power brokers and how these intersections shaped early twentieth-century New York City.

The Committee of Fifteen folded in 1902, following the sudden and unexpected death of its chairman, William H. Baldwin, Jr. A few years later, a similar organization constituted itself with a renewed zeal for cleaning up the "social evil" in New York. This organization, the Committee of Fourteen, inherited the records of the Committee of Fifteen. The new committee, however, failed to thoroughly study the Committee of Fifteen's records and reports. Otherwise they might have been better prepared for the risks involved in using undercover investigators.

THREE

Gender and Undercover Investigation

While working as an undercover investigator for the Committee of Fourteen, Abram Eilperin was dispatched to survey Brooklyn's Williamsburg neighborhood when he stopped into an unfamiliar bar. As soon as he walked in the door, two unknown women waved him over to their table. By way of introduction, one of the ladies declared, "Here is the girl with the big brown naval [*sic*], the cheeks of her ass is as round as a table, the color of her pussy is as red as a rose and how many fucked her christ only knows." She then invited Eilperin "to go out with her to her flat for the purpose of having sexual intercourse."[1] He quickly left the bar, but not in the company of this new lady friend. He did, however, record this experience in a report that he returned to his employers, explaining that he had identified an establishment in Brooklyn that permitted probable prostitutes to solicit in the barroom in direct violation of New York State liquor law.

Not all situations to which the Committee of Fourteen assigned investigators were so clear-cut, as T. W. Veness and Natalie Sonnichsen discovered during their visits to the Harlem River Casino. Immediately upon crossing the threshold, Veness and Sonnichsen determined that the place was "indecent." Veness judged the dance floor to be too small and "much too crowded for decent dancing." As a consequence, the dancers engaged in physically intimate and sexually suggestive dances, such as "the 'nigger,' with some spieling and the 'shivers.'" His report continued, remarking on the "moral degeneracy among the participants." The young women appeared particularly lascivious, "dressed mainly as cheap chorus girls, swimming girls, Buster Browns with bare limbs in evidence." Veness concluded that "as a whole the dance was utterly and superlatively rotten."[2]

Two weeks later, Sonnichsen and Veness returned to the Harlem River Casino to assess its progress (or decline). Sonnichsen observed excessive

drinking and "general rowdyism," which she noted in her report. She, like
Veness, found the young women's attire noteworthy: "Two girls [wore] very
tight knickers." Another young woman "had a very décolleté costume with
practically no sleeves, tights, with very short and skimpy knickers." In addition to the women's revealing clothing, "the character of the dancing
steadily grew worse as time went on. What would happen toward 5 a.m.
it is unpleasant to conjecture."[3] When Sonnichsen and Veness left the Harlem River Casino at two in the morning, the crowd had yet to slow down.
The investigators had not encountered any clear-cut liquor law violations,
however, just behavior they found distasteful. So what precisely was the
problem at the Harlem River Casino other than a preponderance of women
with questionable taste in clothing?

The increasing presence of working-class and immigrant women in public (as workers and as consumers) greatly concerned the newly constituted
Committee of Fourteen because its members considered women's behavior
a harbinger of the city's overall decline. By the first decade of the twentieth century, "ordinary" working-class women—not just "mean" women or
prostitutes—were fixtures in the saloons, dance halls, and cabarets throughout the city (and in most cases, their business was being courted). The Committee of Fourteen wanted to protect these women from the dangers lurking
in such places by restricting their access to leisure establishments, and it did
so by taking interpretation and implementation of New York State liquor
laws into its own hands. It compiled and regularly updated what it called
a Protest List of places that allegedly violated excise laws. This method depended heavily on the use of undercover investigators and the creation of a
new awareness among proprietors and saloon keepers that those investigators were everywhere and saw everything.

The class standing and background of the Committee of Fourteen's members influenced their perceptions of women in public. Its members—largely
white, native-born, middle-class, and Protestant—failed (or refused) to
understand the logic of working-class sociability. They sought to strictly
enforce the provisions of the liquor law, which restricted women from entering bars without male chaperones. Legislators and social activists alike
believed that unaccompanied women went to bars for one reason only:
to solicit men. Many immigrant cultures, however, Irish and German in
particular, considered it perfectly acceptable for women to be in saloons
without male companions.[4]

Moreover, by the early twentieth century, the landscape of commercial
leisure had changed tremendously. The array of amusements available to
the average person was unprecedented, and the cost was democratically

low. A nickel bought a ticket to the moving picture show, where the marquee's dancing lights, promising images of Rudolph Valentino, Mary Pickford, or Lillian Gish, held moviegoers in thrall. Twenty-five cents bought admission to any number of resorts that served dinner, featured live musical entertainment, and offered dancing instruction to neophytes. Without parents around, immigrant and working-class daughters and sons experimented with their sexuality in these venues—through dancing, by sneaking off to a secluded park, or by tiptoeing into the restrooms for nuzzling. Coney Island, dance halls, chop suey houses, moving picture palaces, theaters in midtown Manhattan—in all of these places, young women claimed space and liberation from the world of their parents (and the Committee of Fourteen and its cohort).[5]

Investigators like Eilperin, Veness, and Sonnichsen experienced, perceived, and then represented working-class leisure culture as debauched and immoral, however. The Committee instructed its undercover investigators to look for "tell-tale signs" of moral decline—such as couples dancing in the vernacular style or women swearing, smoking, or wearing too much makeup—to which it assigned a particular meaning. The Committee of Fourteen's undercover investigators levied judgments against the young women they encountered and, through the act of writing their reports, transformed them into moral risks, prostitutes, and myriad other dangerous types. A young woman could live with her parents, attend a house of worship regularly, and be sexually pure, but if an undercover investigator spotted her in a cabaret wearing dark lipstick and lifting her skirt above her knees while smoking a cigarette, she was the equivalent of a whore—and the establishment in which she was found was labeled "disorderly."

Prowling through the city's hotels, saloons, cabarets, brothels, and other assorted resorts in search of "disorder," undercover investigators, through their detailed reports, formed the Committee's picture of conditions in any given establishment. The Committee's combination of undercover investigators and the Protest List system succeeded in creating fear among proprietors that the Committee had eyes and ears everywhere; in this way, the Committee created a new mode of self-policing behavior, a governmentality, among proprietors, their employees, and their patrons. This tactic, based on fear and economic incentives, pushed proprietors into abiding by the Committee's definitions of disorderliness and moral behavior in order to stay in business. The Committee's definition of moral behavior, however, often conflicted with that of immigrant and working-class New Yorkers, who were part of an emergent commercial leisure culture that did not revolve around traditional modes of sociability, such as the family parlor.

Committee members were reaching back to a lost moment in time—one that never actually existed—when women did not work outside of the home and were not found in saloons, and when prostitutes were hidden away from public view in well-appointed brothels.

———————————

In January 1905, three years after the Committee of Fifteen folded, the Anti-Saloon League organized a luncheon to bring together concerned members of New York City's social activist, business, and religious communities to evaluate the ongoing negative effects of the Raines law on the city. The successful summit prompted the City Club to organize a follow-up conference to discuss "appropriate legislative measures and other forms of action necessary to accomplish . . . the abolition of the 'Raines law hotels.'" From this second meeting emerged the Committee of Fourteen for the Suppression of Raines Law Hotels.[6]

Founding members of the Committee of Fourteen included influential and well-placed men and women. Among the founders were George Haven Putnam, of G. P. Putnam's Sons publishing house and former member of the Committee of Fifteen; Rabbi H. Pereira Mendes of Congregation Shearith Israel and the Kehillah; Rev. William Adams Brown, Presbyterian minister and professor at Union Theological Seminary; Lawrence Veiller, secretary of the City Club; Rev. Howard H. Russell, superintendent of the Anti-Saloon League; and Thomas H. Reed, secretary of the Anti-Saloon League (and the first secretary of the Committee of Fourteen). Francis M. Burdick, law professor at Columbia University and president of the Morningside and Riverside Heights Association, was a founding member, as was the Hon. William S. Bennet, a congressman who later coauthored the Mann (White-Slave Traffic) Act of 1910, a candidate for governor of New York State in 1912, and an early supporter of the National Association for the Advancement of Colored People. Mary Kingsbury Simkhovitch from the Greenwich House, and the only woman on the original committee, represented settlement house workers. In 1907, the Committee expanded, adding a Subcommittee on Investigation, staffed by Simkhovitch, Frances Kellor (sociologist, resident of the Henry Street Settlement house, and founder in 1905 of the National League for the Protection of Colored Women), and Ruth Standish Baldwin (cofounder, with Dr. George Edmund Haynes, of the Committee on Urban Conditions among Negroes and widow of William H. Baldwin, Jr., chairman of the defunct Committee of Fifteen).[7] These women conducted research on city laws and neighborhood conditions, and provided the Committee with crucial connections to other settlement house workers, social work organizations, and philanthropists.

The Reverend John P. Peters, vice president of the Morningside and Riverside Heights Association and pastor at St. Michael's Episcopal Church, became the first chairman of the Committee of Fourteen. He was largely responsible for recruiting and bringing Frederick H. Whitin on as the Committee's executive secretary in 1906. Whitin was a Columbia University graduate and a resident of the Upper West Side; he had been a member of the City Club and served on its board of trustees for over a decade, and worked for the New York State Board of Elections. Whitin served as executive secretary of the Committee until his sudden death by a heart attack on the streets of midtown Manhattan in July 1926. Raymond Fosdick, who worked for the Rockefeller-funded Bureau of Social Hygiene and regularly collaborated with the Committee, described Whitin as a "happy warrior" against prostitution and commercialized vice in New York City.[8]

Like its predecessor the Committee of Fifteen, the Committee of Fourteen identified the Raines law as the genesis of many of the city's problems. According to Chairman John P. Peters, the Raines law was "an honestly intended law," but it had unintentionally produced rampant Sunday sales and created a symbiotic relationship between saloon keepers and prostitutes. Peters explained that "if from the outset [the law] had been enforced by well-trained, capable and honest officials, without regard to party politics, primarily as a police measure . . . it might have produced very good results." The law, however, had become primarily a source of revenue and, as such, had turned "the excise commissioner [into] a mere peddler of licenses. His business was to sell as many licenses as possible and to secure as much revenue for the state as possible." Because the licensing process was an important revenue source for the state, rather than a regulatory measure, it "permit[ted] . . . as many saloons as could be called into existence." Moreover, according to Peters, once a saloon had a license, "no [subsequent] inspection was made to ascertain whether . . . it was being run according to the terms of the law."[9]

Whereas the Committee of Fifteen had argued that Raines law hotels needed to be eliminated because of their negative impact on "moral imbeciles," Peters, Whitin, and their colleagues on the Committee of Fourteen claimed that the real flaw of the Raines law was that there were few standards in place for licensing new saloons, and the New York State Department of Excise failed to police licensed establishments to ensure that proprietors adhered to excise law. For instance, in 1913, the state commissioner of excise had only sixty agents working throughout the entire state. The commissioner thought that, in New York City, the police force could and should enforce the liquor laws—an argument that would be repeated during national Prohibition in 1920. Both the mayor and the Committee of Fourteen disagreed, however.[10] The mayor believed that the police had larger concerns than the regulation of saloons, and the Committee of Fourteen feared that using the police to enforce liquor laws would exacerbate a system of payoffs between corrupt police officers and the proprietors of "Raines law hotels" and other excise law violators.

The Committee decided that the solution to the city's excise problems was not to be found in the prohibition of alcohol or the criminalization of prostitution; rather, it wanted to systematically regulate saloons and other leisure establishments and enforce the sections of the excise laws that suited its vision for the city. The Committee approached "vice" as a business problem and tried to avoid its emotional and moral valences. "The social evil in New York is an elaborate system fostered by business interests, a commercialized immorality, not immorality resulting from emotional demand," Peters explained. Therefore, he continued, "what must be fought is not vice per se, but vice as a gainful business."[11]

To wage that fight, the Committee of Fourteen forged cooperative relationships with the national and state brewers' associations, the Liquor Dealers' Association, and the insurance companies that bonded any establishment requesting a liquor license. The Committee provided proprietors and brewers with economic incentives (or, more accurately, disincentives) to clean up the city's barrooms. This style of partnership speaks to the remarkable powers of private organizations in the battle against perceived immorality and corruption in New York City during the Progressive Era. The Committee had abandoned hope that the police and justice system would (or even could) intervene to correct the causes and consequences of Raines law hotels—greed, corruption, and prostitution. It therefore made an end run around the law and the legislature and went straight to the source—the insurance companies and liquor dealers, who were already on the offensive against temperance organizations. Not only did the Committee of Fourteen continue and extend the style of private policing that the Committee of Fifteen had initiated, but it also developed a mode of interest group politics by approaching and accommodating business interests and forcing them to become partners in its (moral) program. The businesses worked with the Committee because it offered them a way to continue to operate. The alternative—an alcohol-free city as imagined by groups such as the Women's Christian Temperance Union and the Anti-Saloon League—was ultimately not acceptable to the Liquor Dealers' Association. The Committee's style of partnership thus succeeded where "morals legislation" would not.

New York State excise law required that all saloons be bonded and insured before the Department of Excise would issue a liquor license. Committee of Fourteen chairman John Peters explained that the surety companies, "by supplying the bonds for these infamous resorts," made "themselves, in a sense, partners in the vice."[12] The Brewers' Association and the Liquor Dealers' Association benefited from their collaboration with the Committee of Fourteen; it made them appear to be interested in cleaning up saloons, which insulated them from accusations by the "drys" and prohibition organizations that they were responsible for the moral decline of the citizens of New York. Whitin noted that "from self-interest [the Liquor Dealers' Association and the Brewers' Association would] support an effort which would tend to reduce the number of small, poor and scattered places (hotels) if those larger ones for which they are responsible and in which the law is generally complied with, were left undisturbed."[13]

These parties worked with the chairman and executive secretary of the Committee to draw up the Protest List, which classified establishments along three broad categories: "too disreputable to continue, needed some improvement, or was running just fine." The Committee of Fourteen then met with the Brewers' Association and the Re-Insurance Association "a month before the Excise Department renewed the year-long liquor licenses" to decide which places to close and which proprietors "needed some intimidation." The brewers and the Committee members pressured the saloon owners, and the surety companies refused to write the bonds until they received Committee of Fourteen approval.[14]

The Protest List was an ever-evolving document. The Committee of Fourteen appointed undercover investigators to visit new places and assess the progress or decline of former offenders. The investigators supplied that information, in the form of a report, to the Committee so that the Protest List could be updated. The Committee required its investigators to look for violations of excise laws. Was food served along with alcoholic beverages? Were there separate toilet facilities for men and women? Was the barroom clean? Did the bartender stop serving alcohol at 1:00 a.m.? In addition, the Committee instructed investigators to observe the behavior of the employees and the patrons. Did the waiters facilitate interactions between male and female patrons? Did the bartender recommend nearby hotels for assignations? Did the proprietor maintain beds in the back room for use by prostitutes and patrons? Any of these violations suggested that the establishment may be supporting prostitution, which could land it on the Protest List.

For example, after Abram Eilperin left the Brooklyn bar where he was solicited, he headed to a bar farther down Broadway. There he joined a woman at her table and purchased her two rounds of drinks. To show her appreciation, she "put her hand between [his] legs and said I'll bet you got some jack!" While still fondling his genitals, she asked, "Why [do] women wear black stockings?" Before Eilperin could respond, she answered: because their legs "are in mourning for all the stiffs that have been buried alive" between them.[15] She then suggested that they go to a nearby hotel and have sex. Eilperin refused. After all, she had (inadvertently) given him quite a bit of work to do. He had to fill out another report, explaining that 879 Broadway in Brooklyn allowed prostitutes to congregate in its barroom and recommending that it be placed on the Protest List.

Saloon keepers who wished to have their establishment removed from the Protest List had to comply with the Committee's disciplinary system, which included a series of humiliating lectures and promissory notes. The Committee extracted promises from the offending saloon keepers that they would control their patrons' behavior; the promissory notes were customized to fit each Protest List saloon's offensive behavior. These included agreements to ban dancing, to refuse to serve mixed-race parties, or to refuse to admit unaccompanied women. The proprietors had little choice as to the terms of these notes, as most did not have the economic or political power to resist these demands; moreover, their suppliers and insurers cooperated with the Committee. Thus the Committee, having already secured the cooperation of the brewers and the insurance companies, maintained absolute control over the relicensing process by deciding what constituted moral or immoral behavior and what, precisely, needed to be changed, monitored, or controlled in any particular establishment.

"The laws chiefly relied upon to regulate the social evil are vagrancy, disorderly persons, and keeping a disorderly house," according to the Committee of Fourteen's report on law enforcement.[16] The Committee employed the logic that the caliber and behavior of patrons indicated whether or not a place was disorderly. By putting the onus on bartenders, waiters, saloon keepers, hotel managers, or landlords, the Committee of Fourteen required them to be ever self-vigilant so that prostitutes, pimps, drug dealers, and other criminals did not use their establishment as a headquarters. Moreover, the particular laws on which the Committee relied were conveniently vague. For example:

Section 1146 of the Penal Law, as amended in 1905 . . . provides that any person who keeps such a [disorderly house] or advises or procures any woman to become an inmate of such a place is guilty of a misdemeanor. Section 899–911 of the Code of Criminal Procedure strengthens the preceding law by providing that any person is disorderly who keeps a house or place used as a resort by prostitutes, drunkards, gamesters, habitual criminals or by other disorderly persons. Section 1530 of the Penal Law, as amended in 1901, defines a public nuisance to include places which offend public decency, or injure the comfort, repose, health or safety of any considerable number of persons.[17]

The imprecision of the language in *The Penal Law* and *Code of Criminal Procedure of the State of New York* left the definition of the situation (such as what, precisely, constituted an offense to "public decency") to the discretion of the Committee of Fourteen and its undercover investigators. If, for example, Veness and Sonnichsen judged the female patrons to have "tough" appearances, or too much makeup, or unacceptably short dresses, the Committee used their reports to define the place as "disorderly," and Whitin would put the establishment on the Protest List.

Investigators working for the Committee enjoyed more latitude in imposing these judgments than did police officers. The New York Police Department's *Police Practice and Procedure Manual* warned that officers must "not attempt to judge a woman by her manner of dress. Just because she has blond hair, has her face powdered, and walks jauntily, she is not necessarily a prostitute. Many innocent girls possess such an appearance without knowing the suspicion it arouses."[18] Because the Committee's investigators did not possess the power of arrest, they did not have to be as confident about their assessments of a woman's moral character as police officers did. If an investigator incorrectly assessed a woman's moral character, the woman would not suffer the consequences, but the proprietor who allowed the woman with blond hair and powdered face to frequent his barroom might. An investigator's detailed description of an immoral woman could help the Committee of Fourteen catch a proprietor they had long pursued. The report need not be entirely true; the woman did not need to be produced as evidence or put on a witness stand. To give their position more legitimacy or credibility with offending proprietors, the Committee exploited investigators' descriptions and knowledge of popular culture when it put together the promissory notes and disciplinary lectures.

Undercover investigators, therefore, served as the foot soldiers in the Committee of Fourteen's campaign against disorderliness and immorality.

Initially, the Committee followed the lead of previous organizations, such as the Society for the Prevention of Crime and the Committee of Fifteen, and relied both on professional private investigators from a detective agency and on the work that individual members of the executive committee could conduct in the evening. For example, in November 1905, the Committee contacted William C. Dodge of Dodge's Detective Agency. He was asked to "inspect . . . all the places which are not obvious bona-fied hotels." The Committee provided Dodge with a list of hotels and instructed him to send two men out together. These detectives were directed to "obtain no legal evidence," which meant that they were not to pick up prostitutes or secure hotel rooms. They were simply to observe and then provide impressions and descriptions—"enough to show to a reasonable man that the place is disorderly."[19] These instances were classified as "observation cases."[20] In addition, the detectives were to obtain the name of the license holder and the brewer supplying the place in question. Then the Committee would approach the leaseholder or the brewer who supplied the offending place, using the investigators' information to justify punitive action.

By November 1907, Frederick H. Whitin, the newly appointed executive secretary of the Committee of Fourteen, had revised the Committee's position on using professional detectives. In a letter to Committee member William Bennet, Whitin explained that the use of "professional" investigators, such as Dodge, was unnecessary. Rather, Whitin preferred unemployed men who "could secure the necessary evidence with a little coaching. They would require little more pay than the rent of the room which room-rent would be saved to themselves."[21] Whitin even crafted a plan for the occasions when "a room was refused to a man unaccompanied by a woman companion." In such cases, "a married man out of work could be employed to take his wife with him. By occupying the room the whole night, there would be opportunity in the early hours of the morning for observation of violations which in the hours of business would arouse suspicions."[22] To Whitin's mind, anyone could gather the evidence the Committee required to move against a disorderly establishment. He was also suspicious that private detectives might not be trustworthy in that they might produce "evidence" that justified their continued employment. Even more significantly, Whitin believed that professional detectives were so corrupted by their occupation that they were less capable of discerning "offenses to public decency" than were ordinary citizens.

Whitin regarded the Committee's use of investigators as crucial to its success, although he preferred that Committee members (the secretary in particular) not "play the part of a detective."[23] During the Committee's early years, however, Whitin ended up conducting a bulk of the investigations himself. By 1912, though, he regularly encountered obstacles when he was out investigating: proprietors and patrons recognized him, and when they did, they sent word around, so that things suddenly became "clean" and "orderly." Whitin determined that he was ineffective as an investigator and could no longer serve the demands of the Protest List system. At this point, he redirected the Committee's strategy and began to cultivate and rely on a stable of temporary investigators. Whitin found it to be "more advantageous to use a large number of men on special nights of the week. This has the advantage of giving us impressions and experiences of men of different types."[24]

In fact, during the Committee of Fourteen's early years, no one worked full time as an investigator; rather, the Committee relied on a group of people, matching individuals to the place requiring investigation.[25] These people were not professional investigators, they were not specially trained for the Committee's goals, nor were they "insiders" from neighborhoods or communities, as the Committee of Fifteen had used. Rather, Whitin selected his investigators because he believed they could "pass" in particular situations or they seemed to fit the neighborhood in question. As Whitin remarked, "The ability to investigate is largely a natural one, requiring powers of observation, deduction and ability to mix with men."[26] In truth, Whitin employed persons who had experience with the New York State Department of Excise, or journalists, or individuals who had worked in settlement houses or similar social service organizations. Unlike the native informants relied on by the Committee of Fifteen, Whitin cultivated a group of investigators who possessed familiarity with the neighborhoods in question and a middle-class mindset that permitted them to "see" the problems, as well as professional skills that were helpful to the work he needed done.

Periodically, though, Whitin sent individual investigators letters commenting on the reports they handed in and offering suggestions for how they could be more useful to the Committee in the future. For instance, Whitin instructed Brooklyn investigator Hugh Doyle to "not waste as much time at a place like Cox's if as in this case, you found nothing doing."[27] Faith Habberton, who worked on the Macy's department store investigation, learned that the Committee preferred "reporting [on] the conversations which you state you overheard which show the general character of the individual and the subjects in which they are interested," rather than an assessment of the efficiency of the physical layout of the sales floor. Whitin eventually had to put "an entirely different person in the store" who, he was "hopeful," could get "closer to the life of her present associates than her predecessor." The better and more detailed reports the individual investigator returned, the more frequently that person was employed.[28]

An investigation was, above all, a performance. Investigators could not simply march into a bar, assume a dour expression, and scribble into a notebook a description of the awful things going on. Rather, the Committee of Fourteen's investigators camouflaged themselves by mimicking the attitudes and customs of the people they investigated. Clarence J. Primm, one of the Committee of Fourteen's investigators, noted that "a shabby investigator with a gum-chewing female partner, by identifying themselves with this neighborhood for a time, would be in a position to make what should be an effective and valuable study of the conduct of the places."[29] Thus, the immediate task of the undercover investigator, upon entering a bar, saloon, or dance hall, was to assess the situation without appearing to be an investigator.

The case of two female investigators for the Committee illustrates this point. Edna Arbing was dispatched to investigate several establishments in Brooklyn, but because she was an "unaccompanied" woman, she was refused service. Arbing reported, therefore, that the places on her list appeared to be law abiding (which was not necessarily the case). Maud Robinson Tombs had a more mixed experience; after being denied entrance to a couple of establishments, she succeeded in getting a seat at Shapiro's, but the waiter refused to serve her. She asked coyly, "Not just one beer?" He said no, but she persisted: "Not just one beer *with* a sandwich?" The waiter agreed to ask the proprietor and returned a few moments later with a smile and a beer. He exclaimed, "You can have *one* drink!"[30] Tombs concluded that this establishment was disorderly because they succumbed to her charms and permitted her, an unaccompanied woman, into the barroom. She noted in her report that while she was drinking her beer, she noticed that she was being "watched from an inner room by two men." As a result, she remarked, "I was very careful how I looked around and seemed interested in the cabaret—applauding it etc." Her concern was not that these men suspected her of being a prostitute but of being an investigator. Something about Tombs gave her away, but it was something ephemeral—her age, her bearing, the way she held her beer mug. Because these men were keeping her under surveillance, they impeded her ability to operate undercover.

In order to succeed, different investigators employed different techniques: some, like Eilperin in the opening vignette, opted to take a seat, order a drink, and wait for patrons to approach them. Others adopted specific poses that they supposed would yield the most information. For example, some male investigators noted that the girls in the room appeared to be "game," so they chose to "flash cash" and act like "men about town." Sometimes the crowd was exclusively male and working class, so the investigator bought a round of drinks for the bar and initiated conversations about women. In either case, the investigator fashioned a persona, drawing on a pastiche of rituals, conversation topics, and behaviors gleaned from previous investigations—about neighborhoods and other establishments, and about how people of a certain class or character behaved in such settings.

The Committee occasionally employed men who worked or had worked in the past for the Department of Excise. For instance, W. K. Van Meter, who conducted investigations for the Committee of Fourteen as an investigator in Brooklyn in 1911 and 1912, was previously employed by the New York State Department of Excise as an investigator charged with enforcing the provisions of the liquor laws.[31] Abram Eilperin came to the Committee in September 1916, also from the Department of Excise.[32] Men from the Department of Excise understood saloons in general and the vagaries of liquor licensing, so they knew how to identify and report on violations of the liquor laws. For the most part, their reports tended to be terse, citing, for example, a blocked fire exit or the absence of separate toilets for men and women. They were not inclined to spin fanciful narratives and tended not to engage as fully in the evening's events, but they could quickly identify violations of the law. In this way, former Excise Department employees were good, but better choices were available.

Because the Committee of Fourteen was particularly concerned with prostitution and sexual immorality in saloons, cabarets, and dance halls, gender was a deciding factor in the hiring and dispatching of investigators. An undercover investigator's gender dictated the pose he or she could adopt in the course of investigating and, in turn, what kind of information was available to the investigator. Whitin worked to find male investigators who met the Committee's investigative needs; the job qualifications included language skills and ethnic physical appearance or race—essentially, the ability to pass in a variety of situations. Male investigators had the opportunity to interact with women or other men during their investigative forays. When they interacted with female patrons, they tended to cross boundaries of moral behavior themselves, often becoming complicit in creating the very conditions their employers were hoping to ameliorate. In interactions with other men, their performances and poses were not about sexual availability but about chummy, homosocial behavior, which often turned on an ability to have conversations about women and sexuality.

An ethnic physical appearance was an important attribute for undercover investigators. If a man appeared to be of the same class background as well as country of origin as those under investigation, the Committee believed he would have greater access to incriminating information. Experience bore out this assumption. For example, Samuel Auerbach, a young Jewish man from the Bronx, worked frequently for the Committee of Fourteen. He typically investigated predominantly Jewish or multiethnic settings, but on one occasion he was sent to a Greek restaurant at 418 Third Avenue in Manhattan. He explained in his report that this venue was essentially a Greek club, a restaurant frequented by recent immigrant men only, at which they also received their mail. It did not employ women and did not appear to be disorderly, although it was selling liquor without a license. He also discovered that the club maintained furnished rooms upstairs for the use of patrons and prostitutes. Because this Greek restaurant was an insular operation—run by and for Greeks—it seems odd that Auerbach was able to gather this incriminating piece of information. In his report, he explained: "After having a meal I entered into conversation with a number of the patrons present and the proprietor." By presenting himself "as Greek, employed in Boston, at present passing through New York City and out for a good time," he earned the trust of the other patrons. Auerbach even went so far as to "deliver compliments" to an imaginary "John Pappas" from his equally imaginary Greek friend in Boston.[33] One clue that Auerbach passed successfully in this milieu was that the Greek patrons offered to help him find a woman for the evening. If they were unconvinced that he belonged, they would have told him nothing (at best) or chased him out (at worst), which occasionally happened to investigators who failed at passing.

Because an integral part of the investigative process involved regularly revisiting establishments on the Protest List to track their progress or decline, an additional part of the investigators' task was to meet other patrons and become "regulars," to be taken into the confidence of bartenders, waiters, and patrons. By cultivating personal relationships, investigators were able to conduct their tasks with more facility. In this way, male investigators might see under the surface and discover just how degraded a suspected "rotten joint" was. (This approach was only effective for male investigators, though, as unaccompanied female investigators were routinely denied entry.) Bartenders could introduce male investigators to "game" girls in the barroom, or offer them hotel rooms, or simply tell them about other "rotten" joints in the vicinity. The patrons proved to be an equally important source of information; moreover, the patrons were often the muscle in some of these saloons, patrolling the borders and keeping out people who were not like them—or who they just did not like.

Another investigator who worked in a number of different ethnic neighborhoods and social settings was David Oppenheim. Oppenheim was Jewish and owned a clothing store on Seventh Avenue in Manhattan.[34] Because of his fluency in Yiddish and German, he was regularly dispatched to Jewish as well as non-Jewish German neighborhoods. For example, he was sent to a number of establishments in Ridgewood, Queens—a predominantly German neighborhood—where he eavesdropped on the proprietors and patrons who spoke German. In addition, he shared confidences with a waiter by telling him "in Jewish that [his date] wasn't a prostitute but if [he] had her in the right place [he] could take her upstairs by telling her its too late to go home but if [he] took her to NY she'd want to go right home and wouldn't want to go anywheres with [him]."[35] His language skills, chummy behavior, and command of immigrant, working-class, barroom culture opened up exponentially more places to investigation for the Committee of Fourteen.

Oppenheim's report of his visit to DeFaust's in Brooklyn demonstrates how he acted "disorderly" to further his task. In his report, he noted a pretty girl at a nearby table. After she returned one of his smiles, he "wrote on piece of paper for her to give me her name and address and when I could meet her." He then gave the paper to the waiter and asked him to give it to the smiling girl. The waiter obliged. Oppenheim then noticed that the "girl then got up and went to toilet . . . when she came out she handed note to waiter which is attached to this report. It stated that she would meet me Saturday night at 8 o'clock in front of Battermans but it had no name or address on it."[36] The investigator now possessed the required evidence that DeFaust's was disorderly: a young woman responded to a man's advances, and the waiter facilitated the interaction. The Committee interpreted this information to mean that the woman was probably a prostitute, and since she had been allowed in the bar, it belonged on the Protest List. But if Oppenheim had instigated this immoral behavior, did that mean the place was immoral? In the Committee's judgment, yes.

In this instance Oppenheim may have had a hand in creating the immoral conditions he observed, but in many other cases the undercover investigators found themselves in truly disorderly establishments frequented by prostitutes, hustlers, and criminals. It was often obvious that an establishment either tacitly approved or openly encouraged such behaviors: the prostitutes solicited openly, the women switched tables frequently, and men and women could be seen kissing and fondling each other. Reports on such establishments tended to be concise, noting the number of alleged prostitutes or the incidents of table switching witnessed in a short period of time. For instance, Eilperin kept his report of the woman in Brooklyn who fondled his genitals brief. His evidence was clear and unimpeachable; he did not need to elaborate. Other investigators, though, found themselves drawn into these situations like moths to a flame. Instead of merely observing conditions, they participated wholeheartedly.

In addition, there remain important questions about the information that investigators provided the Committee. Oppenheim certainly did not write his reports while sitting at the table at DeFaust's. The technology to subtly audio record conversations or take discreet photos of the other patrons did not yet exist. He was not working with another investigator who could corroborate his observations, as had the Committee of Fifteen investigators. Most likely, Oppenheim and other Committee of Fourteen investigators wrote their reports after the fact—the next day, even several days later. Sometimes they reported on several places they had investigated over the course of several days in one omnibus report. Did Oppenheim and the others remember everything correctly? Could he have mixed up one place with another? They drank on the job, after all. Did Oppenheim take creative liberties in writing his reports? Was there a thrill to reliving the evening by writing up the report? Or was it more of a cleansing, confessional act? These reports often read like magazine features articles; could Oppenheim and the others become wrapped up in the artistic aspects of reporting? Maybe adding a little dark lipstick to the girl in the corner gave the report some interest, and when thought of as simply words on paper, that addition was harmless enough, and it might result in an investigator being sent back to a place he or she found interesting. But such a flourish could bring the full force of the Committee raining down on the otherwise innocent proprietor.

David Oppenheim's visit to Martin Busch's cabaret is a prime example of this style of investigating and reporting. Oppenheim entered the barroom around nine in the evening and remarked to Tony the waiter that the place "was dead." Oppenheim explained to Tony that he was supposed to meet up with a woman and asked if she had arrived yet. Tony replied that "there is a lot of c—s come in here but I don't know their names."[37] This remark suggests that although Tony treated Oppenheim a bit dismissively, he did at least "read" him as one of his own, someone to whom he felt comfortable speaking in such colloquial terms. Because Oppenheim had been to Martin Busch's before, Tony recognized him as a local or regular—or at least not as a reformer or someone of whom it was necessary to be suspicious.

Oppenheim told Tony he was going out for a bite to eat and would return later, once the scene picked up a bit. When he returned around ten

INVESTIGATION REPORT

Address 218 East 86th Str.
Cor. betw II nd & III aves
Name of Place Café Artista
Owner Schlesinger
Saloon or Hotel Restaurant

Date May 12th 1917
Hour of visit 1:15 a.m.
Length of stay 15 minutes.
Brewer
License No. no license
Dance Hall no

Conditions observed in Bar Room:

no Bar Room

Conditions in Rear Room

Unescorted women: White	0	Black	0
Unaccompanied men: White	25	Black	0
Couples: White	7	Black 0	Mixed 0

Any soliciting observed? no

Is there changing tables by persons of opposite sex? no

Any entertainment; if yes, what kind? music

Who served you? waiter   Name

Description

State other actions observed or conversations overheard in rear room:

They have music here again.
Prostitutes escorted by their pimps
hang out here.
Liqueres are sold here without
license.

(If necessary use reverse side)

A. K.
Investigator

3. This typical Committee of Fourteen undercover investigator's report cites excise law violations, such as the presence of prostitutes and pimps and the sale of liquor without a license. (Investigation report, 12 May 1917, box 31, folder 2, Committee of Fourteen records, Manuscripts and Archives Division, The New York Public Library, Astor, Lenox, and Tilden Foundations.)

o'clock, he found "20 unaccompanied men, 3 couples, 2 women with 3 men, no unescorted women." In his judgment, "all of the women appeared to be prostitutes but did not act disorderly, some of the men appeared to be pimps, others were pretty tough looking, some of them partly intoxicated."[38] If Oppenheim had finished his investigation at this point, he could have recommended to the Committee that Martin Busch's belonged on the Protest List as a place that "needed some improvement"; even though he did not observe any flagrant violations, he could safely have reported that the place was disorderly because the proprietor allowed drunkards, possible pimps, and people of "low morals" to congregate in his establishment. But Oppenheim remained in the establishment, apparently determined to engineer an interaction with a woman—any woman. In fact, his opening line to Tony about meeting someone there was a fabrication; it was a cleverly designed entrée into this social milieu on this particular evening.

Oppenheim realized that a young woman he had met on a previous visit to Martin Busch's was sitting at a nearby table. Last time, she wrote her address on the back of his card. Her name was F. Stack and she lived at 627 Hart Street. Oppenheim selected a table that permitted him to watch Stack and her friend. He observed that she "kept turning her head to all parts of the room, excepting towards place I was sitting . . . [and] whenever she came back from ladies room, she couldn't help but look towards me on way to her table but as she got near her table she lowered her head so that I couldn't get her eye."[39] Was Stack a prostitute playing coy? Or was she not interested in him? Maybe she was frightened because he kept watching her. Was she glancing at him because he looked familiar but she was having trouble placing the face? Could she have regretted giving him her address last time? Could she have been fearful that he would initiate contact? Perhaps she was a prostitute but not "working" on that particular night and wanted to be left alone.

Stack leaned over and whispered to the young man at her table. Oppenheim noticed this and wrote in his report that "one of her men companions . . . turned around and looked at me. . . . I also noticed that every time I looked up he had his eye on me, he appeared to be watching me."[40] Oppenheim determined that the young man who was watching him must have been her pimp, although he had no evidence of this. Stack had entered Martin Busch's with this young man, but that did not necessarily make him her pimp; he could have been a boyfriend, a cousin, or a brother. Male companions often accompanied working-class women to saloons, and they served to protect them from unwanted advances like Oppenheim's; the presence of a male companion could suggest that a woman's reputation was not questionable. Young women wanted to hang out in bars, but liquor laws (and the social activists who took it upon themselves to enforce them) considered unaccompanied women in bars to be no different than prostitutes. A platonic male companion or relative allowed a woman to socialize in public and protected her—from unwanted male attention, from getting a "tough" reputation, and from the predations of investigators. A pimp, however, would have set up an interaction, not thwarted it.

Whether or not Stack had worked as a prostitute in the past or would work as a prostitute in the future, this particular evening she was not doing anything wrong. She was not unaccompanied, she was not switching tables, she was not smoking, and she was not soliciting. If Stack was attempting to solicit Oppenheim, she might have changed to his table or lifted her dress above her knees to show him "her person." Oppenheim then would have been able to return the necessary evidence to move against this particular establishment because these activities rated as "disorderly." But she did none of these things. Oppenheim noted several times in his report that Stack "saw me but did not give me a tumble" and that she kept "her head turned away from me so that I couldn't get her eye."[41] Oppenheim operated on the logic that if he could induce Stack to switch to his table and the waiter or proprietor did not stop her, then Martin Busch's saloon was disorderly. It was incumbent on the proprietors to prevent table switching and similarly unacceptable behavior.

When Tony the waiter returned to Oppenheim's table and asked him if the woman he expected to meet had arrived, Oppenheim pointed out Stack. He then asked Tony "to kick [her] in the shins and get her to turn around."[42] Tony agreed initially and then changed his mind. He told Oppenheim that he did not know the woman well enough and did not want to risk offending her by treating her like a common whore. But perhaps Tony did not want to get himself in trouble by acting like a pimp. It seems that Tony recognized Stack as a neighborhood girl spending an evening at the tavern; he might have violated an unspoken code or local logic if he had tried to set her up with Oppenheim, even though waiters at other establishments might have done so. Stack eventually left without speaking to Oppenheim. She had a brief conversation with the boss before she departed; she bid him a good night and stated that she would see him the next evening. Did this mean that she was enough of a regular to be on good terms with the proprietor, or did it mean that she was a known prostitute whom the proprietor allowed to work in his establishment?

Stack, Tony, and the proprietor all behaved in an outwardly "orderly" fashion, but Oppenheim remained convinced that the place was disorderly, and his report enumerated the problems with the establishment. Although unescorted women were not permitted and there was "no kissing or hugging," he noted that "some of the women [were] smoking." In addition, Oppenheim wrote, "the men appear to be a rough lot, some of them probably pimps, a few of them were drunk and noisy." But what was supposed to happen in a bar? Were patrons not supposed to get drunk? Ideally, the Committee of Fourteen preferred that, in a bar, a few men would gather after work, perhaps play cards, and enjoy a couple of drinks in moderation. There would be no women at the bar. For example, investigator Nicholas Santella visited the Valente Café, where he "found 3 persons playing cards with the owner of the said place in the rear room. During that time I was in there nothing happened to need reporting."[43] Martin Busch's, however, as represented in Oppenheim's report, did not function as an after-work social club for working men. Most damning, it "allow[ed] unaccompanied men to join escorted women at their tables, [and] Tony the waiter will also take messages from unaccompanied men to escorted women."[44] Of course Oppenheim was one of the men who used Tony to deliver a message, but as the investigator, he could create conditions of disorderliness and immorality that did not accrue to or reflect on his own behavior or character.

The Committee of Fourteen's process required investigators it could trust, but those investigators also needed to be trusted by the people working and playing in the places under investigation. David Oppenheim was the most adept at establishing himself as a regular at neighborhood saloons. He took on an active role; he chatted up waiters, talked about (and with) women, and held forth on horseracing, gambling, and other city pleasures. But an investigator like Oppenheim also presented a particularly interesting problem for the Committee: he became so involved in his performance that he stimulated the very conditions he was supposed to be routing out. His familiarity with the staff in the places under investigation, however, yielded invaluable information that was otherwise unavailable. The Committee of Fourteen readily suspended any ethical qualms about employing Oppenheim in favor of the chance to obtain this prized information.

While Oppenheim's investigative technique focused on picking up women, other male investigators believed that male patrons were the most useful sources of information. These investigators adopted the tactic of using conquest stories and sex talk to facilitate male bonding and, subsequently, their investigative task. Conversations about sexual coercion became the best way for male undercover investigators to connect across class lines. Manipulating a discourse of sexual coercion allowed the undercover investigator to legitimize his pose as a member of the working class and to obscure his "outsider" origins. Moreover, the topic of sexual coercion forged bonds of homosocial camaraderie between the male investigator and bartender or patron, and permitted the investigator to appear to be of the same mindset and culture as the patrons. Perhaps most important, confessions (real or fabricated) on the part of the investigator softened the subjects of investigation, allowing bartenders and patrons to open up and reveal information about prostitution, immorality, or liquor law violations.

Because the Committee was interested in determining whether prostitutes congregated in particular establishments or if the proprietors maintained beds upstairs or in the back room, male investigators often steered conversations in the direction of sex. The investigators were also expected to look for fire code violations and for places that sold liquor after 1:00 a.m., that did not provide separate toilets for men and women, or that did not serve food with drink orders—all in addition to violations that were sexual in nature—so it is significant that the conversation so frequently turned to sex. In the same way that buying rounds of drinks demonstrated to working-class men that an investigator belonged in their social environment, trading conquest stories was another important way for the male undercover investigator to subtly demonstrate that he was trustworthy. Investigators' stories about sexual coercion were not invented on the spot, however; instead, they picked up and circulated stories told by patrons and bartenders. And, unfortunately, these investigators were keeping stories and strategies of sexual coercion in circulation, stories that may have had real—and unintended—consequences for young women.

On the afternoon of July 8, 1913, an investigator who only identified himself in his reports as "L" entered the bar of the Avenel Hotel. A man named Henry was bartending.[45] They greeted one another, and Henry asked L how his girlfriend was "feeling." L replied "that she looked and felt as good as ever." Henry responded, "Still after her, eh! You must like her." L answered in the "affirmative, adding that she was a fine 'chicken,' that [he] had spent all kinds of money on her and would get her in a hotel do or die."[46]

Three weeks later, L returned to the Avenel, and Henry was once again behind the bar. Henry "immediately engaged [L] in conversation . . . asking whether [he] had gotten that 'chicken' yet." L said not yet because he was "afraid to take a chance in the grass or a hallway as she might yell and have me pinched. The only thing to do is to get her in this back-room . . . force her upstairs and then she couldn't squeal." L concluded with a somewhat desperate request, appealing to Henry's manly instincts: "Can you fix it for me, Henry?"[47]

One month later, the Committee sent L back to the Avenel, where he found the barroom empty, save for Henry. The bartender remembered him and, as L documented, "wanted to know what happened with 'my girl.'" L explained to Henry "that she would not enter a hotel for fear of being observed by a friend or an acquaintance and that her speed was in the grass at Clason Point." How did L know to reference Clason Point and similar places? In the spring and summer of 1913, Whitin directed L to investigate saloons that maintained rooms for use by trusted clientele and to follow up on leads of places where sexual immorality was thought to occur. For instance, he was sent up to Clason Point, the "Coney Island of the Bronx."[48] He discovered that the place was "in full swing and the usual rowdy element [was] frequenting the place." By hanging around and talking with other men, L learned "that indecencies [were] being committed and tolerated in at least 2 places."[49] L took this information and used it in his conversations with Henry to present himself as authentic. And it worked. Henry counseled L that "it's easy with cases of that kind. . . . All you have to do is take her upstairs by the 124 St. entrance and she won't be wise." Because L spoke openly of his sexual frustrations and his designs on his hesitant girlfriend, Henry was willing to offer advice on how to have sex with reluctant partners. He even "reminded [L that] he would lend every assistance" so that he may "accomplish [his] purpose."[50] Henry's offer of assistance—namely, a private room—was solid evidence that the Avenel was in violation of excise law.

Apparently this information was not enough for L, who had yet to see anyone head up to the rooms or any possible prostitutes plying their trade in the back. In fact, in four visits to the Avenel, L encountered no women at all. Yet he returned. On July 8, he told Henry that he planned to take his girlfriend to "Pabst's Harlem some night, get her under influence of liquor, take a taxi and rush her into a hotel before she would realize it." L's reference to other popular nightspots demonstrated his familiarity with this social circle, which he imagined made him appear to be a denizen, an "insider." Because of their previous interactions, Henry understood L as one of his own and shared secrets with him. Henry confided in L about Lizzie, a "married woman" he had "walked to Inwood where he forcibly had sexual intercourse with her. Telephoned her three days later and took her to a hotel—after that it was easy." Henry also "reminded [L] how simple it was to 'get to' women who frequent saloons unescorted. In one case he took a salesgirl . . . from back room to hotel in vicinity and had intercourse."[51]

The interactions between these two men suggest a frightening reality for working-class women: if they went out drinking with men, the men considered them sexually available. In these stories, L and Henry were free of the taint of sexual immorality; the unescorted women, drinking in public, were perceived and portrayed as sexually available, whether or not they consented to sexual activity. For the Committee, women needed to be removed from the city's barrooms because then—and only then—would they be protected from "worse offenses," like rape and seduction. The Committee pursued this course as a solution, even though it was unreasonable to expect that young women could or should be kept at home.

The Committee of Fourteen was right about one thing, however: young women experienced sexual predation in this new leisure culture, which wooed them but did not accommodate them. Female investigators often heard stories similar to the ones Henry told L, but from the young women themselves, who were forced to fight off unwanted advances in attempts to guard their reputations. To test the "wages and sin" theory, which held that shopgirls often turned to casual prostitution to supplement their meager pay, the Committee of Fourteen dispatched three female investigators to Macy's department store in 1913. The staff of the Committee worked with the management at Macy's to secure the three women positions as shopgirls. The Committee expected the investigators not only to master their duties at Macy's so as not to reveal their true identities to immediate supervisors and co-workers, but also to befriend their co-workers and get them to open up about boyfriends, sexual encounters and desires, and economic survival strategies.

Whitin was unhappy with the quality of the information the first two investigators gathered at Macy's, so he decided to send in Natalie Sonnichsen. She was the female investigator who appears most frequently in the Committee of Fourteen's records because she was such a versatile investigator, able to pass in a variety of situations. The daughter of a Russian czarist general, she immigrated to New York in the early twentieth century. Professionally, she was a freelance journalist who wrote features for the *New York Times Magazine* and the *New York World*, and she had assisted with the English translation of the anti-Semitic "Protocols of the Elders of Zion." Sonnichsen came to the Committee of Fourteen in 1912 from Belle Israels's Committee on Amusement Resources of Working Girls, for which she often conducted investigations, along with her husband, Albert Sonnichsen.[52] Although Whitin recognized Natalie Sonnichsen's value to the Committee, he had serious reservations about her moral fiber, having once described her as sexually promiscuous and living a "Greenwich Village lifestyle." He remarked, however, that he would continue to employ her because he knew "the lady well enough to . . . correctly read and understand her reports," but that he did "not wish to make that recommendation to or for every one."[53] Whitin also appreciated that she applied her professional skills as a writer to produce fluid, florid, and oftentimes scandalous reports.

Sonnichsen had already demonstrated to Whitin that she was adept at passing in working-class women's social settings. At Macy's, she quickly befriended her co-workers. By posing as a friend and contemporary, Sonnichsen gathered important information about how Macy's shopgirls spent their leisure time. She used a technique similar to L's by asking the women about popular nightclubs, such as Frenze's, which had a reputation as being a rough place frequented by a "tough crowd." Her co-worker Anna said she was not worried about getting a bad reputation if she frequented Frenze's or similar establishments, explaining that "if a girl is decent, nobody will touch her." Her other co-worker, Rose, however, claimed she would never go to Frenze's "because it is enough for a fellow to know that a girl goes there, for him to draw his own conclusions as to her respectability."[54] Nowhere in these conversations do the young women warn each other about how men took sexual liberties, despite a girl's "respectability."

Sonnichsen sensed that Rose might give her the kind of information in which the Committee was interested, so she tested her further. Sonnichsen told her "an imaginary story of a friend of mine who had tripped up" and found herself in a sexually compromised position. Rose reacted with scorn, telling Sonnichsen that her friend was "a fool" and that girls should never "take any chances." When Sonnichsen asked her to elaborate, Rose explained that her practice was to make young men believe she was "fast" in order to get what she wanted materially, but "at the psychological moment she would clear out." Sonnichsen asked her a number of follow-up questions, including if she had ever accepted silk stockings as presents. Rose answered, "No, because they'd want to put them on [me]."[55]

Rose's story illuminates the sexual double standard of the period. Specifically, young women were responsible for policing moral and sexual boundaries, and young men were expected (or allowed) to push those boundaries. If a man succeeded in violating the boundaries, it ruined the young woman's reputation at best, and at worst landed her in the New York State Reformatory for Women at Bedford Hills. The men ended up with a conquest story that served as a coin of the realm in working-class saloons and cabarets. Young women like Rose, who believed that they could "clear out" at the appropriate moment, demonstrate the tension—and vulnerability—that women experienced. These young women may have known their personal boundaries, but did this matter when they found themselves in the company of a man like the young sailor Oppenheim met, who told him of "the last woman that picked him up"? The sailor explained that after he paid for a hotel room, "the woman had [the] nerve to ask him $2 for herself after he kept blowing her [paying her way] all night." The young sailor, enraged by her audacity, "belted her one in the nose instead." As a result of his physical abuse, she "consented" to "stay with him for the rest of the night without asking him for any money."[56] On another occasion, Oppenheim filed a report describing a conversation he had with a Brooklyn Rapid Transit (BRT) employee, who told him that "you could find any number of girls laying around on the sand under the boardwalk about where the . . . bathing pavilion is" at Coney Island. The BRT man explained that "on a Saturday night you find a lot of young girls here dead drunk that men steered here sc— them then left them, he said there [was] hardly a night him and other B.R.T. men don't come over here and get something."[57] No matter how principled the young woman, she might encounter a situation that she could not handle.[58]

These reports on women in public reveal where the Committee's priorities rested and reflect the reality of the legal status of rape as a crime in the early twentieth century. According to the *Police Procedure Manual*, "a conviction cannot be had upon the uncorroborated statement of the person [woman] raped." As a consequence, "the officer whose attention is called to such a crime" must "establish corroboration." The *Manual* advised that "if the crime has been committed in a building, try to find some person . . . who heard the girl protesting or resisting, or evidence of a struggle in the premises." Similarly, the officer could look for "any part of the female's clothing in the room, or her clothing torn or soiled."[59] Because of the difficulty of establishing that a rape occurred, the Committee believed that the most effective way to protect women was to remove them from drinking establishments, which would shield men from the temptation to commit such offenses. Ironically, the positioning of male undercover investigators and their primary goal of passing demanded that they encourage these tales of sexual coercion, which reinforced such behavior.

In August 1912, Committee secretary Frederick Whitin sent Natalie Sonnichsen out to investigate dance halls in Queens, opposite Jackson Avenue Park. At the first establishment, she befriended a man named Mr. Burns, to whom she introduced herself as May. Mr. Burns was quite taken with "May"

and invited her to accompany him to "Martin's Saloon, a large and sumptu-
ous establishment with rooms on the first floor."[60] She agreed. Because she
was open to all of the possibilities the evening offered, Sonnichsen found
herself in a different social circle than the one she was initially sent out to
investigate. This situation proved valuable to the Committee's overall program. Because undercover investigators provided the raw data from which
the Committee of Fourteen operated, Whitin favored reports that read as
colorful, narrative stories, replete with details that he could hone in on and
incorporate into his disciplinary lectures and promissory notes.

Unlike the Committee of Fifteen, the Committee of Fourteen employed
female investigators, although not as frequently as it used men. Whitin characterized the work as "disagreeable" for female investigators, mostly because
he feared they would be corrupted by the situations they encountered, but he
did select women for particular situations. In general, Whitin only hired female investigators from other social activist organizations, which meant they
would have shared the Committee's perspective on the issues of disorderliness and unaccompanied women. Perhaps most important, these women
had to be willing to act in a manner that may not have been in accord with
their middle-class standing and values.[61] Whitin also needed women who
possessed ephemeral "skills": they should look ten years younger than their
actual age, be attractive and therefore desirable to men in leisure establishments, know the argot of working-class culture, and be able to pass easily
among the other young women in dance halls and cabarets.

For example, when the Committee desired information on streetwalking
prostitution, Whitin contacted Mrs. Eula Harris of the Travelers' Aid Society
and instructed her to "appear in war paint on Fulton Street, Brooklyn, and
see if fishing is as good as around Times Square."[62] With this comment,
Whitin demonstrated that he saw women as shiny bait that men could not
resist. His choice of Harris is also telling in that she came from an organization dedicated to preventing young women who came to the city on their
own from falling into prostitution. Whitin regarded Harris—and women
like her—as more able to mimic the kind of women his and other similar organizations were trying to help and therefore were less likely to be corrupted
by the unseemly situations they would have to engineer as investigators.

The unwritten rules of engagement in working-class leisure establishments required women who were not prostitutes to respond to men and
not to take the lead in interactions. Female investigators had to be able to
present themselves as easy working-class girls, capable of being approached.
For instance, as discussed earlier, Edna Arbing and Maud Robinson Tombs

were sent to Brooklyn, unaccompanied, on several occasions. Both returned reports in which they remarked that they were refused entry into a number of saloons, as the establishments did not serve unaccompanied women.[63]

The information Arbing and Tombs gathered indicated that most of the places they visited were not disorderly; for Whitin, however, these details were not enough to justify their continued employment. The Committee believed disorderliness could still exist even if a bartender or doorman refused to serve an unaccompanied woman. Whitin suspected that proprietors denied access to the Committee's female investigators not because they were law abiding but because they did not recognize the women as locals. There were, however, certain kinds of information that only female investigators could gather. So when the Committee of Fourteen engaged female investigators, those investigators were required to behave in the same manner that the Committee imagined a disorderly young woman in a dance hall or cabaret would behave. She was to be sociable, she was to allow men to buy her drinks, and she was to mix with the other patrons. These tactics were used to see whether the proprietor would expel the disorderly young woman or if the men would take the bait.

Upon entering Martin's, Mr. Burns pointed out to Sonnichsen (posing as May) five "fairies" (young men dressed and performing as women who sometimes also worked as prostitutes soliciting a male clientele) and a female prostitute. The fairy named Daisy, who was onstage giving an obscene performance, immediately captivated Sonnichsen. She was transfixed and noted in her report that Daisy made "peculiar, exaggerated gestures" as he sang. Daisy noticed Sonnichsen's gaze, so he approached their table and "began singing directly to" her. She wrote, "When he finished his song he sat down and began talking to me." He "moved his chair nearer to me and continued talking and looking into my eyes." Daisy asked, "Now, dear, you'll give me a kiss won't you?" Sonnichsen replied, "No . . . I never kiss girls." Daisy gave May a "reproachful glance." Burns, who had been carefully monitoring their interaction, intervened. He said: "I think I'd better take you away, May, (myself) before Daisy gets you. I'll bash your head in, Daisy, if you meddle with this girl, the way you did with Lizzie." Sonnichsen recorded that "there was a nasty ring in Mr. Burns' voice." Daisy, with "his eyes glittering," retorted, "I'll have you arrested." The tension between Burns and Daisy over May erupted into an argument that threatened to turn physical. Burns made "an obvious effort to restrain himself" as he explained to Sonnichsen that "only a few weeks ago he had brought Lizzie into this saloon. She was a good girl, but Daisy saw her and seduced her, after which she went wrong, was arrested and is now serving a six month's sentence on [Blackwell's] Island." Burns reiterated his concern that Daisy would also "get" May. Sonnichsen "assured him that [she] could take care of [her]self," but these assurances did not satisfy Burns. He rose from the table and addressed the crowd, loudly exclaiming, "I am going to have a go at Daisy." Daisy also raised his voice, saucily announcing: "You're just jealous, because I won't let you sleep with me." Burns erupted, "By God, Daisy, if you don't clear out and leave this girl alone I'll smash you."[64]

In her report, Sonnichsen presents a remarkable view of sexual rivalry, one in which Burns and Daisy were competing (and had competed in the past) for the affections of the same woman—in addition to what may have been sexual tension or confusion between the two of them. Sonnichsen's representation of these interactions is equally revealing. She wrote and punctuated the conversation as if it were a stage play, suggesting that she understood herself as playing a role in this scene. Conversing with Burns and Daisy as a young woman named May, Sonnichsen had found a way not only to befriend Burns but also to get him to take her to the bar with all of the "fairies." By presenting herself as a young woman who was possibly open to sexual activity, Sonnichsen gained an expanded level of access. She felt confident that her temporary transformation was complete, as she remarked: "Other couples came in, but they seemed to be outsiders."[65]

Sonnichsen's first foray into Martin's pleased Whitin, so he sent her back. Her subsequent report noted that she "recognized a number of the people from the week before." As soon as she entered, Daisy noticed her and "devoted his time to [her], not taking so much part in the entertaining as the two other fairies, Vivian and Elsie, both of whom were in excellent form."[66] Sonnichsen, performing as May, reacted outwardly with delight to the entertainment and Daisy's attention, while Sonnichsen the investigator described the entertainment provided by the fairies (lewd parodies of popular songs accompanied by vulgar choreography) as "obscene."

She noted in her report that when "her crowd" headed upstairs to the private rooms, she opted not to join them. Instead, she followed Daisy out to the parking lot. This was a calculated risk on Sonnichsen's part. She could have been assaulted by Daisy, but she figured that because he was a fairy, he would not be interested in a sexual encounter with a woman. As soon as they were outside, she noted that "a change came over Daisy; he acted as a normal man, dropping his feminine mannerisms. When I called him Daisy he winced, saying that that was not his name." He asked Sonnichsen,

"Don't you understand I am just as human as you are?" Continuing, he declared, "I am not a fairy. . . . It's all a joke—I am only acting. I make my living singing at North Beach." Daisy continued in his attempt to convince Sonnichsen that he was sexually interested in women—her in particular. He explained that he lived in New York and "earned enough for two." He also offered to marry her—if she "were really straight." ("Straight," in the parlance of this period and this subculture, signified a woman who did not work as a professional prostitute. To wit: "Of the two other girls in our company, one was 'straight,' and the other was just starting in as a professional prostitute, having started her career after being taken to a hotel in a drunken condition from one of the dance halls.") Sonnichsen told him that she was straight, but she noted in her report that his offer "refused to move" her. He was persistent, begging to see her again. He invited her to "come to Martin's Saturday evening and he would take [her] to Coney Island." All she had to do was "call up Martin's . . . on the phone and ask for Jim Fielding."[67] She begged off and went back inside.

Following Sonnichsen's last visit to Martin's in August, Whitin determined, from reading her reports, that it was a disorderly establishment that should be on the Protest List. As a result, Whitin called the proprietor in to his Manhattan office and warned him that if he did not clean his place up, the Committee would cause him to lose his liquor license. In October, Whitin sent Sonnichsen back to check on the progress of Martin's. When she arrived, she asked the waiter if Daisy was working. The waiter informed her that Daisy was no longer permitted in the establishment because a "complaint had been lodged" against him. The waiter told her, "Mr. Whitin of the Com. of Fourteen and two other men who had come down said that the complaint was made by a girl, who had been with Fielding [Daisy]." Sonnichsen remarked in her report that "there was only one girl" who had been keeping company with Daisy and "that was me." The waiter returned a few minutes later, leaned over the table, and hissed at Sonnichsen: "You don't think that I don't know that you know that I know who you are?" Trying to maintain her "May" persona and her composure, she "challenged his statements," vehemently denying that she worked for the Committee or that she had lodged the complaints against Daisy.[68]

In her report, Sonnichsen expressed total bewilderment with the way the staff at Martin's treated her on this visit. The waiter told her that his boss "would like to meet the person who made the complaint," adding that the boss "was terrible when angry." The waiter also "enlarged on his own athletic training, saying that he was put in the saloon to make use of it in keeping order. He was simply telling me this so that I should know that I was known." Sonnichsen slowly realized that, when her bosses investigated Martin's, they blew her cover. Despite this state of affairs, she maintained her composure until the very end, sneering at the waiter on her way out the door that "he would find out his mistake in time."[69]

Although she could never return to Martin's, Sonnichsen succeeded in meeting the Committee's goals. Martin's Saloon had resorted to self-policing, which was enforced in two ways: first, the proprietor had fired Daisy and forbad him to return to the establishment; and second, he had hired a waiter who had the "athletic training" to maintain order in the saloon. The staff at Martin's was clearly unhappy with this outcome, however, as indicated by their treatment of Sonnichsen, who was informed in no uncertain terms that she was no longer welcome at Martin's.

As they had done at Martin's, the Committee made numerous other proprietors aware of its powers through its spontaneous "visits" to disorderly saloons. Proprietors found themselves forced to acquiesce to the Committee and its moral code if they wanted to stay in business. Their compliance, however, did not mean that proprietors agreed with or were happy about the arrangements they made with the Committee of Fourteen. Wealthy proprietors who tried to bribe Whitin found him unimpeachable, and proprietors of modest means who tried to appeal to his softer side found him unyielding. As one proprietor explained to Oppenheim, "you've got to do what the committee wants you to [and] if you don't they put the police on you and they break in and frame you up." Oppenheim asked the proprietor how the Committee knew what was going on in any one establishment, and the proprietor explained that the Committee knew about these activities because "they've got their men around and when they see a little bit they make a whole lot out of it."[70]

This proprietor proceeded to explain to Oppenheim that he was trying to keep "this place very strict" and that he spent every evening there, policing barroom conditions. He explained, "I wouldn't let a woman in alone but if a man and woman are sitting together and another man comes in . . . and sits down with them how am I going to stop them? Even if I see the woman giving the man her address can I go over and tell her not to do it?" "If I know the woman is here to hustle," the proprietor made clear, "I keep her out of here."[71] The exasperated proprietor, to protect his economic self-interest, was forced to adhere to and impose the Committee's moral code. He pointed to a problem with the Committee's demands, however: how could a proprietor, an individual, dictate the way other individuals behaved? Surely a proprietor could stop prostitutes from soliciting or hustlers from hustling, but could he tell women not to give out their addresses, or men not to join their friends if they were sitting with women? In short, how could he impose someone else's idea of "proper" behavior on an entire group of people? According to the catchall law of disorderliness and the Committee's power and discretion in interpreting it, proprietors were personally responsible for the behavior of their patrons, and they risked losing their livelihood if they were not vigilant.

The Committee of Fourteen concerned itself with the moral conditions in New York City's working-class leisure sites but pursued a business solution to these perceived moral issues. During this period, the Committee acted with a great deal of power and discretion in defining conditions and determining the punishments that offending proprietors would endure. This power came, in large part, from the Committee's skill and willingness to selectively interpret and enforce sections of the liquor tax laws and penal codes relating to disorderly conduct. In early twentieth-century New York's leisure landscape, the mounting campaign for the prohibition of alcohol and concern over sexually licentious behavior helped the Committee rise to the top, as liquor dealers and saloon owners saw it as the lesser of many evils. Agreeing to ban unaccompanied women from the barroom would not impact weekly receipts as much as an all-out prohibition of alcohol would. Without its undercover investigators' reports and observations, the Committee would not have had the evidence it required to move against proprietors or liquor dealers.

For the Committee, unescorted women were a key indicator of a disorderly establishment. Thus, its investigators relied on and operated under assumptions about how men and women should act and interact in public. Not only did investigators rely on these assumptions, but they also exploited them. Oppenheim tried to get women to "give him a tumble," while Sonnichsen changed tables, flirted with fairies, and danced with several men. Their detailed reports—chatty, compelling, dramatic—were returned to the Committee. Whitin read these reports and acted on the aspects he found relevant. These reports, however, were not objective, and the actions the Committee took were uneven. The proprietor at Martin's had to bar Daisy from returning, whereas the proprietor at Martin Busch's risked losing his business altogether if he did not internalize and redeploy the Committee's discipline. By being in these leisure spaces and inducing table changing or flirting with patrons, the Committee of Fourteen, through its investigators, was complicit in creating disorderliness and moral confusion in the culture that it was attempting to transform.

Brassy blonde hair, a cheap chorus girl costume, an exposed décolleté—all an investigator had to do was report on these or similar items, and the Committee then had enough evidence that a leisure establishment supported disorderly behavior. The mutability and manipulability of the definition of "disorderliness," as used and deployed by the Committee and its investigators, created serious problems for proprietors, who stood to lose their liquor licenses and their livelihoods. It was difficult to muster sympathy for the rapacious saloon keeper who allowed women to be exploited in his barroom as a way to increase his own profits, but when the Committee's definition and deployment of standards of morality and orderliness extended to interracial sociability, the needle on the moral compass shifted significantly.

FOUR

Race Mixing, Investigation, and the Enforcement of Jim Crow

The gaslights in front of Marshall's Hotel, beckoning to potential patrons turning down West 53rd Street, held out the promise of comfortable accommodations, delicious food, cold drinks, and hot jazz. Located in two neighboring brownstones in the heart of the Tenderloin district, Marshall's Hotel featured live music and attracted throngs of fashionable New Yorkers every night of the week. Indeed, the establishment revolutionized social life for black New Yorkers, who began to abandon the older clubs downtown. By 1900 Marshall's was, according to James Weldon Johnson, one of "the centres of a fashionable sort of life that hitherto had not existed." The "actors, the musicians, the composers, the writers, and the better-paid vaudevillians" congregated at Marshall's; white actors and musicians also spent evenings there in the company of their black friends. Luminaries such as Rosamond Johnson, James Reese Europe, Paul Laurence Dunbar, Florenz Ziegfeld, and W. E. B. DuBois all frequented the establishment.[1] In short, Marshall's Hotel was not a gin-soaked, rat-infested, honky-tonk but an important gathering place for New York's black cultural elite.

D. Slattery, special assistant to the police commissioner, confirmed Marshall's reputation. In a written report to the Committee of Fourteen, he explained that Marshall's Hotel, at 127–29 West 53rd Street, operated under an unexpired Liquor Tax Certificate in the name of James L. Marshall. In Slattery's judgment, Marshall's was "conducted in such a manner, that so far it has been impossible to obtain evidence sufficient to substantiate a charge of keeping a disorderly house. Everything possible is being done to prevent cause for complaint at this location."[2]

Yet the Committee of Fourteen kept Marshall's Hotel under surveillance. Although Slattery and the police department offered assurance that the proprietor abided by excise laws and the laws relating to disorderliness, the

Committee regarded Marshall's with suspicion for one reason: Marshall's permitted race mixing. For the Committee, race mixing emerged as the most easily identifiable marker of disorderliness. As a consequence, the Committee required proprietors—black proprietors in particular—to eliminate race mixing from their establishments. As William S. Bennet, congressman and Committee of Fourteen member, explained, "If it is a colored place in which white people were not admitted at all," then it "would seem to me that there is no chance for trouble."[3] For Bennet and his colleagues on the Committee, the "chance for trouble" in commercial leisure establishments that permitted race mixing rested in the increased possibility of sexual activity across the color line, which could potentially overthrow the city's social and racial order. As Slattery noted of Marshall's, "white females frequent the place, with negroes, and it is also visited by white people, while slumming and sight seeing."[4]

Marshall's Hotel was not unique; rather, it was part of a new, emergent leisure culture. In early twentieth-century New York City, a significant number of black-owned cabarets and hotels opened—particularly in the Tenderloin, the theater district, and Harlem. For black musicians and artists, these were important sites of cultural production and consumption; these venues also functioned as the only public places where "respectable" black New Yorkers could meet and mingle with friends. White New Yorkers (particularly those of the bohemian or "sporting" persuasion) also began frequenting such establishments to participate in their "exotic" offerings—the opportunity to listen to jazz, and to dance, drink, and socialize with black New Yorkers.[5]

The Committee of Fourteen used the vagaries of excise and disorderly house laws to maintain surveillance and regulate saloons and cabarets, especially those owned and frequented by African Americans. The extent of the Committee's powers pushed New York City's black bourgeoisie into an untenable position, one that forced them to engage in trade-offs in the quest for both social equality and economic self-sufficiency. The debate that swirled around Marshall's Hotel and its proprietor's treatment by the Committee of Fourteen shows not only the way the Committee perceived and used race as a marker of morality, but also how a private organization imposed segregation in a state with strong antidiscrimination laws.

The Committee of Fourteen did not go unchallenged in its quest for a segregated leisure landscape, however. Despite his own worries about the moral condition of many African Americans, W. E. B. DuBois rejected the Committee's linkage of race mixing with immorality, as well as its solution to the problem—voluntary segregation. The Committee searched for men of "the Booker T. Washington type" to assist them in the goal of creating separate black and white drinking establishments.[6] Moreover, it wanted to avoid the critique raised by DuBois. In response, it created the Colored Auxiliary of the Committee of Fourteen (also referred to as the Committee of Seven) in an attempt to solve the city's "Negro problem" in a manner that satisfied its own moral aversion to race mixing. Black and white Progressives alike and their undercover investigators all worked together (and around New York State's civil rights laws) to usher Jim Crow in through the back door.

Harlem's transformation in the early twentieth century raised the alarm for white middle-class residents of upper Manhattan. Had their Eden come to an end? In 1904 and 1905, the speculative real estate bubble in Harlem burst, leaving investors with empty apartment buildings. To attract tenants, landlords began to offer reduced rents, which allowed many African Americans to move into the neighborhood. The Afro-American Realty Company, founded in 1904 by Philip A. Payton, Jr., purchased many of the empty apartment buildings. Payton regarded the circumstances as an opportunity not only for himself and his investors, but also for the black community; to this end, he advertised for "respectable" and "well behaved" black families to rent apartments in his buildings.[7] Perhaps this wording was intended to guard against the white Harlem Property Owners' Improvement Corporation, which, from 1910 to 1915, tried to combat the influx of black residents to Harlem—to little avail.

By 1914, 50,000 African Americans resided in Harlem. Many had come from other parts of the city, seeking better apartments than could be found in the Tenderloin, as well as less violence ; others were recent arrivals from the American South. As the neighborhood developed, influential black churches moved uptown to be near their recently relocated congregants; a number of popular drinking establishments also chose Harlem as their new locale. In response, New York's black middle class became concerned that Harlem's newcomers did not know how to behave "properly" and would sully Harlem's reputation as a model black community. Black middle-class leaders feared the situation would have a detrimental impact on race relations, wiping out in a single stroke everything for which they had worked. They regarded Harlem as a shining beacon, a community that demonstrated that black people deserved civil rights and economic opportunities. The class distinctions that opened up within New York's small black community unintentionally played into the Committee of Fourteen's plan, which held that voluntary segregation would bring about moral order.

In the perception of the Committee of Fourteen's members, New York was rapidly becoming a black metropolis. Ironically, though, by 1900 only 60,666 black people lived in New York City, accounting for less than 1 percent of the total population. There was a significant upsurge in the number of blacks migrating to New York after the completion of the Panama Canal in 1914, but by 1920 the black population had increased to only 2.7 percent of the city's population. The Committee's outsized reaction to the minute growth in the black population signaled the depth of its members' concern over the possibility of white women consorting with black men in establishments that provided all the necessary preconditions for sexual activity: alcohol, live music, and lewd dancing. Following the same model it had employed successfully in other areas of the city, the Committee of Fourteen dispatched undercover investigators to gather information about race mixing, which it then used as evidence and leverage in the backroom bargains it struck with black proprietors. In the case of black-owned establishments, however, the Committee used its investigators' reports to mold not only a new moral order but also a new racial order out of what it perceived as the rapidly changing racial demographics of New York City.

One April evening in 1911, William F. Pogue, one of the few black investigators employed by the Committee in the pre-1920 period, headed out to investigate a number of black-owned drinking establishments on the Committee of Fourteen's Protest List. He arrived at Marshall's Hotel at about 1:15 a.m., after a few hours investigating and carousing elsewhere. Upon entering, he noticed several white couples in the establishment, and "one of the white women was very much under the influence of drink. During the singing or playing she would get up and sing or try to dance." According to the Committee's definition of disorderliness, this woman's behavior would have been enough to allow Pogue to conclude that Marshall's posed an "offense to public decency" and then depart. Instead, he remained to chat with a young black woman who called him over to her table. Pogue bought a round of drinks for this woman, and she told him that "she came to Marshall's often to solicit among the white patrons. She consented to take me to this hotel for a certain sum of money." By this point, Pogue had gathered evidence that prostitutes solicited in Marshall's establishment, which was enough to mark the place as "disorderly." Pogue, however, stayed. He bought more drinks for the prostitute, the change from which he "put . . . in one pocket." After a while, his lady companion "excused herself." After waiting "about a half hour for her to return," Pogue realized that he was missing "three dollars from [his] pockets." He wrote, "She had taken it and made her 'get away' she had been putting her arms around and over me and evidently that was her scheme to get it."[8]

Resigned, Pogue decided to leave. On his way out the door, however, he "met several friends coming in and was invited to go back in by them. Which I did I stayed there until 4:45 a.m. at that hour they were still dancing and drinks were being sold."[9] Even before he ran into his friends, Pogue had solid evidence that Marshall's Hotel was disorderly: the proprietor and employees permitted prostitutes to solicit in the barroom and drinks to be sold beyond the legislated hour. In his report, Pogue's investigative tasks and personal social life intersected; he condemned Marshall's for serving alcohol until nearly five in the morning, but he was little concerned that he was engaged in disorderly behavior himself. The mantle of "investigator" protected him from the label "disorderly" and actually made him even more of an asset to the Committee's program.

George Francis O'Neill, a white investigator for the Committee of Fourteen, had a very different experience at Marshall's. To facilitate his investigative task, O'Neill adopted the persona of a white "slummer." He hired a "touring car" and chauffeur, explaining that "in places of this character, the word 'auto' is the open sesame whereby evidences of a disorderly character are more readily obtained." Despite his best efforts to appear to be a habitué of clubs of this character, O'Neill was treated with suspicion at Marshall's. He noted that they refused to serve him "at ten minutes of one," and he was "duly informed that owing to the excise law [he] could get no intoxicating liquors." James Marshall, the proprietor, "would, from time to time, go about the place and look about same to see that no disorder would manifest itself." Had O'Neill not had the good fortune to run into his acquaintance Patrick, a black entertainer, his "observations" may have stopped with the fact that Marshall abided by excise laws and patrolled the barroom to ensure that his patrons behaved themselves.[10]

O'Neill waved Patrick over and offered to buy him a drink, but the assistant manager intervened and called Patrick out into the hallway. When Patrick returned, he explained to O'Neill: "they were afraid of you, and didn't want to let me drink with you, but I want to fix you right here; I told him you were all right. Let me introduce you to Marshall, so that when you come in again, everything will be all right." Patrick, by virtue of his color and reputation, brought O'Neill into this inner sanctum, sanctioning him as "all right" and bestowing "regular" status upon him. In fact, O'Neill noted that "after Patrick had vouched for me, things seemed to brighten up in the place and Marshall contented himself by sitting down with a party of people." Shortly thereafter, O'Neill observed that "two negro men, a negro woman, who was holding a maudlin drunken man, entered and sat at a table near me, and the negro woman began to caress the white man."[11] Unlike a couple hours earlier, Marshall did not intervene to put a stop to this behavior. At that precise moment, he became guilty of running a disorderly establishment.

In his report on Marshall's, O'Neill noted that he observed "a party of eight colored folks, two of whom were colored women and one white woman, who was of the degenerate type as far as I can judge, and who I ascertained indirectly, of course, was the lover of a rather light colored Negro, who was in the party." Not only did O'Neill guess that the white woman was the partner of a black man, but he also surmised that "the white woman was evidently a habitué of the place from the fact that she was on very familiar terms with the colored entertainer and would from time to time applaud very boisterously their very mediocre performances." By using the term "habitué" in his report, O'Neill summoned up a specific image; undercover investigators frequently used the term to refer to people who engaged in debauched behavior—drinking, doing drugs, and frequenting cabarets. O'Neill also noted that the white woman enjoyed the "mediocre" performances of the black entertainers, indicating either a lapse in her judgment brought on by the influence of alcohol or a general lack of good taste.[12]

Many of the Committee's undercover investigators, when writing about mixed-race couples, emphasized that the white women appeared to be under the influence of alcohol, which allowed the investigators to interpret a woman's questionable behavior as a product of her intoxication. The Committee's efforts to segregate leisure establishments in New York City were in part about protecting the morality of white women. White women were portrayed as "victims"—of alcohol or seduction, or of their own bad judgment—but only when it was convenient to the Committee's overall plan. As discussed in the previous chapter, these were not women the Committee cared about deeply, however. Rather, by removing white women from mixed-race leisure establishments, the moral problem of race mixing, as understood by the Committee's members, would vanish. So the Committee used intoxicated white women in black-owned establishments as justification for sanctioning black proprietors.

O'Neill concluded his report by stating that he had "entered Marshall's thoroughly without prejudice . . . and the report I make is still without prejudice and I might say I consider the place fair in moral tone." Although O'Neill insisted that he did not suffer from racial prejudice (to discourage anyone from assuming that any negative reports he generated on Marshall's could be attributed to such an attitude), he remarked that "frankly, there were not evidences of disorder in the strict legal sense, but I have my own peculiar ideas of any place in which black and whites are entertained."[13]

Indeed, so did the Committee of Fourteen, as suggested by the number of undercover investigators who did *not* express the same kind of dismay when they encountered all-black establishments, or mixed-race establishments that served men only. For example, black investigator Pogue visited Bowman's Café at 135th Street and Fifth Avenue in Manhattan and observed "about fifteen persons of both sexes all negros drinking at the different tables. Here I observed nothing out of the ordinary going on."[14] Undercover investigators who visited supposedly disorderly establishments that were frequented by both men and women often made note of table switching or women smoking. Pogue's report suggests that what black men and women did together was not of consequence to the Committee of Fourteen.

A more critical report of an all-black leisure establishment, the Green Cup Café at 6 Carmine Street, noted that the barroom was occupied by four "'buck negros' and 2 wenches," one of whom was "standing in the middle of the room arguing with the other wench who was seated on top of a table with her clothes half way up her back. The profanity and obscene language used by these wenches in their discourse was unbelievable." Shortly after the investigator took a seat in the barroom and ordered a drink, he noted, "the wench who had occupied the center of the floor followed me out and . . . drank a gin with me." The woman then "commenced to nag the bartender, 'Phil,' for a pinochle deck, saying, 'I'se gwine to hab nothing to do wif no man tonight; I'se gwine to play pinachle all night.'" The investigator was appalled at the behavior he witnessed, as evidenced by his need to represent the black woman's pronouncement in dialect. The investigator, though, asked the bartender his opinion of the patrons and the environment. Phil replied, "they're great people . . . always happy, no matter what happens." The investigator noted that he "argued" with Phil about his assessment of the clientele and then left the establishment.[15] Clearly, this particular white investigator had disdain for the black men and women he found in the Green Cup Café, and he did not share Phil's judgments regarding his customers. This investigator, however, did not describe the establishment as disorderly or as one that required watching. His report suggested that because all of the patrons were black, there was no real reason for the

Committee to intervene as the black women did not need to be saved from black men. His report surely would have been different if there had been white women in the establishment.

Similarly, investigators who encountered black and white men socializing together in public expressed no concern in their reports. For example, David Oppenheim returned a series of reports from investigative junkets through Brooklyn in December 1915. At the first establishment, he counted "4 black men, 6 white men in barroom very noisy, 4 men in sitting room, 1 was sleeping on table saw no women here, 3 men playing checkers in sitting room." In the next establishment, he observed, "in barroom 5 colored men 4 white men, no women here, were not disorderly."[16] Although the issue of race mixing was gendered, a problem only existed if women—white women—were present. To the Committee and its investigators, homosociability among men—drinking, playing cards after work—in a mixed-race environment did not set off alarms. Moreover, it did not threaten the established gender or racial order in any significant way. The presence of white women and black men, however, threatened to beckon in a mongrelized future. Whitin admitted in a letter to Ruth Standish Baldwin, his ad hoc adviser on issues relating to black New Yorkers, that there were "certain places to which both races go and sometimes a very light colored girl is taken for a white woman with a colored man and . . . this arouses much antagonism."[17] Whitin and other Committee members hid behind the notion that white women needed to be protected—from becoming drunk, from seduction, from predatory black men.[18]

Although the mingling of the races in public was not illegal in New York City or State, the Committee of Fourteen used its considerable (unofficial) powers to enforce the separation of the races in public accommodations and amusements. It effectively ushered Jim Crow into a city that historically has not been thought of as a segregated place—in fact, in a city and state that had strong provisions against discrimination and that had no antimiscegenation laws.

In 1873, New York State passed its first civil rights act, which guaranteed "'full and equal enjoyment of any accommodation, advantage, facility, or privilege furnished' by public conveyances, innkeepers, theaters, public schools, or places of public amusement."[19] In 1895, 1905, and 1909, the state expanded the original statute, granting all persons "full and equal rights and privileges" in all "places of public accommodation and amusement."[20] By then, New York State possessed one of the most extensive civil rights codes in the United States, which covered a wide range of facilities, including hospitals, amusement parks, schools, and restaurants. In 1913, the Levy law established that "accommodations, advantages, facilities and privileges" could not be "refused, withheld from or denied to any person on account of race, creed, color or national origin."[21] In addition to adding "creed" to the statute, the Levy law instituted fines or prison sentences for anyone found guilty of violating the law.[22]

Despite these extensive civil rights codes, the Committee of Fourteen found a way to enforce the separation of the races, which it imagined would restore moral order. The Committee of Fourteen's agenda was part of a larger trend in New York City. By the end of 1913, the Carswell Act, which prevented the marriage of blacks and whites, was introduced (but not passed) in the New York legislature; the New York State Boxing Commission instituted a rule prohibiting blacks and whites from sparring with each other in licensed boxing clubs; and the New York National Guard refused to start a black regiment.[23] The Committee of Fourteen operated on the logic that if one of their investigators could engineer an interracial encounter in an establishment run by a black proprietor, then any man could. For instance, Oppenheim's investigation of the Anstel Hotel in Brooklyn could have been brief. From the outset, Oppenheim had good information that the Anstel Hotel was disorderly: women under the age of eighteen were being served alcohol in violation of excise laws, and this approach was the easiest and most legitimate way to revoke a proprietor's license. He could have noted the excise violations and moved on to another establishment, but Oppenheim opted to stay and descend further into the events.[24]

Foots, the assistant waiter, sat Oppenheim at a table with three unescorted women. Oppenheim bought drinks for the three women, and one of them, Martha, asked him if he was drinking alone; he replied, "I got to, no one wants to drink with me, she said I will, but I didn't take her hint, I thought there was nothing doing with her because from the conversation at the table I found out one of the girls was her sister."[25] Oppenheim initially believed that these three unescorted women were prostitutes out working together, but when he discovered they were sisters, he decided that they could not possibly be prostitutes. He abandoned his interaction with them and worked on getting himself invited to another unescorted woman's table.

In the meantime, Oppenheim managed to get "pretty friendly" with Celia, a woman at another table, and she gave him her address. She lived in a boardinghouse with several other girls, who, she said, went "out hustling" together. When Martha noticed that Oppenheim was paying a lot of attention to Celia, she became jealous. While Celia was in the restroom, Martha slipped her address to Oppenheim, and they made a date to spend an afternoon together. She warned Oppenheim not to tell any of the other girls that they had made plans, however, because they would get angry with her. Martha explained that the other girls, including Celia, were "out for the dollar and they always blame her for stealing their men away."[26]

Martha explained to Oppenheim that, unlike her friends, "she ain't out for the dollar but is as game as the rest of them, and if she likes a white man, she'd go the limit with him, she wouldn't expect any pay for it but if she needs a pair of shoes or [shirt]waist she'd expect him to buy it for her."[27] Martha distinguished herself from her friends who worked as prostitutes and expected monetary compensation for sexual favors; Martha happily accepted goods in exchange for her services.[28] Moreover, she did not consider herself a prostitute; rather, she participated in a barter system that would get her what she needed. Martha also suggested to Oppenheim that her friends, who were black prostitutes, regarded white men simply as opportunities to make money and that they saved their personal intimate encounters for black men. Martha, though, was willing to sleep with white men simply because she liked them, and the material benefits were an added bonus.

Oppenheim explained in his report that despite Martha's warnings about the other girls, he "got tangled up with both women," and "each of them wanted me to go home with them." Oppenheim, ever the gallant gentleman, explained that he would "have to see Martha home [because] she lives" far away "and there are no trains running." As an undercover investigator for an organization that was trying to reduce prostitution, Oppenheim bore no professional responsibility to escort these—or any—women home safely. He could have disengaged and walked away; instead, not only did he insist on seeing the young women home, but he also accepted an invitation from another woman to "get a couple of pints of whiskey and come down to [her] bungalow." So this woman, her male companion, Oppenheim, Martha, and Celia "went to 42 Carlton Ave, where we found another couple (Jule and a man that she is not married to just living with him) another blk. man also came in a little later, he was looking for some blk. girl."[29] The Committee of Fourteen, despite its moralism regarding other realms of people's lives, was unconcerned with the goings-on in private homes. There was no logical, professional reason for Oppenheim to continue reporting these events. But he was a persistent and curious investigator.

After having finished the liquor at this impromptu house party, Martha, Celia, and Oppenheim returned to Martha's boardinghouse. Oppenheim remarked in his report that "there was no way of getting out of it"; he *had* to go. Once back in Martha's room, he reported, "the 2 girls undressed and went to bed and waited for me to get in with them[.] I said I would as soon as I finished smoking. I made no attempt to undress till they finally fell asleep, I had to sit in the chair all night as all doors were locked and I couldn't make my getaway."[30] What must have been going through Oppenheim's mind as he sat in that chair all night, smoking? Did he actually join the two young women in bed? Why did he proceed to record all of this information for Whitin, when he had acquired ample evidence hours earlier, upon crossing the threshold of the Anstel Hotel? Could the act of writing the report have served as a cleansing ritual for Oppenheim? By purging himself of the experience, by dumping it into the narrative framework of a report, was he saving himself from charges of immorality while also getting to experience the thrill of transgressing racial and moral boundaries? What must Whitin have thought when he read this report? The manner in which Oppenheim explained that he had to escort these two women home, that he could not escape the room because the doors were locked, betrays a sense that he was concerned with how the Committee may have regarded his behavior. In fact, by going home with two prostitutes, Oppenheim was guilty of supporting disorderliness and sexual immorality. Fortunately for Whitin and Oppenheim, the system of economic blackmail that the Committee of Fourteen employed meant that Whitin did not have to worry about putting his investigators on the witness stand.

On the basis of undercover investigators' reports, the members of the Committee of Fourteen had a picture of the disorderliness at Protest List establishments and could tailor their responses and punishments accordingly. To be removed from the Protest List, proprietors were forced by the executive or general secretary to attend a lecture and perhaps sign a promissory note. These promissory notes usually required proprietors and their staff to observe excise laws, but the content of the letters was modified to cover violations particular to the establishment in question. In the case of black proprietors, the Committee tailored the promissory notes to address interracial mixing. Proprietors promised that they would serve black and white patrons in separate rooms or refuse service to white patrons entirely. For instance, William Banks, the proprietor of a club at 206 W. 37th Street, signed a promissory note in 1908. Afterward, he stated in a letter to Whitin that he had "punctiliously adhered to the exclusion of the Caucasian and the Negro. I have not permitted them to mix. . . . I have, however, refused admittance invariably to either a colored man and a white woman or white man and colored woman."[31]

The Committee enacted its agenda through more than extralegal promissory notes. By having its investigators regularly appear in black-owned establishments in predominantly black neighborhoods, the Committee spread the fear of the promissory note and the attendant economic reprisals for those who did not follow the Committee's rules. The investigators succeeded in creating a new self-policing mentality among black proprietors, who stopped seeing dollar signs when they looked at a white patron and instead began to see the white customer as a reason they could lose their livelihood.

For example, Whitin dispatched investigator David Oppenheim to black-owned and black-patronized establishments in Brooklyn to determine if they permitted race mixing. When Oppenheim arrived at Rickey's (which he mistakenly and consistently referred to as Richey's) at midnight on October 23, 1915, he was let in without question and did not have to resort to any of his "tricks" for getting into black establishments, such as telling the doorman that he was not white but Cuban.[32] He entered the "sitting room," where he "found about 50 people . . . about 15 couples, 10 men, 6 unescorted women all blacks and 1 white man sitting with a black man. Most of the women were smoking cigarettes." Oppenheim sat down and ordered a drink, but as soon as the waiter brought it to him, the proprietor chastised the waiter:

> Mr. Richey said to him, why man this is one of Whitin's men and you serve him with drinks, the waiter said I saw him here several times before and that's why I am serving him, the waiter then made an attempt to take drink back I said all right take drink away but knock that idea of me being Whitin's man out of your head. Richey then said well as long as you brought it let him have it.[33]

For Rickey, allowing unescorted black women into his barroom was a calculated risk, but serving white men—and getting caught—would definitely get him called into the Committee's office. (Ironically, Oppenheim employed the same tactic that the local branch of the National Association for the Advancement of Colored People used to gather evidence to prosecute discrimination cases.)

Notwithstanding the fact that Oppenheim implored Rickey to disabuse himself of the notion that he worked for Whitin, Rickey remained suspicious—and rightly so. He returned to Oppenheim's table and asked for his name and card; when Oppenheim obliged, "he said yes that's the name you told me last time." Rickey softened a bit, and Oppenheim engaged him in a conversation. Rickey told him that he was "trying to run his place respectable . . . he pointed to a sign on the wall (no women allowed without escorts) and said that was to keep out the prostitutes." The topic of the

Committee's policy on race mixing came up. Rickey claimed that "Mr. Whitin told [me I] could serve white people but to try to discourage them from coming again."[34] How a proprietor was to go about enforcing that policy remained unclear.

About a month later, Oppenheim visited Chadwick's Novelty Café. Chadwick seemed to succeed in discouraging white patrons where Rickey had not. Oppenheim "knocked at door, colored man on inside motioned me to go away." Perhaps this would have deterred an ordinary white patron, but not Oppenheim. He asked the bouncer to send out his boss. Oppenheim noted in his report that "a few minutes later a colored man came out. I said to him I have been here several times and I don't see why you don't let me in, he said we don't let any white men in here unless we know them." Oppenheim persisted, quite possibly to see if he could get Chadwick to break the agreement he had made with the Committee to refuse service to white patrons.[35]

Oppenheim continued: "I told him . . . that I was known all over Harlem. I told him I could go to any colored place in Harlem and they would let me in," and he mentioned "Baron Wilkins, Leroys and a few others." Chadwick explained that "he was not acquainted with the people in Harlem and that he couldn't take any chances on letting [Oppenheim] in." Oppenheim was hoping to use his familiarity with other black-owned venues as a wedge to open this door, but the proprietor would not budge. Chadwick replied, "I don't doubt you are all right but I can't let you in unless some one I know introduces you." Oppenheim replied, "well if you won't let me in I guess I'll take a ride to Richey's on Dean St." Chadwick perked up a bit, asking "do you know Rickey"? Oppenheim replied that he did. It was probably clear to Chadwick that Oppenheim did not know Rickey that well, seeing that he got his name wrong. Chadwick seized on this opportunity to get rid of Oppenheim, though. He told Oppenheim that "Rickey is a very good friend of mine, if Rickey comes down with you I will let you in or else have Rickey phone me. I asked him his name, he said Chadwick I said when I get to Rickey I'll have Rickey phone." Oppenheim asked Chadwick if he ever let white men in; Chadwick explained that "he lets some white men in but they are friends of his that used to go to school with him."[36]

Four years later, Oppenheim attended the Al Reeves Beauty Show at the Casino Theatre on Flatbush Avenue. The Committee instructed him to look for uniformed servicemen under the influence of alcohol, in violation of the Selective Service Act. As the "lady usher" showed him to his seat, he started a conversation with her about conditions in Brooklyn. She told him that "there ain't a cabaret around here where any colored person could go out for fun" ever since "they close up Richeys."[37] It may have taken a while, but the Committee of Fourteen, working off of Oppenheim's information, did it. They put Rickey out of business.

The members of the Committee of Fourteen suspected that they would encounter some opposition to their agenda from black New Yorkers, and so they attempted to find black allies in order to forestall that opposition. In September 1911, Whitin and other members of the Committee embarked on an outreach campaign to round up some African Americans of the "better class and reformer type." Whitin had been casting about for black associates—to little avail—for a few years. In 1909, he wrote to Ruth Standish Baldwin, member of the Committee of Fourteen and personal friend of Booker T. Washington, expressing his concerns "as to how to treat fairly and wisely the troubled places of the Negroes."[38]

Ruth Standish Baldwin was active in civil rights in New York, and she easily became Whitin's point person on all issues pertaining to African Americans in the city. His letters to her were candid—in that they expressed his confusion over how to deal with the "race problem"—in a way that his exchanges with "race leaders" were not. He remarked that there were "not many" black-owned establishments in New York, "but it is difficult to get satisfactory inspection and I find something of a sentiment, oh, well, they are niggers why trouble about them, either as to character or attempted cleaning up. This does not help me."[39]

Whitin intimated that his white investigators were incapable of returning the necessary "evidence" of the immorality of these spaces, but that so long as these establishments were run exclusively for African Americans, he saw no reason to waste his Committee's limited resources. Whitin also suggested, however, that to *not* attend to such establishments was equally unacceptable. His solution to this moral quandary was the creation and maintenance of clean, orderly, single-race leisure establishments. Whitin appealed to Baldwin for help on this matter, asking her if she knew "any colored man in this City who is of the Booker T. Washington type who would be willing to discuss the problem with me."[40] Whitin assumed that a "Booker T. Washington type" would assist him in preventing race mixing in public accommodations, and that this person would share the contention that "in all things that are purely social we can be as separate as the fingers, yet one as the hand in all things essential to mutual progress."[41] Whitin wanted to see separate barrooms and cabarets for blacks and whites—"separate as the fingers"—and he hoped to work with this person, "one as the hand," to enforce what amounted to Jim Crowism and outright racial discrimination.[42]

Whitin and the Committee of Fourteen hoped that if they could announce to black proprietors that other black men found their establishments to be disorderly, then these offenders would believe that the Committee's evidence was unimpeachable and would acquiesce to its demands. The members of the Committee also believed that black proprietors' critiques of their policies were based on the fact that the Committee did not have enough black men to investigate black establishments and that that was the sole reason its evidence was skewed. The Committee did not understand that criticism by black proprietors was aimed at its overall social vision: segregation in New York City's world of leisure. Black allies, Whitin imagined, were necessary to lend his organization credibility and authority in matters pertaining to black establishments.

On August 14, 1910, Booker T. Washington wrote to "my dear Mrs. Baldwin" and begged off on direct involvement with the Committee of Fourteen, citing a busy schedule. He wrote, "Bear in mind that I am not a citizen of New York and that I should not 'dabble' in many of these matters which are purely local. Anything that I can do, of course, to aid the work you are engaged in I am always willing to do, but purely local questions I think I ought not to take up."[43]

Whitin devised an alternate solution. He invited a few prominent African American men, some of whom had been recommended by Baldwin, to attend a meeting at the Committee of Fourteen's offices. The invited included Dr. William Lewis Bulkley, founder in 1906 of the Committee for Improving the Industrial Condition of the Negro in New York, and Dr. W. H. Brooks, pastor of St. Mark's Methodist Episcopal Church and a founder of the National Urban League.[44] Professor George Edmund Haynes, who had earned his Ph.D. in sociology from Columbia University and was a cofounder of the National Urban League, was also invited.[45] It was Fred R. Moore, however, editor of the *New York Age* and founding partner in the Afro-American Realty Company, who became the Committee of Fourteen's most valuable ally among "respectable" black New Yorkers. Moore knew Ruth Standish Baldwin from the National League for the Protection of Colored Women, of which he was chair in 1910, and through his involvement with the Commission for Improving the Industrial Conditions of Negroes in New York and the National League on Urban Conditions among Negroes.

Under Moore's editorship, the *New York Age* expressed and exemplified a northern, urban version of the conservative social vision of Booker T. Washington, emphasizing concepts of self-sufficiency and uplift.[46] In 1907,

Washington had purchased the *New York Age* and appointed Moore editor.[47] Critics quickly dismissed the paper and its editor as entirely under the thumb of Washington. Although Moore was widely considered Washington's right-hand man in New York, he was more independent than this characterization suggests and accomplished in his own right.[48] Moore was also the general manager of the National Negro Business League, a partner in the Afro-American Realty Company, and in March 1913 was appointed minister and consul general to Liberia (although he resigned shortly after taking the oath of office). Under Moore, the *New York Age* developed into a widely influential newspaper within and beyond New York's black community; it was not merely an organ of Washingtonian thinking. During Moore's tenure, James Weldon Johnson became an editor in 1914, and from this position he wielded significant influence as an advocate both within and for the black community.[49]

By taking the point of view that some black New Yorkers were better equipped to lead the race than others, the *Age* emphasized the class differences in New York's black community. In so doing, it enabled a segment of the black bourgeoisie to trap itself in the tensions and contradictions of "uplift" ideology. Uplift emphasized "self-help, racial solidarity, temperance, thrift, chastity, social purity, patriarchal authority, and the accumulation of wealth." Class differentiation within the black community came to be viewed by black elites as a marker of "race progress."[50] These efforts to point to the creation of a black bourgeoisie, one that mimicked the class structure of white society but with none of the attendant material benefits, was an attempt to supplant "the racist notion of fixed biological racial differences with an evolutionary view of cultural assimilation."[51] The *New York Age*, with Fred R. Moore at the helm, exemplified uplift ideology.

In 1909, for example, the *Age* published an editorial titled "Conduct on the Corners." In it the author remarked that "we are constantly mortified by the conduct of our young people in various parts of the city . . . and especially do we call attention to the very bad habit our young men have of congregating on the corners." The problem, according to the author, was that such "offensive conduct hurts the race." It was not only the public socializing that the author found so objectionable but also the visible evidence of unemployment. The article concluded that these were "the little factors of the race problem which we ourselves may easily remove."[52] This mindset put the obligation of racial uplift on every single black New Yorker; every action became politicized and had the potential to contribute to either the success or the demise of the entire race.

In January 1910, the *Age* ran an editorial called "A Fulfilled Need?" which explained: "There are a hundred thousand Negroes in Greater New York who do their shopping and attend the theater who are likewise lost for places of first-class restaurant accommodations."[53] Thus, for New York's black bourgeoisie, not only was there a need for more first-class accommodations, but there was also a need for places like Marshall's Hotel to be run according to the letter of the law so that they could remain open. The editorial board of the *Age* hoped that places like Marshall's would demonstrate to the Committee of Fourteen (and its allies in government, as well as the insurance, business, social work, and social activist communities) that African Americans were worthy of civil and political rights because they too had a law-abiding segment of the population who knew how to behave "properly" and had the financial means to shop, attend the theater, and stay in nice hotels. The coalescence of these impulses made Fred Moore an important ally of the Committee of Fourteen. Although this alliance was a shrewd one for black New Yorkers of a particular class standing and outlook in a particular moment, it ended up damaging the cause of civil rights. Ultimately, it did not overthrow the structure of racism but was instead handmaiden to it.

On the program for the Committee of Fourteen's first meeting with its black allies was the issue of "saloons and hotels conducted by colored men, or to which persons of that race resort." The guests would be presented with "the reports . . . received from the investigators, of conditions found by them."[54] The Committee hoped that "as a result of the conference and the examination of these reports . . . a just and effective way will be determined upon which to correct those conditions, which have been found objectionable."[55] As a result of this meeting, the Colored Auxiliary of the Committee of Fourteen, also known as the Committee of Seven, was created, with Fred R. Moore at the helm.

On September 15, 1911, Walter G. Hooke, executive secretary of the Committee of Fourteen, wrote to Fred R. Moore that he "view[ed] with the greatest hope, the result of your meeting, and trust that you as a member of the committee in charge, will be able to impress upon the proprietors of the colored places, the necessity of maintaining decent conditions."[56] Hooke and the Committee of Fourteen believed that someone of Moore's stature in the African American community would be able to exert influence—by dint of his "position"—on black proprietors.

Hooke also felt compelled to assuage any fears Moore had of a racist agenda on the part of the Committee. Hooke wrote: "Our greatest protest against these places is in no sense due to the fact that they are kept by colored men. I consider, however, that young colored women and men of the community are entitled to the same safe guards, and protection that we try to provide for the white young women and men."[57] These "safe guards" to the black community translated into separating white men and women from black men and women. The Committee figured that it would be easier to convince African American proprietors to bar white patrons from their establishments if it were an African American issuing the edict and enforcing the rules.

The Committee of Fourteen, therefore, charged its new "associate committee" with "assist[ing] . . . in the work of regulating colored saloons and hotels."[58] Fred R. Moore as chairman, Dr. P. A. Johnson, Dr. E. P. Roberts, Counselor James L. Curtis, and George Haynes comprised the Colored Auxiliary of the Committee of Fourteen, which planned to begin meeting regularly with Hooke early in September 1913. Perhaps not surprisingly, Lucien H. White, the theater and arts reporter from the *Age*, began to work as an undercover investigator for the Committee in 1914.[59]

Moore gladly upheld his end of the bargain with the Committee of Fourteen by publicizing and explaining their joint effort to his readers. On November 2, 1911, the *New York Age* ran an article on the front page titled "About Committee of Fourteen." The article began with Hooke's statement denying "that the committee is extending most of its efforts to the closing of colored saloons and hotels in New York City." Rather, it noted that the Committee was "devoting its attention to any and all saloons, etc., not conducted along respectable lines." Hooke attempted to forestall any criticism issuing from black New Yorkers by stating that the Committee had been "more lenient with the colored saloonmen and hotelkeepers than with the whites" because its members recognized that "the colored people have less places to go to than the whites, and we have not objected to rathskellers run by Negroes, with music and singers, so long as the places were orderly and within the bounds of propriety."[60] What Hooke did not explain was that, for the Committee of Fourteen, race demarcated the "bounds of propriety."

Elements of New York's black establishment initially responded positively to the Committee of Fourteen's appeals to assist in controlling "disorderly Negroes"; the paradox for the Committee of Fourteen's black allies, though, was that by cooperating with the Committee, they were complicit in expanding Jim Crow throughout New York City. By joining forces with the Committee of Fourteen, these black men lent the imprimatur of "black New York" to this system of separate-but-equal leisure conditions. They tacitly accepted the Committee's decision to ignore state civil rights laws and did not subscribe to the "slippery slope of discrimination" argument that W. E. B. DuBois would raise the following year. Because the members of the Committee of Fourteen's Colored Auxiliary perceived and explained the plans as "uplift," as a service to the race, they did not view this partnership as a traitorous alliance.

The key to understanding the position taken by Moore and other like-minded men rests in their understanding of the importance of black-owned businesses. The main tenets of uplift ideology—particularly this northern, urban variant—were leadership, moral stewardship, and business success. As such, the men of the Colored Auxiliary seized on this unique opportunity presented by the Committee of Fourteen. They would be in charge of disciplining recalcitrant black saloon keepers and encouraging those who maintained orderly establishments—those who were a credit to the race.

Simultaneously, black saloon keepers organized for their own protection and to control moral conditions in their saloons. On June 8, 1911, the *Age* ran an article on the front page about the formation of the Negro Liquor Dealers Association of Greater New York. The piece stated that the "reform wave has struck the colored saloonkeepers of New York City and Brooklyn." The "principal reason for organizing is to put the saloon business on a higher plane and command more respect from the public." The first meeting of the association was held on June 5, 1911, at John W. Connor's Royal Café in Harlem. In attendance were Gib Young, Barron D. Wilkins, Walter Herbert (of the Criterion Café), Leroy Wilkins, Percy Brown, and Edmund Johnson, among other proprietors.[61]

The black men who created this organization owned and operated popular cabarets and casinos throughout New York City. Not coincidentally, the Committee of Fourteen frequently investigated their establishments. In 1909, for example, Barron D. Wilkins signed a promissory note stating that he would not "admit male whites to any part of the licensed premises to which colored women are admitted; That [he would] not at any time admit any white women."[62] Herbert's and Young's establishments were also under the Committee's periodic surveillance.[63] The *Age* celebrated the entrepreneurial spirit of the black saloon keepers—not only for running their own businesses but also for creating an organization to protect and police themselves.

By December 1911, the "colored saloonmen" were meeting with the Colored Auxiliary of the Committee of Fourteen to arrive at mutually agreeable conditions. The *Age* ran an article titled "To Raise the Moral Tone of Local Saloons: New York Colored Saloonmen to Organize to Better Conditions: Conference Held Saturday: Associate Committee to the Committee of Fourteen to Co-Operate with Saloonkeepers."[64] The article reported that the two groups—the Colored Saloonmen and the Colored Auxiliary—pledged to cooperate with one another, and that "there was not a saloon man present who did not express a desire to eliminate some of the features that have been declared objectionable by the Committee of Fourteen." Although the article did not explicitly state those features, it suggested that these saloon men would maintain establishments for "their race" only.

In particular, the black proprietors of Harlem pledged to "make an effort to decrease the number of drunks among colored men." These black businessmen were fighting for the moral uplift of black New Yorkers from behind the beer taps. The tasks of racial uplift and Washingtonian self-sufficiency coalesced in Harlem barrooms, as the Negro Liquor Dealers Association also hoped to ameliorate the "tendency of Negroes to support saloons and other business enterprises managed and owned by whites in Harlem . . . and plans will be made to equalize this support among the colored business institutions."[65]

Was it foolish of Fred Moore and his cohort to think they could win their arrangement with the Committee of Fourteen? The relationship between the Committee of Fourteen, their Colored Auxiliary, and the Negro Liquor Dealers was an uneasy one and resulted in a Faustian bargain for black proprietors. While the Committee of Fourteen drove the agenda by insisting that the separation of the races in saloons and leisure spaces was a way to prevent immoral behavior, the "colored saloonmen" seized on this opportunity to encourage black New Yorkers to support black businesses. Through cooperation and voluntary action, the black proprietors believed that they too could benefit if they helped the Committee of Fourteen solve the "problem" of race mixing. The black proprietors sought to use this situation to encourage, create, and maintain more black-owned, black-operated, and black-patronized drinking establishments.

Whereas the Committee of Fourteen wanted to create and maintain single-race leisure establishments in the interest of a racist and ephemeral "morality," the Negro Liquor Dealers Association seized on this moment to create more opportunities for black business ownership. Although the goals seemed similar superficially, the ideological underpinnings were not. The black saloon owners understood themselves as taking up the mantle of reformer; from behind the bar, they would police the moral conditions of their patrons and their neighborhood, and this endeavor ought to, in effect, broadcast to white New York that African Americans were moral, upright people who were worthy of being granted equal civil, political, and social rights.

The Committee of Fourteen and their African American allies arrived at a delicate balance, one in which each group's goals were nominally met. White patrons would be kept out of black-owned establishments, which satisfied the Committee's goal of a voluntarily segregated leisure landscape. The Negro Liquor Dealers Association took this opportunity to consolidate the power of African Americans engaged in commercial ventures in Harlem. Frederick Whitin and Walter Hooke must have breathed a sigh of relief, believing that finally they had the "Negro situation" under control. In September 1911, however, W. E. B. DuBois contacted Frederick Whitin regarding the Committee's treatment of James Marshall.

For DuBois, Whitin and the Committee of Fourteen represented a powerful force in New York City; as a group of supposedly "progressive" New Yorkers, they were pursuing a retrograde segregationist policy that stood in the way of the work of the National Association for the Advancement of Colored People (NAACP). In addition, the Committee had teamed up with a visible and influential group of black New Yorkers, which was lending its authority to this racist program.

DuBois explained in his first letter to the Committee of Fourteen that he had patronized Marshall's Hotel for nearly ten years, and he found it to be "a well run hotel, and on the whole as it seemed to me improving." He was confused as to why the Committee of Fourteen refused to recommend Marshall's for liquor license renewal, explaining that "as compared with other hotels in New York, white and colored, it seems to me that Marshall is unusually well run, and as a patron who is loathe to lose about the only place where a colored man downtown can be decently accommodated, I would be very glad to know the reason for the Committee's action."[66] DuBois implied that the grounds for the Committee's recommendation were not the actual conditions at Marshall's Hotel but perhaps were something else, something unseemly.

One year later, DuBois contacted Frederick Whitin and the Committee of Fourteen on the subject of Marshall's, reiterating the points made in his earlier letter. In addition, he said that he was "sorry to hear" that the Committee was still refusing to recommend Marshall for a liquor license and asked "if this decision of the Committee is because of any violation of the law on Mr. Marshall's part or is it for other reasons."[67]

The following day, Whitin replied to DuBois. He argued that the problems at Marshall's were not of the kind "which the casual diner in the place might observe." DuBois, pioneering sociologist, clearly had powers of observation superior to those of the casual diner, but Whitin proceeded to elucidate the Committee's logic anyway. He explained that Marshall's was "a place which if it could be conducted for either your race or mine, undoubtedly would not be objectionable. In addition to being on the border line of entertainment places, it has that unfortunate mixing of the races which when the individuals are of the ordinary class, always means danger."[68] Whitin operated from the assumption that, despite being of different races, he and DuBois would share opinions on the subject of the "common classes" because of their own respectable class positions. Marshall's Hotel offended Whitin because black and white patrons were allowed to sit together, were served together, and danced together. He assumed, wrongly, that DuBois would agree with him.

DuBois challenged Whitin. "If the objections against Mr. Marshall's place are on account of the races being served together there as you say in your letter," wrote DuBois, "then the Committee of Fourteen is seeking to violate the laws of the State of New York, which expressly declare that discrimination between races must not be made in places of public entertainment." He warned Whitin that he would be gathering "further information on the subject" as he was "loathe to believe that the Committee of Fourteen is ready to take any such illegal position."[69]

Whitin expressed surprise and confusion that DuBois did not share his position, yet he remained steadfast in his convictions. He believed that he possessed "true" and accurate information pertaining to Marshall's because of the information gathered by his investigators—and because he believed that he was doing a service to the black race by attempting to clean up "their" lower class.[70]

Whitin explained to DuBois that, in negotiations with Marshall, he maintained the position that if Marshall (indeed all black proprietors brought into his office) were to refuse service to white patrons, then the offending establishment would be removed from the Protest List. Whitin continued, expressing surprise at the position DuBois was taking: "With regard to the law of discrimination the point which you suggest is rather the reverse of the ordinary, a discrimination against the white man. The law was passed as I understand it to secure justice to the members of the negro race and was not intended to be used as a means to permit that which both races agree is objectionable."[71] Whitin saw the civil rights laws as steps toward the erosion of moral order in New York City—that they would permit (and perhaps encourage) mixed-race sociability like never before. But it is on this point that Whitin erred; he seemed to think that because the members of the Colored Auxiliary were willing to help him separate the races, they shared his point of view on the moral aspect. Whitin made another mistake when he conflated the ideological position of the Colored Auxiliary with that of DuBois.

DuBois responded with horror to Whitin's interpretation of the state laws. He pointed out that "the state law in question is not simply to protect colored men, it is to prevent discrimination on account of race or color and has been invoked in behalf of white men and sustained by the courts."[72] Whitin countered that DuBois's logic was the same as that used by desperate proprietors. Whitin cited the "the hotel law [which] requires hotel keepers to admit all persons who are in proper condition and able to pay for the accommodation." Hotel keepers, however, were not supposed to admit unaccompanied women, and Whitin pointed out that that "could also be called an unlawful discrimination."[73] Using this reasoning, Whitin rejected DuBois's interpretation of the antidiscrimination laws.

DuBois enlightened Whitin on the meaning of discrimination. "It would be illegal for your Committee to force any colored man to refuse to entertain white persons in his place of business or compel any colored man to promise any such discrimination," he wrote. DuBois then remarked that if the Committee continued to pursue this policy, "the matter will not be allowed to rest where it is."[74] Whitin realized that, despite the cooperation of his Colored Auxiliary, he truly had a conflict with the "colored" race. He had imagined that his position was simple to enforce: make Marshall and other black proprietors stop serving white people, and then leave the problem of immorality in the black community to black leaders.

Whitin replied to DuBois, asking if they could meet to discuss the problem at length. In terms of discrimination and immorality, Whitin explained that he saw the issue as "a question of which of the two laws is more important." As such, the solution was simple for Whitin. He attempted to set out his reasoning for DuBois, arguing that "if we find that the association of the two races under certain conditions results in disorderly conditions and their separation results in a discrimination based on race or color, we must choose between the horns of the dilemma. I naturally hold a brief for the point that disorderly is worse than discrimination. It seems to me that you will hold a brief for discrimination."[75] Indeed, in the worldview of Whitin and his cohort in the Committee of Fourteen, sexual immorality was the ultimate concern. Therefore, they believed that if they could prevent black and white men and women from mingling in places where alcohol was served and dancing encouraged, they would be taking one large step forward in cleaning up Gotham.

DuBois replied to Whitin, stating that he would be glad to have a conversation on "the question of racial discrimination as a means of stopping immorality."[76] DuBois's phrasing of this clause casts light on the fact that Whitin *was* willing to break civil rights laws to end "immorality." DuBois explained that while he too wished "to reduce the immoral conditions in New York to a minimum among all people," he was only willing to cooperate with the Committee of Fourteen "if Marshall's or Rector's or any other restaurant in New York is breaking the law or encouraging illegal or immoral conditions."[77] And then, he concluded, such offending proprietors should have their establishments "closed or improved," not pushed into violating antidiscrimination laws as a solution to immoral or illegal conditions.

Whitin failed to persuade DuBois that Marshall's was especially immoral and deserved to be denied a license. DuBois refused to accept that black proprietors should be forced to institute a policy of discrimination. Although DuBois agreed that immorality was a problem, he did not see this immorality as a direct result of black and white people socializing in the same establishments. Moreover, he pointed to the fact that, despite New York State laws, Jim Crow lived in New York; there were few establishments where people of his race and stature could have a meal. Black New Yorkers had access to juke joints like the Green Cup Café. But would DuBois take someone like Jane Addams there for dinner? Or even go there himself?

In the final extant letter between DuBois and Whitin, Whitin promised to telephone DuBois so they could meet to discuss "how this Committee can correct the conditions which it was organized to suppress and yet to avoid as far as possible other unfortunate conditions of equal or less danger."[78] Here Whitin tipped his hand: discrimination, he conceded, was an unfortunate condition, but surely not as deleterious to American society as "immorality," which, in this case, functioned as code for "miscegenation." This communication is the final word in the debate between these two men; it is unclear whether they ever met personally.

Even with the money and influence James Marshall possessed within his own community and social set, he could not fight the Committee on his own. Despite DuBois's intervention, James Marshall finally succumbed to the Committee's pressures in October 1912. He was summoned to the Committee of Fourteen's office, where Frederick Whitin presented him with the damning evidence, gathered by his undercover investigators, and forced Marshall to submit to a humiliating lecture on how to improve conditions in his establishment.

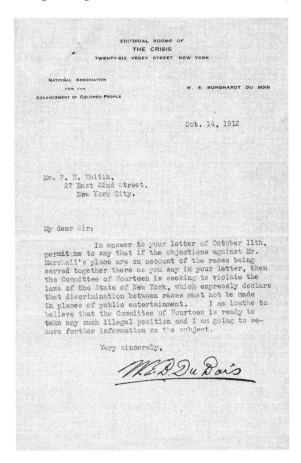

4. In this letter to Committee of Fourteen secretary Frederick Whitin, W. E. B. DuBois indicted
the Committee for violating civil rights laws in New York State. (W. E. B. DuBois to
Mr. F. Whitin, letter dated 14 October 1912, box 11, folder "DuBois, W. E. B.," Committee
of Fourteen records, Manuscripts and Archives Division, The New York Public Library,
Astor, Lenox, and Tilden Foundations.)

The next day, Marshall sent Whitin a letter in which he consented to
"live up to the said agreement." In addition, he agreed: "The dining rooms
to remain the same exclusively for colored people. Where the 2 large private
dining rooms are they will be made into one large room for private dancing
and entertainment *exclusively* for my white patrons only. . . . We will have
and run a strictly first class place for the Negro as well as one for the whites—
hoping that this will meet with your approval."[79] This agreement did not ask
Marshall to refuse to serve anyone but merely had him provide "separate
but equal" accommodations; it therefore avoided direct violation of New

York State's civil rights laws. Because of the considerable power the Committee of Fourteen wielded with the brewers and insurance companies, men like Marshall—otherwise wealthy, successful, powerful businessmen—were left in powerless positions. Marshall had to agree to the Committee's terms and abide by the promissory note at all times because he could never know when the white patrons seeking entrance were actually Committee of Fourteen investigators. Marshall, and others in similar positions, had no choice but to comply or risk having their liquor licenses revoked. Marshall's promissory note (and those signed by other black proprietors) resulted in the forced separation of the races in public accommodations—in part because of the cooperation of the Colored Auxiliary and the Negro Liquor Dealers Association with the Committee of Fourteen.

In 1914, the *Age* ran an editorial titled "Too Many Saloons in Harlem," which estimated that black proprietors operated only nine of the seventy saloons in the neighborhood. The editorial referred to white saloon keepers' practice of allowing patrons to run a tab: "The bigger the 'tab' he lets you run the better you like him. Consequently, there are many 'popular' white saloonkeepers." The piece concluded that white proprietors were responsible for the poor moral conditions in Harlem, and therefore they needed to be driven out of the neighborhood. "The white dealer in liquor has no interest in the morals of our women," and for this reason, white saloon keepers should be "put out of business, or be compelled to change their ways to an appreciable extent." For the editorial board of the *Age*, the benefit of having black men running businesses in and for the black community was that these individuals would presumably have a vested interest in the moral health of the neighborhood and community. Thus, they should be willing to "see to it that conditions are greatly improved and that less temptations are put in the way of unsophisticated young men and women."[80] Running a bar in Harlem was a race enterprise, and all black proprietors should have felt the ethical imperative to police their patrons and provide a space where the best moral conditions could thrive (never mind that good moral conditions may have meant smaller receipts at the end of the night). Indeed, given the influence of the Committee of Fourteen, running or patronizing a drinking establishment in New York City in the early twentieth century was more than a business; it was also a political exercise.

In 1913, the Committee of Fourteen's annual report provided limited details on its continued relationship with its African American allies. The report noted that, with the assistance of Fred Moore and the Committee of

Seven, the executive secretary was "advised in his regulation of places conducted by colored men, by members of that race interested in the Committee's problems." It concluded: "Such places as were purely dives have been eliminated, and the remaining saloons are being conducted in a much more respectable manner."[81]

Aside from this brief mention, there is little correspondence and few records from the Committee of Seven. Was the Colored Auxiliary merely the Committee of Fourteen's attempt to add an air of authenticity to its program for the "Negro sections" of the city? This seems to be the case, as evidenced by the fact that the annual report noted that black men interested in "the Committee's problems" offered their assistance. Still, black New Yorkers continued to criticize the Committee of Fourteen, which points to the fact that African Americans in New York were not of one opinion on the matter.

Gilchrist Stewart, chairman of the New York Vigilance Committee of the NAACP, became embroiled in a conflict with the Committee of Fourteen over an establishment owned by Gibeon L. Young of the Negro Liquor Dealers Association. The Committee of Fourteen charged that Young's establishment was disorderly. Stewart and the NAACP disagreed with this assessment, so they conducted their own investigations of the Young establishment—"both in the night, day, evening and early morning between one and five, for seven consecutive nights." Stewart maintained that his Vigilance Committee's investigation was an "impartial one," as opposed to those conducted by the Committee of Fourteen, and therefore his information represented what was "truly" occurring at Young's. Stewart asserted that Young was "a public spirited man whose place of amusement you are closing up and bankrupting upon the word of some colored paid investigators whose testimony would not be worth two cents to an impartial jury."[82]

For Stewart, the "character of a colored man which [the Committee of Fourteen] could hire to act as a stool pigeon to secure evidence of a colored place" would be entirely suspect, therefore rendering his evidence useless. Such a man, according to Stewart, "would have to be a detective and you know what detectives do when you hire them. They get the kind of evidence they think their employer wants. They either are broke or think a certain kind of evidence is necessary to the security of their employment."[83] According to Stewart, the men employed by the Vigilance Committee, on the other hand, engaged in such work for the benefit of the entire race.

Fred Moore, aware of Stewart's "stool pigeon" charge, drafted a letter to be sent out to all offending black saloon keepers. Moore explained that for black proprietors, "living up to the rules laid down" was of utmost importance. Moore continued: "A voluntary cooperation is preferred to our having to resort to punishment, or you to be closed because you do not comply with the reasonable requests we have made of you from time to time."[84]

On the issue of "stool pigeons," Moore argued that proprietors could "be the means of doing away with stool pigeons as they are called. . . . By exercising strength of character sufficient to convince your patrons that indecency is not going to be permitted—no complaints would then be made against you and your records would be a guarantee of proper treatment." Moore emphasized that "the Committee of Fourteen only asks that you conduct your places decently, remember, no colored place has been closed and many white places have been; and the warnings given them have been fewer than those given you."[85] Hooke, however, crossed out the "stool pigeons" comment in Moore's letter before the Committee allowed it to be sent out. The Committee of Fourteen may have been willing to cooperate with African Americans and delegate some responsibilities, but giving up the undercover investigators was out of the question.

Despite Gilchrist Stewart and Fred Moore's concerns regarding "stool pigeons," undercover investigation remained essential to the enforcement of the Committee of Fourteen's racial program. For them, it was not enough to send an observer, as Stewart's Vigilance Committee had done, into an establishment to check up on the moral conditions. The Committee of Fourteen believed that if conditions could be *created*, then proprietors were guilty of violating its policies.

The Committee of Fourteen had found tools to prevent race mixing in commercial amusements: economic blackmail and fear. Black proprietors were forced to bend to the Committee's demands or risk losing their licenses and thereby their livelihoods. Men such as Rickey and Chadwick were required to run all-black establishments, even if it did not suit them personally. Black businessmen were made unwitting and unwilling hosts to Jim Crow. Although the Committee's members and their black allies may not have understood their project as repressive, proprietors such as Marshall, who was forced to comply with the Committee, or Rickey, who was forced out of business, experienced it as such.

FIVE

Children and Immigrants
in Working-Class New York

Edward M. Barrows, field secretary for the People's Institute's Department of Recreation, argued in a letter to the board of trustees that how New Yorkers spent their leisure time had a direct impact on the "community good" and so was worthy of the Institute's resources. As an example, he pointed to a troubling rise in criminal activity among boys and the "social evil" among girls. He explained that, for instance, fighting, stealing, committing assault and battery, and destroying property were all "distorted attempts to play, on the part of the children." This situation resulted from the "morbid environment" in which the children were forced to live; it did not derive from inherent evil on the children's part. Barrows insisted that children turned to crime as play because the municipal government and social service agencies neglected their needs. With "wise forethought and supervision," Barrows argued, play could become "an incalculable force for good."[1] His department in particular and the People's Institute in general were well positioned to lead that fight.

Founded in 1897, the People's Institute organized public lectures, concerts, reduced-rate theater tickets for workers, holiday parties, and other similar events that appealed to a cross-section of New Yorkers. The offerings were based on the social vision of the Institute's founders, who had worked extensively as social workers, settlement house workers, educators, and advocates.[2] Charles Sprague Smith, former member of the Committee of Fifteen and professor of Germanic languages and comparative literature at Columbia University, founded and served as managing director of the People's Institute until his death in 1910. Smith and his colleagues envisioned the People's Institute as an entirely new kind of organization, one in which men and women of all classes and affiliations joined together to address the issues affecting "the people" of New York.

Early supporters of the People's Institute included activist and journalist Jacob Riis; Felix Adler, founder of the Society for Ethical Culture; Lillian Wald of the Henry Street Settlement; and Mary V. G. Simkhovitch of the Greenwich House Settlement and the Committee of Fourteen. Michael M. Davis, Jr., came to the Institute from the Russell Sage Foundation, for which he performed and supervised extensive investigations of the city's commercial amusements, dance halls in particular; he had also worked with the Committee on Amusement Resources of Working Girls. Others represented on the Institute's advisory council included American Federation of Labor president Samuel Gompers; James Bronson Reynolds, former chairman of the Citizens Union and headworker at the University Settlement Society; ministers William Rainsford and Lyman Abbott; Jewish philanthropist Jacob H. Schiff; and Edwin R. A. Seligman, also of the Committee of Fifteen.[3]

The People's Institute had faith in the ability of government to do good; moreover, its members recognized that Tammany Hall provided real benefits to its constituents by supplying services such as jobs, places to live, and emergency loans to recent immigrants, the unemployed, the injured, and the vulnerable. The People's Institute did not appreciate that Tammany expected votes in exchange for those social services, however, so it sought to supplant the importance of the political machine and to disaggregate politics, saloons, and elections.[4] Frederic Howe, director of the People's Institute from 1911 to 1914, explained that he "lean[ed] unaccountably to the Irish view of things," referring to a state "that did things for" the people. According to Howe, the Irish "warmed the state into a human thing, made frank demands on it for things they could not get for themselves."[5] Howe and his colleagues believed that the government in New York City could function as "a human thing" that met the needs and demands of its residents.

Armed with data collected by undercover investigators and social surveys, the People's Institute presented a convincing case about the lack of safe, supervised amusement resources available to those in the tenement districts and its consequences to the municipal government—once a sympathetic mayor and other high officials were in office with whom they could collaborate. City officials then moved to centralize the departments that attended to recreation resources, and the city and the Institute came to work together in a humane partnership that in many ways reflected the highest ideals of the Progressive movement. The New York City Committee on Recreation, created at the behest of the People's Institute, represented "constructive" work—not repressive or punitive, but instead ameliorative, addressing the difficulties experienced by immigrant and working-class New Yorkers. The People's Institute extended the reach of the state into immigrant neighbor-

5. The Cooper Union housed the People's Institute for its entire thirty-seven-year history. This exterior view features posters advertising upcoming events, including a People's Institute–sponsored lecture on health insurance by Pauline Newman, a concert by the Beethoven Musical Society at P.S. 63 (another People's Institute initiative), and a lecture by Eugene V. Debs. ("Cooper Union Exterior," no. 4 in 83, box 64, People's Institute records, Manuscripts and Archives Division, The New York Public Library, Astor, Lenox, and Tilden Foundations.)

hoods, through government appropriations for recreation and education programs, while simultaneously curtailing the state by demonstrating the deleterious effects the police had on children in these neighborhoods.

It was through their work with and on behalf of children that the members of the People's Institute came to realize that immigrant adults in New York City's tenement districts also had unaddressed needs, particularly in regard to leisure time and recreational spaces. Describing their work as "constructive," the members of the People's Institute aimed to develop alternative community institutions to engage the creativity and "native" talents of immigrant and working-class men, women, and children. The People's Institute provided alternatives to the dissipated lifestyles created by the conditions in tenement neighborhoods.

The power and authority of the People's Institute rested in its expertise with "objective" methods (which, its members believed, gave them an intimate understanding of the needs of immigrant and working-class people), and the conclusions those methods yielded. With information gathered by undercover investigators and trained social surveyors from the social work departments of the City University of New York and New York University, the People's Institute collected data and then provided the city government with focused energy and expertise for addressing seemingly overwhelming problems—problems that were "human" and yet ignored by the government apparatus. In this sense, information provided the basis for the advocacy work of the People's Institute.

The People's Institute's theorists identified leisure—where it happened, and how it happened—as urban America's most pressing problem, and they understood themselves as allied with their subjects in a way that the Committees of Fifteen and Fourteen did not. By building on existing community structures and traditions, the People's Institute created "constructive" alternatives to saloons, dance halls, and the streets, for immigrant and working-class New Yorkers living on the Lower East Side, Hell's Kitchen, the Upper East Side, and Gramercy Park. By conducting surveys of immigrant and working-class neighborhoods and compiling information supplied by undercover investigators (their own as well as those working for other organizations) on the "leisure problem," the People's Institute nurtured existing social forces and connections within the neighborhoods and gave residents the sense that they had a stake in something other than the local watering hole or Tammany man. By breaking the ties among corrupt ward politicians, the saloons, and Tammany Hall, the People's Institute hoped to birth a healthier democracy in New York City. Buried within the Institute's plans and assumptions was a desire to re-create, within the modern metropolis, a village ethos complete with the social control that comes from living in a close-knit community.[6] This aspiration became more of an imperative once the impact of the Great War was felt in the United States.

In the mid-nineteenth century, social reformers began addressing the needs of New York City's children. Despite the creation of organizations like Charles Loring Brace's Children's Aid Society in 1853 and Elbridge T. Gerry's Society for the Prevention of Cruelty to Children in 1874, little had changed for poor children—boys in particular—by the early twentieth century.[7] In the 1870s and 1880s, existing organizations attempted to deal with poor and immigrant boys' use of their leisure time and their presence on the streets by establishing and deploying mechanisms of social control, such as the Children's Aid Society's Newsboy Lodging Houses. At the same time, New York City's justice system took a "get tough" approach toward juvenile criminals and addressed the issue of criminality among boys by sending increasing numbers of them to prison for longer periods of time.[8] Child welfare advocates argued that this increasingly punitive approach to juvenile criminality backfired because the lodging houses and jails unintentionally provided boys with opportunities to hone their techniques and learn specialized criminal skills from each other. It is no accident that residents of the famed Five Points neighborhood referred to the Tombs prison, which sat in their backyard, as City College. Many of the neighborhood's young men were sentenced to the Tombs for a few years and came out with new skills and knowledge—all criminal in nature. Moreover, a stint in the Tombs or at Sing Sing often made the young man a local celebrity and natural leader when he returned to his neighborhood and his gang.[9]

Charitable organizations' attempts to "rescue" children were no more successful than the justice system's, largely because immigrant and working-class New Yorkers found their approach to children unacceptable at best and frightening at worst. Irish immigrant families in New York City referred to charity workers as the "child snatchers" because of the capacious definitions of "criminal" and "orphan" on which they operated.[10] For instance, in the late nineteenth century, the Children's Aid Society regularly sent orphans and street children, who were predominantly Irish Catholic, to the Midwest, where Protestant farm families adopted them. Unfortunately, many of those families regarded their new sons as little more than cheap labor. As a consequence, the children and their families developed a reasonable suspicion of reformers—on top of the fear and suspicion they already felt toward law enforcement.

Many social activists, including those affiliated with the People's Institute, considered children the future of American democracy. In the tenement districts of New York's immigrants and working class, however, children—boys in particular—regarded the government as their enemy. In neighborhoods like Hell's Kitchen, peopled by immigrants from Ireland, Italy, and eastern Europe, the first (and often only) contact boys had with municipal government occurred when they were arrested for playing kick the can in the alley or baseball in the street. As a result, the children of Hell's Kitchen developed a suspicious attitude toward agents of the state. Instead of learning a valuable moral lesson from their arrests, children realized that arrest must be avoided, and that propelled them into an actual criminal relationship with the state. As People's Institute employees John Collier and Edward Barrows argued in *The City Where Crime Is Play,* "If the Hell's Kitchen children are trying to be good citizens though the conditions will not allow them to be, then so are the rest of the city's children. If the Middle West Side needs a neighborhood and social programme, then so does New York City as a whole."[11] The Institute devoted part of its energies to claiming public space in Hell's Kitchen and other neighborhoods to create a supervised environment dedicated to children's play. Armed with information gathered by undercover investigation and intensive social surveys, the Institute devised what it believed was the most feasible solution to the "no place to play" problem.

Into this quagmire stepped the People's Institute, which operated from a different understanding and approach to the problems New York City's children faced. According to the Institute, children were not innately evil, nor were they creating problems; rather, children were being victimized by their environment. After all, boys and girls of the tenement districts in New York City—Hell's Kitchen in particular—played in the streets because there was nowhere else to play. The "logic of urban progress" worked against the development of neighborhood parks because, as the population grew, habitable land increased in value.[12] Neither parks nor playgrounds could house people or produce revenue, so few in the booming city prioritized their creation.

In addition, tenement apartments offered no space for children to play. For example, if the mother did outwork for the garment trade or rolled cigars in the kitchen, a child underfoot could ruin a week's worth of income with one careless move. Therefore, children were turned out onto the streets to play. Mothers favored this arrangement because the children could be seen easily from the apartment window; they were also within view of neighbors, shopkeepers, and others who could intervene in the event of danger.[13] Social activists and settlement house workers, however, took a dim view of this practice. On the streets, they believed, children were introduced at a young age to the underworld; they witnessed half-naked prostitutes soliciting from tenement windows, and brothel keepers hired them as cadets and lookouts. Activists argued that these children were transformed into vandals, petty criminals, and thieves because the neighborhood presented these activities as legitimate forms of entertainment.

In the early twentieth century, social activists began to reject moralistic interpretations of the problems facing young people in favor of environmental explanations. For example, Jacob Riis theorized that boys turned to gangs and broke windows for sport because they had nowhere to play and nothing else to do.[14] In fact, many of the children in the immigrant and

6. The People's Institute employed photographers to document conditions in neighborhoods like Hell's Kitchen; it was particularly interested in capturing conditions experienced by
children. This group of boys was playing kick the can in the alley amid the dirt and garbage.
(Krohn and Kaldtz Photographers, "Kick the can for which many youngsters are arrested,"
no. 39 in 83, box 64, People's Institute records, Manuscripts and Archives Division,
The New York Public Library, Astor, Lenox, and Tilden Foundations.)

working-class districts of the city did not attend school or dropped out at an
early age, so they literally had nowhere to be all day long. By the early twentieth century, settlement house workers and parks-and-playground activists
realized that children loitered in the streets, gambled, and made mischief
because of the lack of dedicated, organized play spaces available to them.

Assistant director of the People's Institute Lester F. Scott provided a similar interpretation: the absence of adequate play space led children "in the
poorer sections of the city" to "petty gambling such as crap-shooting and
card-playing . . . in the rear of cigar and candy stores." He explained that
"city children are no more naturally depraved than children brought up in
the country. They are simply forced to live pinched lives."[15] John W. Clark
of the Amity Church Settlement, which had participated in the Association
of Neighborhood Workers' survey on November 18, 1906, of adults and
children who played the dice game craps in the street, noted that it was the
"lack of 'something else to do'" that explained why "many boys take to crap
playing—especially the older ones."[16] Gaylord S. White of the Union Set-

tlement Association also observed that games like craps and marbles could not simply be suppressed; they were popular for a reason, and therefore something had to be provided in their place. White proposed that "opportunities for wholesome amusement and recreation—the means of more rational living—such as are furnished by the settlements, the boys' clubs, the playgrounds and recreation centres are helpful and should be greatly multiplied."[17]

It took the People's Institute three years to arrive at the reasoned (and reasonable) conclusion that the children in neighborhoods like Hell's Kitchen were not criminals but that they turned to criminal activity because their environment provided them with few other opportunities. This conclusion came only after an undercover investigator took an apartment in Hell's Kitchen in 1910, became a member of a gang, and a regular at the neighborhood saloons. People's Institute special investigator Edward Barrows succeeded in passing as a "denizen" of the street corners, "which year after year [were] the meeting places of gangs."[18] The neighborhood's residents slowly came to trust him and even to regard him as a friend and an ally. He recognized that these relationships were crucial to the success of his "field work," which became central to the People's Institute's larger goal of addressing the interrelated issues of child crime and the "leisure problem" in New York City.[19]

Edward Barrows's constant presence in and slow ingratiation into the neighborhood of Hell's Kitchen and its culture helped him to earn the trust of gang members and allowed him an intimate perspective on the causes and consequences of the neighborhood's problems. Unlike the Committee of Fourteen's David Oppenheim, however, Barrows never brought the authorities in to punish his "friends." Barrows's investigations did not result in the adoption of a new self-policing mentality by Hell's Kitchen residents, but they did bring play streets and social centers to the neighborhood for the residents' use. Yet these things were a mixed blessing. Barrows indeed brought services to an underserved "slum" neighborhood, but these services brought the government into the neighborhood, innocently enough at first. With these activities came supervision, however, and eventually surveillance.

Barrows had impeccable Progressive credentials: his authority stemmed from his experience working on "child crime" issues for the National Child Labor Committee, his work as an investigator for the Russell Sage Foundation, and his position as secretary of the West Side Recreation Committee. When he took on the investigation for the People's Institute and moved into Hell's Kitchen, his mission was to gain an understanding of the relationship among "juvenile crime and street gangs and street play."[20] He wanted to figure out why "juvenile crime [was] multiplying."[21] By living in the neighborhood for an extended period of time, Barrows ensured that he would have a different relationship to his subjects than did the "child snatchers" and that he would be interpreting his evidence and observations accordingly. Barrows was sympathetic to the boys in Hell's Kitchen; he understood the neighborhood as more than just a breeding ground for the next generation of Sing Sing inmates. Instead, he approached his task from the perspective that boys in the tenement districts had no choice but to use the streets as their playground because no alternatives existed. Rather than look at the children's use of the streets and arrive at a judgment about their morality or their parents' fitness as guardians, Barrows searched for a solution to the "no place to play" problem.

Because the boy gangs viewed adults in general and outsiders in particular with suspicion, Edward Barrows used an undercover technique to ingratiate himself into the culture of Hell's Kitchen. The neighborhood residents' mindset meant "that no investigator who is known as an investigator can find his facts. Still less can an 'uplifter' find his facts or do his work if he is known as an 'uplifter.'"[22] Instead, as Barrows and John Collier explained in *The City Where Crime Is Play*, he presented himself in the neighborhood as "a free-lance newspaper man and good fellow generally." A "good fellow," in the argot of this subculture, was a person who refused to cooperate with law enforcement officials and would not testify against another thief; moreover, a "good fellow" might even take the fall to protect another criminal.[23] Barrows explained that his "good fellow" pose worked with "the hundreds of adults and children with whom [he] became intimate in that neighborhood," and all were "still without an inkling as to [his] professional identity."[24] In addition, Barrows earned a gang's trust by presenting himself as a local, one who did not identify with the "adult" world of discipline and repression.

For Barrows, earning the boys' trust meant that he witnessed firsthand the way the police treated children, for example, arresting them for obstructing public passages or trespassing.[25] According to the *Police Practice and Procedure Manual*, police officers were supposed to

arrest and charge with Improper Guardianship any child actually or apparently under the age of sixteen years . . . who is abandoned or improperly exposed or neglected; who is in a state of want or suffering . . . who smokes or in any way uses any cigar or cigarette or tobacco in any form in a public place; or who frequents the company of thieves, prostitutes and vicious persons, or who does not subject itself to proper restraint or control by its parents.[26]

Individual police officers exercised enormous discretion in their interpretation of children's behavior and situations. Police officers who encountered "rowdies" on their beat sometimes took to meting out punishment themselves in the form of stern lectures or even beatings; still others regarded arrest as an intervention, saving a child from bad parenting and a bad environment.[27]

In Barrows's interpretation, though, the children did not violate the law; the law violated the children. For instance, through his extensive research in Children's Court records, Barrows discovered that the same section of New York City's penal code that punished burglary also punished baseball. He discovered that approximately 12,000 children were arrested annually in New York City, and most of those arrests were for playing games. For these young lawbreakers, Barrows noted, the "first arrest [was] normally a punishment for the attempt to play, and to play in ways that [were] intrinsically good."[28]

From the statistics, Barrows created a more complete picture of the "no place to play" problem. He separated child arrests into two categories. His first category included children who were arrested for playing "games which are against the law *only* because they are played on the street," such as "baseball, football, jackstones, singing and marbles." Barrows explained that the law (and law enforcers) did not understand that these children were just trying to find places to play their games. Instead, police officers treated the children as young lawbreakers, not children with special problems that "a morbid street environment" had created. Because the city government had "not provided play space" for children who lived in crowded tenement districts like Hell's Kitchen, Barrows ominously concluded that "in the streets of New York, under present conditions, play is crime and crime is play." Barrows's second category encompassed children who were arrested for playing "games which through their nature involve[d] an infraction of the penal code." These included "stealing, fighting, destruction of property and similar violations of the code of social procedure." Boys engaged in this kind of deviant or criminal behavior as a form of recreation.[29]

By arresting children, police officers ended up treating "good" and "bad" play in the same way. Barrows explained that, in the eyes of the law, "crap shooting [was] identical in terms both of punishment and of why the punishment is given, with chalk games, or ring-around-the-rosy, or kick-the-can. The arrests for gambling and for chalk games alike are treated as cases of street obstruction." As a result, these children did not know that there was a moral distinction between gambling and chalk games because they were taught (and learned) that they could be arrested for either. It was the lesson of the arrest and not the lessons of the game (like establishing and following mutually agreed upon rules) that stayed with these children. The tragedy, in Barrows's view, was that play was supposed to be "an alternative to crime—a cure for crime," yet in New York City these things were conflated and became synonymous.[30] Under these circumstances, how could play serve as a natural bulwark against crime? How was play to serve as the site where children learned how to cooperate, how to function in a group, or how to handle conflict? In essence, how were city children to learn early lessons about citizenship in democratic society?

Barrows discovered that his second category of play evolved out of the first. Because the city did not provide recreation spaces, children played in the streets and were arrested for it. As a consequence, boys formed protective societies—or gangs. The boy gangs were initially based on "the co-operative evasion of necessary law on the part of children."[31] For example, because the boys knew that they would be arrested for playing baseball in the streets, they stationed lookouts around their game to announce when the police were coming so their friends could scatter and avoid arrest. Barrows understood their logic but saw the practice as part of a progression; this collective evasion of the law in the service of baseball games was a slippery slope, as the gangs eventually turned to crime for entertainment.

Barrows learned that "gang stealing" developed naturally out of the gang members' desire for entertainment. In gang stealing, the boys posed as employees of local grocery stores and went "from tenement to tenement . . . taking orders from the housewives for fruits, vegetables, groceries." Barrows explained that once the boys had "a sufficient number of orders," they would spread out and "by a series of organized raids" on neighborhood grocers, "secure the goods which the housewives have ordered." The boys would then deliver and sell the stolen "goods . . . on a regularly established scale of prices." After the boys collected their money, they would "retire to their 'hang-out' where the money is divided into equal parts." The boys would then "shoot 'craps'" until one of them had won all of the money. "This boy divide[d] the winnings into two parts, one of which he spen[t] in treating the other members of the gang. The other half he is permitted to keep and spend for himself."[32]

Nothing illustrated the impact of the morbid street environment on children quite like gang stealing. The boy gangs devised resourceful ways to entertain themselves in their limited environment. Gang stealing fulfilled boys' needs economically, as the rules required the winner to spend half the money on his friends—usually for a trip to the movie palace or ice cream parlor. The process also provided a way for city boys to amuse themselves and fill their idle time, and it also gave them a certain amount of psychological comfort in an uncertain environment, not unlike the Chinese immigrant men who joined tongs. For Barrows, gang stealing did not mean that these children were hopeless; rather, he saw that "children tend[ed] to develop play leadership" that, he theorized, with "a little adult encouragement and guidance," could be coaxed in the right direction.[33] He advised that cities establish "play streets," which simply required the "allotting of streets which are little used by traffic, to be used by the children for play with the minimum of adult guidance and police supervision." He believed that this would encourage normal development in children and rewrite play as "an enemy of crime" rather than "the fountain-source of crime"—all at little expense to the city.[34]

Barrows's conclusions and proposed solutions convinced the People's Institute to undertake an additional study to corroborate his data. The Social Center Committee of the People's Institute devised a larger survey of play conditions, which they referred to as an "instantaneous" or "flashlight survey." For the purposes of the survey, they divided New York City into twelve districts. In each district, a "responsible civic organization . . . assume[d] direction of the survey." Participating organizations included the Progressive Party, the College of the City of New York, University Settlement, the Public Recreation Commission, and the South Harlem Neighborhood Association. On April 19, 1914, the People's Institute dispatched approximately four hundred "civic workers, who had been carefully drilled in advance, with tabulation sheets, maps" to the twelve districts to count the number of children and adults gathered in the streets. The surveyors were instructed to classify the games the children were playing and to determine whether the adults fraternizing with the children were a positive or corrupting influence.[35]

The data collected in this survey, used to supplement "the intensive studies of Mr. Barrows," confirmed his conclusions. The flashlight survey gave the People's Institute an instantly developed picture of the leisure landscape in New York City on one particular day. The Institute then used its data to extrapolate to the circumstances in the city writ large, as well as to those in other major American cities. The People's Institute understood the play problem as a social problem, but it was one that was quantifiable. The surveyors observed where and how children played; they counted and tabulated their observations and then made rational, dispassionate claims—based in "social science"—on behalf of the children in immigrant and working-class neighborhoods. Ultimately, they determined that "street play is deeducational in its tendency—cutting short the normal evolution of children's play interests which would, if society cooperated with them, lead the child upward toward social relationships."[36] The findings indicted the municipal government and its role in the perversion of the natural human impulse to positive social organization.

With this evidence in hand, the People's Institute approached the municipal government about its failure to provide recreation for its most vulnerable residents—and for its complicity in creating a permanent underclass. In this way, the flashlight survey challenged, rather than accepted, the city's suppositions about children's criminality. What kind of civilized society arrests innocent children for playing baseball? Demonstrating that the city created the child crime problem by not investing in play spaces and by deploying the full force of the law against children, the People's Institute argued that the city acted irrationally in its attempts to combat crime in the tenement districts. The People's Institute rendered the needs of the powerless concrete; by using the numbers and evidence its workers compiled, the People's Institute offered the city an opportunity to create new, alternative play spaces for children and made itself integral to the functioning of the modern, progressive city.

The members of the People's Institute sincerely believed that the city's lackadaisical approach to the human needs of its residents victimized the children in the working-class and immigrant quarters, but they also knew that arguing that the city was responsible for creating little criminals would not win them advocates in government. Instead, the Institute chose a dispassionate and "scientific" approach to the problem, and it presented its evidence and the possible consequences as being easily addressed through "simple solutions." When approaching the municipal government, the "efficiency" argument was the most compelling. For example, in her article titled "Why Play Streets?" People's Institute community worker Helen Ruth Richter relied on statistics to make this point. She noted that the "120,197 children who tried to satisfy their natural, healthy desire for play did so in the streets. No other recreation ground was convenient." Richter then moved into an exegesis of the dangers of street play. She noted that traffic was an "obvious" danger, as this "cruel reality" was evidenced by the "average of 300 children . . . killed every year while playing on the street." Although the vehicular manslaughter of children was of universal concern, Richter avoided the easy emotional appeal. Instead, she noted that the real problem with the number of children who were killed while playing in the street was that they were "a big loss to the city in dollars and cents. Up to the age of fourteen a child is a liability, cared for at the city's expense. . . . If 300 healthy children die every year through street accidents . . . but why continue? It is a simple problem in arithmetic."[37]

Richter and the People's Institute's members were not the only ones who noticed that children died in street accidents at alarmingly high rates;

settlement house workers also used this evidence as they lobbied the city for the creation of playground space. What was unique, though, was the People's Institute's solution to this "arithmetic problem." The People's Institute knew that there was no money in the city's coffers for the creation of playgrounds, so it proposed "play streets." "Why not close certain streets in each district of the city daily in the late afternoon, and let the children play in them, guarded from evil?"[38]

The People's Institute posed this very question to the city government and found a valuable ally in police commissioner Arthur Woods, who agreed to cooperate. Woods arranged to close five streets to traffic from three until six o'clock on weekdays. He also stationed a police officer at the end of each of these streets.[39] By1913–14, the Institute and the police department were cooperating on the play streets project. Three streets were opened in Greenwich Village; one on the Lower East Side, at East Fourth Street between First Avenue and Avenue A; and one in Hell's Kitchen (the Middle West Side), at West Forty-seventh Street between Ninth and Tenth avenues.[40] To each play street the People's Institute dispatched representatives who supervised the activities and kept older children from preying on the younger ones. In addition, the play streets allowed the gang presence to be neutralized because each representative made "use of the natural 'gang' leaders" to start group games and patrol the other children's behavior.[41] Finally, by having policemen keep vehicular traffic out of these streets, the People's Institute imagined (and hoped) that the children would come to regard the police as friends rather than enemies.

The circumstances in which Barrows lived in Hell's Kitchen while gathering his data and his intimate relationships with his subjects raise important questions: How many crimes were committed of which Barrows had foreknowledge? How many times did Barrows turn a blind eye and not report to the police? How many pilfered apples did he purchase from boys? Barrows's sympathies rested with his subjects, whereas investigators like Natalie Sonnichsen or David Oppenheim remained committed to the Committee of Fourteen. Oppenheim's and Sonnichsen's "transformations" were temporary and were in the service of repression, punishment, and a higher moral tone in New York's commercial leisure establishments. Barrows, however, worked in the interest of data collection and accumulation of knowledge. He wanted to understand the special challenges that faced young people in the tenement districts, and if he had called in the authorities, his real identity and purpose would have been revealed and his experiment short-circuited. He then would have found it impossible ever to help these children.

7. The plan for "play streets" was among the People's Institute's most successful programs. In this photograph, a large group of children are surrounded by police and adult supervisors; the children will presumably begin to play in a safer environment than their counterparts playing kick the can in the alley. (Krohn and Kaldtz Photographers, "Children playing in Street under adult supervision," no. 37 in 83, box 64, People's Institute records, Manuscripts and Archives Division, The New York Public Library, Astor, Lenox, and Tilden Foundations.)

Following on the success of the play streets project, the People's Institute expanded its reach to include adults in tenement neighborhoods with its creation of social centers. The People's Institute's Social Center Committee proposed an experimental plan: "to try out the public school as a self-governing recreation center and peoples' club house." "Self-governing" was critical to the success of this plan. The People's Institute took pride in the fact that their social centers were to be run by a committee from the community, not a head worker from the Institute. Each social center would "develop its own recreation and co-operatively manage and support its own activities."[42]

To this end, before the People's Institute's New York Social Center Committee opened its first clubhouse at Public School 63 on East Fourth Street in 1913, it sent Clinton S. Childs into the Lower East Side. Over the course of three months, Childs "spen[t] his days and nights in the streets, stores and gathering places around School 63," observing, talking, and listening to the neighborhood's residents. At the end of that time, he organized "a meeting of the neighbors, who organized a local governing body to finance and manage the community enterprise of School 63."[43] On the basis of their needs and desires, Childs assisted the local community in developing programs and moving neighborhood social life ("for the most part spent upon the streets, in the saloon and in the dance hall") into "a club house, town hall and democratic center for the life of the community."[44] These social centers were designed to provide alternatives to commercial dance halls and saloons, and ideally would protect the family and community from erosion by providing the social controls of a small village.

The social center at P.S. 63 grew out of an extant community organization. As Childs explained in "A Year's Experiment in Social Center Organization," the Wednesday Neighborhood Club ("an adult club organized by a volunteer worker of the Public Education Association") already existed and had founded a dancing club, which sponsored dances in the open courtyard of P.S. 63. The dancing club charged dues ("fixed at five cents per week") and issued membership tickets; it served not only to provide a supervised alternative to commercialized amusements but also to raise money to support its own activities and organization. The dancing club was the "nucleus" from which a "local self-governing committee was formed."[45] The money that the dancing club raised was "turned over for use in the Center, and the community organized was well on its way toward looking after its own social problems."[46]

After the success of the social center at P.S. 63, the People's Institute planned additional surveys and studies to determine how people were using recreational amenities in "typical neighborhoods" throughout the city. Included in this study were settlement houses, philanthropic institutions, and educational facilities, in addition to "commercialized amusements" such as dance halls and movie theaters. To pursue this wide-ranging and important work, the People's Institute recruited students from the sociology departments of the College of the City of New York and New York University, who received course credit for participating in this project. The Institute sent the student investigators into five different neighborhoods in Manhattan; they made "weekly reports to this office and their work will be a basis of further neighborhood study along this line."[47] Barrows, who headed this inquiry, explained that the new survey would provide the People's Institute with a better idea of the city's existing parks and playgrounds, as well as "undeveloped play spaces, of school buildings, armories and other possible public buildings, of recreation piers, public gymnasia and libraries, to meet the recreational demands of the people." After the study was complete, Barrows explained, "We propose to carry on a wide campaign for the adoption of this program as a whole by the city."[48]

In late 1915, the People's Institute presented the New York City Board of Estimate and Apportionment with its new collection of dispassionate, objective data. The Board of Estimate's responsibilities included, among other things, the city's budget. Convinced by the Institute's evidence, the board decided to "make an official investigation of the subject for the purpose of reorganizing the recreational life of New York, the readjustment of appropriations and the utilization of unused properties." In December 1915, it created a Committee on Recreation to do just that.[49] The stated purpose of this new municipal Committee on Recreation was the consolidation of the city's "playground and recreation work." Because the city was so large and the agencies dealing with play and recreation so numerous, the Committee on Recreation served as a clearinghouse, or "central committee," which oversaw the work of those "various departments."[50] The People's Institute worked closely with the city's newly formed special committee and declared victory in one battle in the larger war for leisure alternatives.[51]

During the first few months of 1916, the municipal Committee on Recreation implemented some of the People's Institute's recommendations and strategies. For example, New York City was the first city in the United States to create a "definite standard" regarding how much play space individual neighborhoods needed based on the density and distribution of the population and the age and number of children. This "definite standard" helped the committee to assess existing parks and playgrounds in particular neighborhoods, to avoid "duplication between play facilities," and to relocate duplicated facilities.

The city's Committee on Recreation, persuaded by the People's Institute's data collection techniques and studies conducted by "settlements or other local bodies" in individual neighborhoods, set out to assess the recreation resources of these neighborhoods. This municipal study was the first conducted in New York City to analyze "how many square feet of playground space is needed . . . what per cent of the need is being met by the present use of present property to the limit of its capacity, what per cent could be met by the temporary use of vacant lots and reserved streets in that neighborhood, and what are likely to be the needs in the future for that locality." The committee also began working with private agencies "to conduct summer playgrounds in order that public playgrounds need not duplicate those conducted by philanthropic bodies."[52] As a city agency, the Committee on Recreation had an advantage over charity organizations and other private groups: it could make "budget recommendations" for developing a recreation program to serve the entire city. This policy represented a significant step forward by the municipal government toward streamlining and rationalizing its approach to children's leisure; the city never took significant action in terms of adults' leisure needs until the war years, however.

As Americans became more preoccupied with the Great War, the Americanization of immigrants took on greater importance—for the People's Institute as well as the municipal, state, and federal governments. In fact, wartime proved to be an important period for the People's Institute, with the city coming to rely more on the Institute because the municipality did not have the human or financial resources to address the "immigrant problem." But failing to Americanize or assimilate recent immigrants came at a much higher cost in 1917 than it had in 1907.

"Americanization" meant very different things to different people and organizations. Settlement house worker (and member of the Committee of Fourteen and the city's Committee on Recreation) Mary Simkhovitch described the quandary of the immigrant in America and Americans' attitudes toward immigrants: "It is not that the immigrant does not desire to become American, but rather that a cordial welcome . . . is lacking in the attitude of Americans toward him. The first persons to Americanise therefore are ourselves. If we protect the immigrant from exploitation, if we insist on a better standard of training, of sanitation, of education, of public recreation, the immigrant will be a good American."[53]

People's Institute members believed that they were Americanized in the sense that Simkhovitch described; they were sympathetic and experienced in providing social services and therefore were in a good place to help immigrants become Americans. Through their work on behalf of children, the People's Institute had developed a method for working with public agencies and the government to solve social problems. In addition, through its work with children in the Irish immigrant community in Hell's Kitchen and the Italian and eastern European immigrants on the Lower East Side, People's Institute members became alerted to the problems all immigrants faced once they settled in the city. They believed the federal government actually created some of the immigrants' problems because federal authorities treated immigration as a process that was confined to Ellis Island: screening, processing, admitting, rejecting. The People's Institute argued that immigrants confronted problems once they were settled in the city and that services for immigrants should extend beyond the physical site of the immigrant landing depots.

The People's Institute succeeded in persuading the government to address the human needs of its new arrivals and aspiring citizens, and carved out an important place for itself in this new style of public-private partnership. In this way, the People's Institute stood in contrast to the Committee of Fifteen and Committee of Fourteen. Although all three organizations used undercover investigators, the People's Institute perceived itself as an advocate for the most vulnerable members of society, those who were victimized by ill-conceived and poorly implemented laws and those for whom the government operated primarily as an agent of repression. The People's Institute used undercover techniques to acquire knowledge, which it took directly to the appropriate departments of the municipal government, formalizing its ability and power to work as an advocacy group. The Committees of Fifteen and Fourteen identified the municipal and state governments as hopelessly corrupt; therefore, working around such government bodies was honest and ethical. By contrast, the People's Institute established partnerships with the same governmental authorities, a technique that came to full flower in terms of the working relationships the People's Institute forged with the municipal and federal governments in addressing the "immigrant problem."

Throughout 1917, various branches of the municipal, state, and federal governments tapped the People's Institute to assist in "secur[ing] the home front" through participation in and creation of a variety of Americanization campaigns. For example, the Committee on Aliens of the Mayor's Committee on National Defense approached the People's Institute's newly founded Training School for Community Workers and asked its leaders to develop and implement a series of "special courses for volunteer and professional workers in Americanization." The course of study began on October 1, 1917, and ninety-one students enrolled. The Training School for Community Workers proved well suited to the task of Americanizing immigrants in a humane fashion. Distinguishing itself from other schools of social work, the Training School for Community Workers claimed that its curriculum did not "overcrowd the minds of the students" with theory and academic studies; rather, its students were given practical experience and "immersed in civic situations."[54]

Aspiring community workers had five courses from which to choose, titled Industry, Co-operation, Recreation, Health, and Government. All of them focused on immigrants' needs and problems. The goal of training community and volunteer workers had as much to do with the government's concerns about disloyalty as it did with the People's Institute's concern for the needs of the immigrants themselves. These trained volunteers would permit "hundreds of thousands of immigrants [to be put] in constant touch with the more significant influences of American life."[55]

The city turned to the People's Institute and its community workers for help with its own programs directed at immigrants. During the 1916–17 academic year, the New York City Department of Education established and ran eighty-four Elementary Evening Schools for Foreigners. An estimated 40,000 immigrants attended these schools, but there were at least 250,000 more "who need the ministrations of the evening schools." Whereas the city did not understand why its evening schools for immigrants were failing, the People's Institute immediately recognized the problem: the schools did not engage the needs and interests of the immigrants, mostly because the city established the schools to satisfy administrators' concerns about loyalty on the home front, not out of actual concern for the immigrants themselves. Distressed by this fact, Henry E. Jenkins, district superintendent in charge of the evening schools, approached the People's Institute for assistance in turning the schools into places immigrants sought out.[56] He asked that People's Institute–trained "community workers" be placed in the city-run "night-schools for foreigners." The Institute readily agreed, claiming that the goal of this cooperative effort "was not merely to give the newcomers book-training, but to introduce them to American ways . . . and to give them a neighborhood consciousness."[57]

The People's Institute believed that municipal officials had initiated the night schools for foreigners with little to no knowledge of the prospective students. The Institute described a typical scene at a city evening school, providing an explanation for the 70 percent drop-out rate: "After toiling all day . . . these men and women come to evening school and, for two hours, sit wedged in between a seat and a desk built for a child of ten, and patiently struggle with the English language. No opportunities for relaxation or social intercourse are provided for them and they go out at the close of the term almost as strange to each other as when they came in." The Institute's members explained that their schools were successful because they adopted a different orientation toward their students. Rather than bringing the immigrants in and drilling English into their heads, the school run by the People's Institute represented the "first attempts to extend to [the immigrants] the hand of fellowship and to greet them, not only as students of English, but as human beings and future Americans."[58] By giving students control over their school, the Institute gave them an investment in their new homeland.

City officials had been aware that the evening schools needed to be improved, but they were unclear about what to do. By contacting the People's Institute, the city was tapping into a body of specialized knowledge, one acquired through the Institute's vast work in the field. The Institute stepped in, fine-tuned one of the city's schools, and transformed it into something truly successful, with success defined as a school that immigrants wanted to attend.

Employing the lessons learned at the social centers about bringing the community on board and tailoring the program to its needs, the People's Institute entered into an experimental educational partnership with the board of education. District superintendent Jenkins selected P.S. 40 because it already hosted a community social center and city-run evening school serving more than three hundred men who spoke as many as fifteen languages.[59] A member of the People's Institute and a student from the Training School for Community Workers assumed control of the evening school experiment. They immediately organized a "Students' Council" to give the students a voice, rather than running an authoritarian school that did not provide for the community members' stated needs or that provided only what city government imagined immigrants needed. When students were asked what they wanted from their evening school experience, "physical training and social dancing" were at the top of the list. In addition, the students decided they wanted their school to be coeducational, so women were invited to enroll.

By putting this evening school under democratic and student control, "the change was magical in its effects. . . . Like the puppets in the Russian ballet, the sober, silent rows of tired men sprang to life." The Institute found that as the students were permitted more unstructured time, they began to talk to each other "in a quaint jargon of a dozen different tongues and, strange to say, proceeded to learn more English in their recreation hours than in their classes." As the experimental term drew to a close, "the students manifested their reluctance to disperse and a plan was worked out to continue the school under the People's Institute, on a self-supporting basis with a fee of ten cents an evening." The school at P.S. 40 was so successful that the city gave the People's Institute control of the evening school at P.S. 32 in Chelsea.[60]

The People's Institute introduced a new kind of authority into the immigrant neighborhoods—one the people had not necessarily invited, despite the Institute's claims to the contrary. With limited resources available to them, the neighborhood residents used the social centers, evening schools, and play streets, thereby ratifying the People's Institute's programs, which led to the expansion of the Institute's claims to authority and therefore its work. The city and federal government's trust in the People's Institute and their willingness to use its resources—and the Institute's willingness to collaborate—brought an increased governmental presence to ordinary people's lives. In this case, it was in the form of social services; later, it assumed the form of policing.

The People's Institute engaged in "war work"—in the shape of schools, and through public health campaigns and Americanization programs—that was constructive. It also cooperated with the municipal and federal governments to carry out philanthropic, rather than repressive or punitive, projects. The Institute continued to address the human needs of immigrants in New York City by participating in an education and Americanization campaign that, perhaps subtly, brought immigrants to consider the United States their home by courting their loyalty. Ultimately, the events at home during World War I created a changed political environment that both tolerated and required an enhanced policing mechanism run by and through the state—and that mechanism needed the efforts of private organizations to carry out the government's plans and agenda. Members of the People's Institute would not have directly supported such repressive measures; they preferred to have friends and neighbors convince the socialists or anarchists in their midst to have faith in the American system, to come dancing and learn English. The Institute's partnership with government agencies, however, inadvertently contributed to the extension of political surveillance.

SIX

Public-Private Partnerships during World War I

On October 13, 1914, a bomb exploded in St. Patrick's Cathedral in New York City. On November 11, the anniversary of the Haymarket executions, the Bronx Court House was bombed. Three days later, Magistrate John A. L. Campbell of the Tombs police court, who had sentenced New York anarchist Frank Tannenbaum to one year in prison for leading a march of the unemployed, narrowly missed being blown up.[1]

The New Year did not bring any relief; in fact, the situation worsened. On March 5, 1915, an explosion in the DuPont munitions plant in Haskell, New Jersey, killed five. On April 4, bombers targeted a freight depot in Pompton Lakes, New Jersey. A blast ripped through the DuPont plant in Carney's Point, New Jersey, on May 10, injuring six.[2] The same fate was visited upon the Central Railroad grain elevator in Weehawken, New Jersey, on July 15, and the DuPont plant in Wilmington, Delaware, on August 29.[3] Between March 6 and July 9, 1915, ten explosions occurred on steamships in New York harbor. In October 1915, the New York Police Department's Anarchist and Bomb Squad arrested six men "for conspiring to destroy merchant ships in New York Harbor by attaching bombs to the rudders."[4] Several Germans were arrested in 1915 for conspiring to blow up munitions plants or for building bombs and concocting explosives in their apartments.[5]

After nearly two years of monthly bombings in munitions plants, explosions aboard ships in New York harbor, and the arrests of German, Austrian, and Italian immigrants for bomb making in their apartments, New Yorkers thought they had seen the worst of wartime activity on the home front. But the most devastating attack was yet to come. In the early morning hours of Sunday, July 30, 1916, a massive explosion shattered thousands of windows throughout Lower Manhattan, and some as far north as Times Square. The rumble was felt as close as Jersey City and as far away as Philadelphia.

Millions of tons of war materials and explosives, stored on Black Tom Island in New York harbor, exploded. Investigators initially blamed spontaneous combustion; the search, however, conducted in large measure by the New York Police Department's bomb squad, eventually zeroed in on Michael Kristoff, a citizen of the Austro-Hungarian Empire.[6] The earlier bombings of 1914 and 1915, culminating in the Black Tom explosion, highlighted a problem: the federal government was incapable of securing the home front against acts of sabotage during wartime. As a result, the federal government began to rely more heavily on private organizations to monitor and control political subversion and, perhaps more surprisingly, prostitution.

During the war, as a consequence of and in response to the weakness of federal police mechanisms, private organizations were either deputized by agencies of the government or deputized themselves to fill the gaps in the policing system. These private organizations conducted undercover investigations of prostitutes, immigrants, "slackers" who failed to register for the draft, and radicals. The undercover agents' reports were sent to the proper authorities, who had the power to make arrests, begin deportation hearings, or initiate criminal proceedings. The exigencies of war, the increased presence of sailors and soldiers in New York City, and the fact that "attacks" regularly occurred on the home front resulted in a system of cooperation between these private organizations and public agencies—a system that was useful to the government in suppressing domestic political subversion and prosecuting and deporting "dangerous radicals" who might commit crimes against the United States.

While the federal government made efforts to expand its own police powers and agencies during the Great War, private organizations and their undercover investigators wholeheartedly joined in these efforts and became vital partners in the national security agenda on the home front. Rather than curtailing their activities, the war allowed social activists to expand their reach. Public officials turned to these private organizations, like the Committee of Fourteen, and delegated to them unprecedented authority. In the extreme case of the National Civic Federation (NCF), the organization assumed authority, deputized itself, and forged a secretive and informal partnership with agents of the military and the federal government. Private organizations responded to the military and the federal government's concerns about the presence of prostitutes and the activities of immigrant aliens by dispatching undercover investigators to the "affected" areas. Although it is difficult to discern truth from fiction in the reports on prostitutes and anarchist cells from the war years, the reports illuminate the anxiety provoked by several factors: immigrants (and the failure of the immigrant screening processes), loose women, law breakers, and bumbling law enforcement officials, all of whom seemed to be enemies of America and were conspiring to destroy the nation from within.

Two New York City–based organizations provide important case studies of how social activists adapted to the wartime environment—and the ways in which they and government agencies adapted to and exploited each other. To protect soldiers and sailors from immoral entertainment and its consequences, the Committee of Fourteen, long committed to researching and routing out liquor law violations and their relationship to prostitution, was the logical choice to assist the federal government. After the United States declared war in April 1917, Secretary of War Newton Baker established the Commission on Training Camp Activities (CTCA), whose main goal was to protect the troops from venereal disease by substituting wholesome entertainment for booze and brothels. Throughout the country, the CTCA struck up partnerships with local antivice societies both for their local expertise and their staff. In the New York metropolitan area, the War Department authorized the Committee of Fourteen to police and apprehend prostitutes, soldiers, sailors, and proprietors in the New York metropolitan area who violated provisions of the Selective Service Act. Unlike Committee of Fourteen investigators, those who worked for the National Civic Federation found themselves in the precarious position of prioritizing knowledge gathering over crime preventing once the conflict erupted in Europe. The war dramatically changed their role.

Founded in 1900, the National Civic Federation (NCF) brought together men and women from three areas of society: business, labor, and social activism, with this last sphere represented mainly by academics and clerics.[7] The NCF emerged from an 1899 meeting on combinations and trusts in Chicago, hosted by the Civic Federation of Chicago. The Civic Federation of Chicago had been founded in 1893 by moral reformer William T. Stead, author of *If Christ Came to Chicago*; banker Lyman J. Gage; and Bertha Honoré Palmer, a philanthropist, women's rights advocate, and president of the Board of Lady Managers of the Columbian Exposition in Chicago. Progressives such as Jane Addams were involved from the beginning, as were prominent Chicago industrialists. The main goal of the NCF, as stated in its founding prospectus, was "to provide for study and discussion of questions of national import affecting either the foreign or domestic policy of the United States, to aid in the crystallization of the most enlightened public sentiment of the country in respect thereto, and, when desirable, to promote necessary legislation in accordance therein."[8] Its overall goal was not only to create "departments to study national problems," but also to "provide a national forum, by means of which representatives of all these great divisions of society may come together and discuss the problems in which all have a common interest."[9] The NCF's president, Ralph Easley, envisioned it as "a practical agency for establishment of industrial peace," but "without unduly enlarging the size of the national government."[10] By approximately 1915, though, Easley turned the organization's attention to the presence of immigrants in the greater New York area, mainly because of his concern with activities in war munitions plants. Easley feared that Italian, German, and Austrian immigrants provided support to the German war machine from *within* the United States.

Both organizations—the Committee of Fourteen and the National Civic Federation—used undercover investigators to assist the federal government in improving policing of the home front, in the hope that they could prevent a national security breach. Whereas the War Department directly recruited the Committee of Fourteen to assist in carrying out its wartime goals, the department officially rebuffed the National Civic Federation but then secretly accepted its help. The War Department, however, never publicly acknowledged the role played by the NCF in securing the home front. These public-private partnerships offer a mixed legacy. Before the war, private organizations filled gaps in the architecture of the state. During the war, immigrants and streetwalking women acquired ever more dangerous qualities, in the minds of the private organizations, and so the need for surveillance and policing increased. The private organizations became extensions of the government—either working from within, as supplements to municipal or federal authority, or from without, as vigilantes.[11]

With the proliferation of bombings and the perceived increase in immigrant radicals and anarchists in the New York metropolitan area, the Great War arrived on the home front. The bombings were but one way disloyal and disaffected immigrants threatened the American nation and war effort. But a quieter and perhaps more insidious threat roamed the streets, infiltrating barrooms and bedrooms in all five boroughs of New York City: loose women with venereal diseases enticed innocent soldiers and sailors to get drunk and pay for sexual intercourse. The War Department became concerned about whether enlisted men would be prepared to fight for democracy abroad if the pleasures of the city destroyed them before they even left the training camps.

In reality, the number and presence of military personnel in New York City increased dramatically after 1915. With a naval yard in Brooklyn and army encampments in the Bronx and Queens, sailors and soldiers in uniform became a familiar sight on city streets. In addition, New York City developed into the most popular destination for military personnel before shipping out, while on leave, or upon return from the front. For social activists and some neighborhoods, soldiers and sailors on the streets were disturbing not because they were a reminder that the world was at war, but because their presence hinted at the real increase in prostitution and the number of other women looking for sexual encounters. Prostitutes were not simply regarded as immoral women who corrupted others in the dance halls and cabarets of far-flung Brooklyn and Queens. Instead they were transformed by the wartime environment into walking scourges, women who could decimate the entire American military machine with venereal diseases.

Shortly after the United States' declaration of war on April 2, 1917, Secretary of War Newton Baker established the Commission on Training Camp Activities (CTCA), which was responsible for ensuring "moral" conditions around military encampments, as well as for providing wholesome recreation to soldiers and sailors. Connected to the creation of the CTCA was the Selective Service Act (which Congress passed on May 18, 1917), sections of which criminalized the sale of alcoholic beverages to uniformed servicemen and limited their access to prostitutes and "women of low morals" in order to protect the men from venereal diseases.[12] Baker appointed Raymond B. Fosdick chairman of the CTCA, whose previous experience included work as an investigator for the Rockefeller-funded Bureau of Social Hygiene, conducting research and surveys of policing in the United States and Europe. These investigations had launched Fosdick's national reputation as a social hygiene advocate, and in 1916, Baker asked Fosdick to conduct a full-scale investigation of training camp conditions at the Mexican border.[13] Fosdick approached the problem of camp conditions from a constructive rather than repressive perspective: the soldiers and sailors required alternatives to supplant the supremacy of alcohol and sex in and near the training camps. Under his direction, the CTCA busied itself with providing these alternative activities for the men stationed at the thirty-two U.S. Army and National Guard training camps within the United States. In addition to recruiting the YMCA and similar organizations to help inside the camps, the CTCA turned to private organizations to help enforce the bans on the sale of liquor and sex in the areas outside military encampments.

Fosdick explained that, in striving to meet its goals for the camps, the War Department did "not desire to create any more additional machinery than is absolutely essential." Rather, inside the camps, the CTCA relied on organizations like the Young Men's Christian Association, the Knights of Columbus, and the Jewish Board for Welfare Work to provide leisure activities. Fosdick elaborated on the positive work undertaken in the camps; for example, the American Library Association established libraries in each of the thirty-two camps, and the YMCA provided educational, recreational, and musical programs. Fosdick then mentioned that the troops had to be protected from "the evils to which they have been exposed for years and years": saloons, red-light districts, and immoral women. He reassured his audience that all of the neighborhoods near military camps were "undergoing a process of continual scouring." After all, as Fosdick averred, "an army is not a fighting army until it is a contented army," and the CTCA's goal was "to create a fighting machine. We never lose sight of that."[14]

The CTCA also joined with the Young Women's Christian Association to open "hostess houses" near bases, where men and women could visit one another in a supervised environment. Fosdick emphasized that all of these activities were directed at one goal—protecting soldiers from venereal diseases. It was "a matter of efficiency, let alone morals." The United States could not afford to lose any soldiers to "preventable causes," and the fighting men must "come back . . . victorious, and with no wounds except those gloriously won in honorable conflict."[15] The War and Navy departments would be able to explain why a young soldier had returned home with a missing leg, but syphilis would be more difficult to explain to a mother or sweetheart.

Although Fosdick briefly acknowledged that government and voluntary organizations expended great effort and expense to provide leisure alternatives "because we have got to put something *positive* in the place of the things that for years have been traditionally associated with armies and army camps," he neither elaborated nor directly identified that negative alternative. Nor did he mention the CTCA's partnership with the Committee of Fourteen, which worked primarily in New York and New Jersey (but also sent investigators to Connecticut and as far away as Canada) to clean up the areas surrounding army and navy encampments.[16]

Despite the Committee of Fourteen's experience in matters related to liquor sales and immoral sexual behavior, the situation during the war years posed new problems for its members and investigators. During this period, the Committee never abandoned its undercover investigations of disorderly leisure establishments and continued to survey the sexual behavior of working-class, black, and immigrant men and women. At the start of the war, however, its investigators began to note conditions that diverged from earlier trends. For example, undercover operatives began noticing "possible prostitutes" working the streets near the Brooklyn Navy Yard, which suggested to both the investigators and the Committee that streetwalkers had moved beyond their regular territory of Times Square and other Manhattan districts.[17] On a separate investigation of a barroom in Queens, an undercover operative found seven sailors in uniform, one of whom was quite inebriated and playing the piano and singing for a small crowd.[18] Investigator Eula Harris had a similar experience; she entered a barroom where she "found a tough looking girl piano player . . . [and] three nice drunken sailors." Unfortunately for Harris, "no one liked [her] looks enough to flirt with [her]," so she continued on her way.[19]

The investigators encountered unforeseen difficulties in the areas around training camps. Before the war years, the Committee's male investigators were adept at determining the immorality of an establishment by seeing if female patrons could be "made," which, in the argot of the time, meant a woman was willing to engage in sexual behavior. By wartime, however, young women's attitudes toward casual sexual encounters had changed. "Game" girls were less likely to chat with men in civilian clothing in drinking establishments near military encampments. Instead, they preferred to engage in sexual activities with men in uniform, which they construed as "patriotic." Other women, though, had different reasons to cease soliciting men in civilian clothing, as investigator David Oppenheim discovered.

In May 1916, Frederick Whitin dispatched Oppenheim on a reconnaissance mission to the area of the Brooklyn Navy Yard. He started on Sands Street, the main thoroughfare running out of the Navy Yard toward the Brooklyn Bridge. Upon arrival, Oppenheim quickly spotted "14 professional street walkers and 5 on Washington St." Oppenheim noted that he "tried to 'make' several of these women but they wouldn't give me a tumble, but solicited the sailors openly." He remarked that although there was a police presence in the area, the patrolmen ignored the women, despite the fact that he "saw several of these women solicit sailors." Oppenheim even witnessed prostitutes and sailors making arrangements, commenting that "one woman solicit[ed] 2 sailors, they stopped and spoke for a few minutes then the woman went across the street and picked up another street walker and brought her over to these 2 sailors, the 4 of them then went away together, I followed them as far as the Borough Hall Station of subway." He even followed several other couples to various subway stations; the last streetwalker he staked out solicited a sailor on Sands Street. He followed the couple down Adams Street; another sailor joined them along the way, and eventually they entered a saloon on the corner of Adams and Myrtle Avenue.[20]

While stalking prostitutes and sailors through Brooklyn, Oppenheim slowly came to the realization that, as a civilian looking to pay for sex, he no longer appealed to prostitutes. Was his money no good in Brooklyn? Actually, a seismic shift had occurred; as the risk of incarceration for prostitutes dramatically increased during the war years, they became less likely to solicit civilians. A news agent at the Long Island Depot reflected to Oppenheim, "There are plenty of women on the streets but they are all scared and will not talk to a man on the streets unless they know him, said the cops are after them, they have all been chased away from here, a lot of them have been picked up and locked up and sent to the workhouse or jail."[21]

The CTCA and its adjuncts were engaged in a massive roundup of women—not just prostitutes—suspected of having (or who could be accused of having) venereal diseases. The CTCA worked with organizations like the Committee of Fourteen to apprehend prostitutes, but it also appointed 150 women as "protective officers" who were assigned to patrol streets in and near army encampments and naval yards, looking for young women who appeared to be runaways or camp followers. In addition, these protective officers compelled women to submit to venereal and psychological testing; if they were found to be infected or mentally incompetent, the protective officers committed the young women to hospitals, reformatories, or prison.[22] The CTCA also arrested known prostitutes in areas around military encampments, and if the arrested women were found to have a venereal disease, they could be detained and quarantined during the entire course of their treatment. Uninfected women were also often quarantined, however, and infected women were often detained after their infection cleared. Between 1918 and 1920, the CTCA and its partners incarcerated more than 18,000 women—and not just prostitutes or those with sexually transmitted infections.[23]

In 1919, Oppenheim embarked on an investigative junket to the area around the Brooklyn side of the Williamsburg Bridge, which the Committee considered notoriously "dissipated." As he walked the streets, Oppenheim was struck by the absence of women. He asked a man who had lived in the neighborhood for over a decade what was going on. The man explained that "theres [sic] nothing doing around here at all any more." Although he confirmed Oppenheim's initial impression that the area had dried up, the man could not explain why. Perplexed, Oppenheim continued farther north in his quest for prostitutes. He proceeded to the corner of Lorimer and Broadway, an area he knew as fertile ground. Alas, there were no women there either. He encountered a Brooklyn Rapid Transit inspector and asked him what had become of the women who used to solicit in the area. The

BRT man explained, "They all got jobs now . . . you will find a lot of them working on the cars as conductors."[24] The war presented some working-class women with safer and better-paying jobs than prostitution. Still, although the wartime economy afforded some employment opportunities for some women, large numbers continued to walk the streets, and under more dangerous conditions than they had previously encountered.

Despite the Committee of Fourteen's increased powers, prostitutes' fear of arrest created new difficulties for the Committee's investigative method during the war years. Many of the Committee's male investigators noted the changed circumstances and attitudes of the soliciting women, and observed that they themselves were "unsuccessful in picking up girls" in the area around the Brooklyn Navy Yard because "the girls are looking only for sailors." Investigator Harry Kahan encountered the same problem during an investigation of the Metz Hotel in Rockaway Beach. While at the hotel, he overheard a conversation between two men who were lamenting the fact that in the past they had "visit[ed] quite often Metz Hotel purposely to pick up women, professional prostitutes are operating here and some of them were recognized by these two men and they tried to get them over to their table, but couldn't do it, because the uniformed men got them first."[25]

What was happening? For the prostitutes, the uniformed men represented not only a "patriotic" choice but also a safer choice. Prostitutes knew that the uniformed men had cash and disposable income. They also trusted the uniformed men not to turn them over to the police or other authorities. Because both the prostitutes and the soldiers were running afoul of the law by consorting with each other, they also protected each other. Committee of Fourteen executive secretary Frederick Whitin explored the possibility of having his investigators wear "sailors' clothes," but "the Police Department [said] that such clothes would be considered a disguise and would be unlawful."[26]

Despite this unspoken trust between servicemen and prostitutes, even uniformed men noticed they had an increasingly difficult time finding both prostitutes and hotels that would cater to them. A young sailor at John Herbst's told Oppenheim that "there used to be a lot of [prostitutes] hanging out in here but they are not here any more." Oppenheim asked, "Where could I take them if I did pick something up?" The sailor confessed that "he didn't know of any hotels there, the only one he knew was on Washington St and that's closed up."[27] The Committee of Fourteen, in partnership with the War Department's Commission on Training Camp Activities, had succeeded in spreading fear among prostitutes and uniformed men seeking sex. This time the Committee of Fourteen did not have to use backroom bargaining or economic threats to enforce its standards; rather, as an official agent of the War Department, it brought the full powers of the government to bear on individual prostitutes.

Even though the Committee of Fourteen worked in an authorized partnership with the CTCA, Whitin decided not to push the issue of putting his undercover investigators in military uniforms to entrap prostitutes. Ralph Easley of the National Civic Federation, however, was largely unconcerned with the fact that his organization did not have permission to pursue its agenda. Starting around 1907, the National Civic Federation began sponsoring "studies" of what it termed "subversive activities" in the United States. These studies continued through the 1910s and intensified during the period of World War I. Easley also openly battled "subversion" and warned others of its deleterious effects during this period. For example, he used the official publication of the organization, the *Review*, to argue against socialism, writing articles himself and hiring specialists in the field of antiradicalism to submit pieces for publication. He even dispatched undercover investigators to the meetings of other Progressive organizations, such as the National Consumers' League, suspicious that they advocated socialism. During the war, Easley perceived the situation as becoming increasingly dire, so he created a "secret service bureau" within the National Civic Federation and fashioned an information pipeline to the military and federal government in an attempt to get them to implement policies and procedures designed to protect the nation from political subversives.[28]

Easley was not alone in his concerns about radicalism. Samuel Gompers, president of the American Federation of Labor, contacted him and explained that he believed that the large number of strikes and disruptions in the munitions plants were "instigated" not by loyal trade union men but by Germans trying to disrupt the Allied efforts against Germany. He needed help proving his hypothesis, however, so Easley agreed to lend a hand. Easley approached Henry P. Davison, a member of the National Civic Federation's executive committee and a partner in J. P. Morgan's bank, to present his concerns. Easley convinced Davison that the domestic situation required the NCF to have its own secret service bureau, which could be used to investigate strikes and other disruptions. "Such a bureau, of course, would necessitate considerable expenditure—at least $25,000 in the beginning," Easley explained.[29] Davison was amenable to the idea and agreed to contact ten different manufacturing concerns to raise the money, which was used to create the National Civic Federation's Subversive Activities department.[30] This bureau was never known (or intended to be known) to the public and was never officially sanctioned by the rest of the National Civic Federation's board members. In fact, when Andrew Carnegie and others major donors to the NCF found out about the secret service bureau and Easley's zealotry, they rolled back their donations to pre–World War I levels.

Before the war, the National Civic Federation was fighting a battle on two fronts. It opposed groups like the National Association of Manufacturers (NAM), which wanted the government to protect small business interests from competition at the hands of large corporations and the demands of organized labor.[31] The NCF also wanted to prevent socialists from making incursions into elected offices and the unions. As Easley explained in a letter to labor leader and socialist Morris Hillquit, "the president of a very large corporation" stated that "had it not been for The National Civic Federation, we (the manufacturers) would have smashed every union in this country two years ago."[32]

The National Civic Federation established itself as an intermediary and devoted its efforts to fighting organized labor's enemies.[33] The enemies were unenlightened employers—those who ostensibly had refused to participate in the NCF's program—and radical labor organizations—those that did not fit into or comply with the craft-based model of trade unionism as represented by the American Federation of Labor. In fact, at the 1911 convention of the American Federation of Labor in Atlanta, Duncan McDonald of the United Mine Workers presented a resolution calling for condemnation of the National Civic Federation "as an enemy to organized labor, and to demand that labor officials connected with that organization shall sever their connection therewith." The resolution further argued that "the civic federation is composed of men the majority of whom are antagonistic to labor's interest, is financed largely by such men, and that labor men should have nothing to do with it." John Mitchell, former president of the United Mine Workers, promptly resigned his National Civic Federation position; Gompers, however, refused. He claimed that this resolution was just another effort on the part of the socialists to "bring about the disruption of labor organizations and to block the labor movement in its progress." Gompers continued to work with the NCF because he believed it was the best way to secure workers' rights.[34]

Gompers's decision to remain aligned with the National Civic Federation was in part an attempt to clear his own name. In November 1911, he was actively trying to distance himself from two particular incidents. First, he had been was accused of delivering his 1911 Labor Day speech while standing on an American flag, and the photographic "proof" was first published in the *Los Angeles Times* on October 1, 1911. This allegation of flag desecration put Gompers on the defensive; he explained that "any statement or picture purporting to say or show that I did or would desecrate the flag of our country is false and a misrepresentation. The fact is on Labor Day in San Francisco there was an ordinary table festooned with the American flag. Its edges were tacked to the edge of the table." Although the photograph (and another one that appeared later that same year, claiming to show the footprints Gompers had left on the flag) was a forgery, this scandal tarnished Gompers's public image.[35]

To make matters worse, in December 1911 John and James McNamara, the two brothers arrested for the 1910 bombing of the *Los Angeles Times* building, confessed. James revealed his involvement, and John admitted his complicity in dynamiting the Llewellyn Iron Works. Gompers and the AFL had been heavily involved in the defense of the McNamara brothers; they had raised approximately $100,000 and secured Clarence Darrow to defend them. After the McNamara brothers confessed, the U.S. Department of Justice launched an investigation into the American Federation of Labor and Samuel Gompers, charging that Gompers and the AFL had had a hand in the dynamiting.[36] The charges were eventually dismissed, but Gompers's reputation suffered further damage. By aligning himself with Easley and the NCF and undertaking investigations to drum out disloyalty among immigrants, workers, and labor unions, however, Gompers believed he would be exonerated and would prove he was 100 percent American. He would also help advance the cause of politically moderate organized labor.

During the war, the War Labor Board secured collective bargaining rights through a system based loosely on the ideas of voluntary associationalism and cooperation pioneered by the National Civic Federation. As a result, the Federation's goals were partially achieved. But the era of World War I was one of labor militancy, with more than a million workers striking annually between 1916 and 1920. Gompers claimed that "foreign" elements had infiltrated American Federation of Labor unions, and they were solely responsible for these undisciplined strikes and walkouts. He wanted to expel these agitators and reestablish union and AFL legitimacy in the eyes of the American people. To accomplish this goal, Gompers teamed up with the NCF, and together they embarked on a crusade against socialists and radicals—within the labor unions and beyond.[37]

When Ralph Easley and Samuel Gompers considered the rash of bombings in New York City in 1914, they concluded that a powerful conspiracy to disrupt the industrial component of the American war effort existed among Germans, Italians, anarchists, and the Industrial Workers of the World (also known as the IWW or the Wobblies). It was not this feared conspiracy alone that worried them; they were more concerned that the federal government was not equipped to deal with this dangerous new threat. To create a safety net, Easley forged alliances among the National Civic Federation's Subversive Activities department, the New York Police Department, and the Military Intelligence Division (MID) of the War Department. Although the National Civic Federation's secret service bureau was not officially sanctioned by these government agencies, Easley nevertheless regularly sent them reports of its investigations of spies and saboteurs. The concerns and anxieties of the war years allowed a private organization like the National Civic Federation to seize unprecedented powers as the government and military divisions stepped up their efforts to ensure loyalty and security on the home front. Unlike the Committee of Fourteen, the National Civic Federation functioned simultaneously as ally and critic of the federal government. It took up the extra policing the war required, but did so in order to point out to the federal government that it needed to expand federal police powers. The wartime environment indeed required additional and expanded police mechanisms, and after the war, the government pointed to the reports of groups like the NCF as evidence that the government needed to become more serious about domestic subversion, which eventually it did with the Palmer Raids, mass deportations, and the passage of peacetime criminal anarchy statutes.

A. Bruce Bielaski, the Bureau of Investigation's director from 1912 to 1919, noted that he did not have enough agents to carry out all of the additional work required during the war. The army, navy, and State Department employed no investigators; rather, they were forced to rely on secret service agents employed by the Department of Justice and the Treasury Department.[38] R. H. Van Deman, the officer in charge of military intelligence for the War Department during World War I, had expressed to Easley that he was frustrated by the limited amount of money and manpower budgeted for domestic intelligence work. According to Easley, after he informed Van Deman about "the scope of the work" the NCF's investigators were conducting of anarchist camps, Van Deman "became very enthusiastic about having the assistance of the Federation." Van Deman believed that "organizations such as the Federation with its power and influence with men in official life and especially with members of both houses of Congress, can be of the greatest value to the Government in working with the Intelligence Bureau."[39] For Van Deman, private organizations like the NCF could compensate for the Military Intelligence Division's deficiencies—namely, the requirement that soldiers wear uniforms while on duty and when conducting investigations of subversion among enlisted men (which made undercover investigation impossible), and the prohibition against investigating civilians, which had obvious limitations.

The New York Police Department (NYPD) had fought the most successful and least constrained battle against foreign elements and subversion since 1906, when it created its Italian Squad. The NYPD organized this squad when the illegal activities of Italian secret societies known as the Black Hand increased to the point that the police department's "small force of Italian detectives" became insufficient to combat and investigate the rising number of kidnappings, briberies, bombings, and murders. In response, Commissioner Theodore Bingham authorized the organization of a secret service squad whose sole purpose was the elimination of the Black Hand. All of the detectives were drawn from among the Italians already on the force, and the identities of these men were concealed—"not even those [who were chosen] know all who have been or will be chosen."[40] The Italian Squad, headed by Detective Joseph Petrosini, did not even operate out of police headquarters; rather, it was located in its own office "on Elm Street, a hundred yards or so from Headquarters."[41] Petrosini's force worked entirely underground in order to catch the brigands of the Black Hand off guard.

After the Italian Squad's first few years, the NYPD increased the squad's responsibilities to include crimes committed by socialists, radicals, labor unions, Wobblies, and gangs.[42] The expansion was the result of its members' familiarity with and expertise in investigating crimes involving dynamite. The Black Hand frequently dynamited the shops of Italian merchants who refused to pay protection money, so when the rash of anarchist bombings began in New York in 1914, this police squad was the obvious choice to take the lead in investigations.

On August 1, 1914, "the day after war was declared by Germany," the New York Police Department officially expanded the Italian Squad and renamed it the Anarchist and Bomb Squad; the squad was put under the police commissioner's direct supervision, with Lieutenant Thomas Tunney in command.[43] According to an untitled report from the NCF's subversive activities files, the Anarchist and Bomb Squad began to gather evidence by dispatching detectives "of various nationalities" to infiltrate groups of Wobblies and anarchists. Tunney, in addition to instructing the detectives in how to act, also made sure that none of the detectives knew each other. "This was done for the purpose of obtaining different reports and also that in case one of them was suspected he could be withdrawn without giving away the identity of the others."[44]

In 1917, the NCF report explained, the Anarchist and Bomb Squad sent out detectives to find and "secure evidence against about one hundred alien enemies, who were subsequently turned over to the Federal Authorities and interned. Thousands of communications relative to alien enemies and spies and propagandists have also been investigated by the members of this Squad."[45] Despite the success and reach of the NYPD's Anarchist and Bomb Squad, its operations were confined to the city of New York. No wide-reaching federal system existed for finding and punishing political dissidents, spies, or saboteurs. In essence, the enforcement of the Espionage Act of 1917 and the Sedition Act of 1918 fell largely to local law enforcement agencies, private citizens, and their organizations.

Both the Bureau of Investigation and the Military Intelligence Division of the War Department turned to "volunteer private assistants" to assist in finding spies and saboteurs.[46] The American Protective League (APL) was the best-known example of this public-private policing partnership. In the spring of 1917, Albert M. Briggs, the founder of the APL, approached Bureau chief Bielaski and proposed the creation of a citizens' auxiliary. Bielaski accepted.[47] The APL functioned as a semiofficial adjunct to the Justice Department; members investigated "disloyal acts and utterances" in their communities and reported back to the attorney general and Bureau of Investigation.[48] In reality, APL agents' reports on sedition and disloyalty consisted of little more than rumors and unfounded information, based on personal antipathies and ethnic hostility.[49] Created to function as the eyes and ears of the Justice Department, the APL, by the end of the war, had expanded its activities: conducting highly publicized "slacker raids," checking to see that people were purchasing Liberty Bonds, and enforcing rations on food and fuel.

The NCF's undercover investigations were not dissimilar to those undertaken by the APL; however, whereas the APL functioned as a *posse comitatus*— intercepting and opening mail, arresting "offenders," and even physically assaulting dissenters—the NCF maintained a lower profile.[50] The first of the NCF's investigations were "for the purposes of helping Mr. Gompers to find out whether the German saboteurs were causing strikes, explosions and so forth in the factories," but their scope quickly expanded to include "the whole general field" of radical activities. Easley began to "suppl[y] the Government with the information obtained [by his investigators], thus aiding in very many important situations."[51] Easley and Gompers went beyond simply collecting information through their undercover investigators and then using it internally to guide policy; rather, the reports of these investigators were selectively passed out of the NCF and into the hands of those in positions of power.

The National Civic Federation's secret service bureau worked to gather information that those who wielded actual power might find useful—if the information hit the right notes or pushed the right buttons. The NCF's investigators, as private citizens, used techniques that employees of the federal government never could; uniforms and government rules did not dictate the limits of the NCF investigators' activities. Easley forwarded the information gathered by his investigators to agencies such as the Military Intelligence Division of the War Department, the Bureau of Investigation, and the Bureau of Immigration, which initiated deportation proceedings.[52] By employing a variety of men, including "a German reservist who was in a position to get into the Kriegerbund and form contacts with Saegerbunds and other German-American societies," "an Italian who engaged in Black Hand work for Police Chief Bingham," and "other experts in various lines," Easley had access to munitions plants and factories, anarchist camps, Italian neighborhoods, Austrian and German social clubs, and meetings of the Industrial Workers of the World.[53] Easley concealed his secret service agents' identities, "except to the government officials who should be informed of the source from which each report is received."[54]

Precisely how many undercover investigators worked for the NCF on this project is not clear, but two men are identifiable by the code names they listed on their reports: F and Mr. X. B. F. Garland, alias Mr. X, came to the National Civic Federation's secret service bureau as a freelance investigator. He had worked previously as an investigator for the Bureau of Investigation and the federal Secret Service.[55] The other agent used by the NCF in its investigations of anarchists was Felix Periera, known in his reports simply as F. Periera had worked for the NYPD's Italian Squad. Although his written English was barely adequate—the handwritten reports he returned to the NCF were rife with grammatical errors—Periera spoke Italian. Together, Periera and Garland made a formidable team. Paired to investigate areas that Easley and Gompers had identified as harboring anarchist camps, F and Mr. X infiltrated these organizations and uncovered plans to bomb powder and munitions factories, as well as papal conspiracies and plots to assassinate world leaders.

Easley used the information gathered and reports filed by F and Mr. X to compile three major reports about anarchist activities in Paterson and Passaic, New Jersey, titled "Anarchists," "History of Anarchists," and "Chronology." Easley, in these three mediated reports, drawing on the raw data returned by his investigators, imposed a narrative structure and provided interpretation in order to construct a history and record of activities of anarchist enclaves in nearby New Jersey. His reports also unintentionally illustrate and expose the paradox of undercover investigation as a regulatory strategy. Throughout their investigations, F and Mr. X became involved in, and sometimes encouraged, the very activities they were supposed to ameliorate. Easley used their activities to produce "evidence" of the bizarre, disturbing, and chaotic world of immigrant New York and New Jersey, evidence intended particularly for those inclined to believe in conspiracies among anarchists, priests, Germans, Italians, and Wobblies. Easley then forwarded his renarrated and repackaged reports to the War Department's Office of the Chief of Staff with the caveat that "care should be taken to keep [the report] secret, and to use care and judgment as to who reads it."[56] Easley explained of his reports: "Nothing in fiction surpasses these actual occurrences."[57] As it turns out, the reports themselves may have been works of fiction.

According to a report filed by Mr. X, most Americans believed that "the anarchists, as an organization, have amounted to nothing in this country since a number of their leaders were hanged as a result of the Haymarket Riots in Chicago in 1886." "This belief is erroneous," however.[58] In the wake of Haymarket, Mr. X explained, anarchist leaders reorganized their executive committee into a "triangle" ("one German, one Italian, and one English-speaking man") to ensure the survival of their movement. With a leader in Chicago, another in St. Louis, and another in New York City, the Triangle operated on the logic that their records "would never be complete, as they were divided into three parts;—hence if one part is found and the key to the cipher is obtained, no one can make anything out of the capture until the other two parts are located in as many cities."[59] Rank-and-file anarchists and local camps of anarchy had to seek the approval of the Triangle, whose members had to receive permission from the anarchist leaders in Europe before any major bombings or activities could be undertaken.[60]

Anarchists were indeed located all over the United States, but it is unlikely that such a Triangle ever existed. As historian Paul Avrich has explained, in the United States, anarchists' organizations were local and connected to particular towns and communities; anarchist newspapers and the speakers who crisscrossed the country were the closest anarchists came to a "national" organization. Therefore, Easley's and Mr. X's description of a highly centralized organization appears to be an exaggeration designed to arouse readers' concern.[61] In addition, in his three mediated reports, Easley employed literary tropes and exaggerations similar to those found in contemporary fiction that depicted anarchist activities, such as Henry James's *The Princess of Casamassima* (1886) and Joseph Conrad's *The Secret Agent* (1906), both of which posited that anarchists did in fact have a leader. The NCF reports were in part propaganda and as such required drama to be convincing. Easley thus created a mélange of fact and fiction, drawing on tropes and stereotyped characters from these or other fictional accounts of anarchists and the information provided by his investigators.

Two key figures in F and Mr. X's reports on anarchists in New Jersey were "The Doctor" and "The Professor." "The Doctor" was an Italian physician who provided medical care to injured anarchists and other radicals, which kept them out of hospitals and official channels. "The Professor" (who bears a striking resemblance to the anarchist professor in Conrad's *The Secret Agent*) was a German immigrant named Von Steinmetz, who was in close touch with the Triangle. The main character, though, is Father Alfonzo D'Angelo, whose function in these reports is to represent the entire Italian anarchist problem in the United States. An immigrant from Italy and a member of a "well-known and well-to-do Italian family closely connected with the Roman Catholic Church," Father D'Angelo studied for the priesthood in Italy, and while in service to a rural parish, he converted to the tenets of anarchism. He immigrated to New Jersey "several years before the outbreak of the European war to promote the interests" of anarchism.[62] While in the United States, D'Angelo "renewed his acquaintance" with a German named Franz Von Papen, "military attaché of the German government in Washington, D.C." and "formerly in charge of the Royal Guard Secret Service at Berlin."[63] When these two rekindled their relationship, Von Papen allegedly convinced D'Angelo and his comrades to "assist in carrying on German sabotage work in this country and in Canada."[64] The NCF document titled "Anarchists" explained the relationship among Von Papen, D'Angelo, and the Triangle:

> The Triangle organized a force of four squads of two each, consisting of the most scientific and trained experts in the handling of explosives and the performance of dangerous acts, whose work was to promote explosions in large munition plants and docks and other places where damage could be done to the cause of the Allies. . . . The anarchistic agents who are blowing up factories under the orders of the Triangle in America deal only with large concerns. . . . Not one of the eight men who have been at this work under the Triangle for the past year has been arrested.[65]

This description, based on the evidence collected by the NCF's undercover investigators, painted a horrifying picture of a vast syndicate of disloyal people operating within the United States, who were conspiring to undermine American industry as a means of promoting German victory. This revelation would have been frightening for the target audience of this report, which included men like Easley, Gompers, and R. H. Van Deman. The report, by pointing out that "not one of the eight men who have been at this work . . . has been arrested," suggested that if unauthorized civilians were capable of discovering this information, why had the government not been able to apprehend any of these people? Was it because the government never gained the same degree of access to anarchists? Or perhaps it was because government agents simply did not have Easley's flair for the dramatic when it came to reportage.

MID reports tended to be more sober than those produced by Easley. MID agents did not dramatize or interpret their subjects; rather, they retold conversations and recommended practical action. For example, the MID employed an agent, known only as Operative #40S on his reports, who was dispatched to investigate the Workers' International Industrial Union in Niagara Falls, New York. Operative #40S wrote that he left the union meeting in the company of a man named Sirriano, who, after being forced to flee Italy for plotting to overthrow the monarchy, had settled in Niagara Falls, where he had been living for the last two years. Sirriano explained to #40S that "in Italy he was a big factor in the Socialist Party and that in April 1915 he assisted in overthrowing the Municipal Government and in place put a Socialist Government."[66]

Operative #40S sensed that he had located a person of interest. He prodded his subject on a number of issues, including religion. Sirriano ranted to Operative #40S, "Religion is composed of a lot of black robed hypocrites, militarism is the life of a dog. It is forced on the people by the Capitalists. That it [sic] what we are fighting against now, in the course of time the people will see that our cause is right and they will back us up. We will then be able to establish socialistic Governments all over the world." Operative #40S did not editorialize about the dangers posed by Sirriano; rather, his report ended on a comparatively restrained note. He explained that he had conveyed the information about Sirriano to immigration inspector Baldwin, stationed in Niagara Falls, hoping he could "take some action concerning this man."[67] Perhaps the difference in style between MID and NCF reports was attributable to the fact that Operative #40S possessed authority and an ability to take decisive action against a dangerous individual. Easley, by contrast, was engaged in a propaganda campaign to convince the federal government of a problem that required extensive federal intervention.

Like MID Operative #40S, NCF investigators F and Mr. X successfully infiltrated meetings. They focused on the anarchists in Paterson, New Jersey, which was, according to their report, "the headquarters of the Anarchists of the United States."[68] New York City was increasingly inhospitable to anarchists and radicals due in part to the NYPD's Anarchist and Bomb Squad, which had conducted a number of raids and successful crackdowns, putting the radicals on the defensive. New Jersey became increasingly more attractive to anarchists not only because of its physical proximity to New York City, but also because large numbers of working-class German immigrants, many of whom created anarchist groups with ties to New York City, already called New Jersey home.[69] Moreover, a large number of munitions plants were located in New Jersey.

The NCF's investigators discovered that meetings were always held on Saturday nights in "a saloon in the German district of this city."[70] The topic of conversation at the first meeting attended by the NCF operatives was anarchist opposition to the war. At this meeting, the anarchists decided that the only way to prevent the United States from officially entering the war was either to assassinate President Woodrow Wilson or bomb munitions plants. After much discussion, the anarchists rejected assassination, in part because "the anarchists have for many years been taking little, if any, part in public assassinations." Therefore, they decided to "interest themselves in the removal of those who are guilty of perpetuating the war, as all agreed that if the United States put a stop to the sale of munition supplies the Allies would have to surrender." They blamed John D. Rockefeller, J. P. Morgan, and other corporate leaders, who, they believed, "made it possible for the Allies to buy war supplies."[71] This anarchist cell even gave members F and Mr. X an important assignment: to gather information on the comings and goings of these wealthy industrialists, information that would assist in planning future actions.

Shirking their homework assignment, Mr. X and F instead set out on a reconnaissance mission to identify the leading anarchists and Wobblies in Paterson, New Jersey. They discovered that 73 Prospect Street was the printing office that produced the *Independent Workingmen World*, which they described as the "official organ of the I.W.W. end of the anarchists." According to their report, this office opened in Paterson after the New York City police shut down "the Berkman printing office," where Alexander Berkman and Emma Goldman produced their journal *Mother Earth*.[72] During the course of conversation, the investigators learned that this printing office also served as a "clearinghouse" where bombs were manufactured for fellow anarchists located elsewhere in the United States; the anarchists placing the orders, however, "*must call at the printing office for them, as it is against the rules of the main camp of anarchists to risk shipment*" of bombs and explosives. In the rear room of 73 Prospect Street, the local anarchists had their meeting room, which contained a "shrine" to their "martyr," Gaetano Bresci, the assassin of Italian king Umberto in 1900. The proprietor shared with the agents that this was the very room where Bresci "drew the marked slip which designated him as the one to remove the king of the land that gave him birth, and he did so."[73] The language used in the report was revealing. To describe the task of King Umberto's assassin as removing "the king of the land that gave him birth" suggests that Bresci in particular and anarchists in general were the sort of people who could not feel an allegiance to their own homeland, let alone their adopted country. Therefore, could they ever feel an allegiance, a love and appreciation, for America? Implicit is the suggestion that no amount of supervised dancing clubs or evening schools for foreigners would cleanse the immigrant anarchist scourge from America's shores.

The two investigators continued to wander freely about these anarchist "joints," and the people they encountered readily offered privileged information. How did Mr. X and F succeed in gaining entry into these camps and bringing anarchists into their confidence? In other words, how did they remain above suspicion themselves? These investigators each developed a distinctive pose to carry out their mission. Felix Periera introduced himself as a "leader in the Black Hand of New York City," and B. F. Garland claimed to be "a camp member from Harrison [New York]." Father D'Angelo was impressed by their connection to the Black Hand, perhaps because the investigators bragged that they could easily "pull off a few murders at any old time."[74] This shared language of violence, danger, and illegality made it possible for these men to understand and trust one another. Not only did they share a subculture of violence and destruction, but they possessed equally damning information on one another. Perhaps anarchists and Black Handers quietly respected each other, or maybe D'Angelo and Periera's Italian heritage was sufficient to forge this relationship. In any case, these poses worked as an "open sesame" for the investigators, and brought them into the confidence of D'Angelo and into the inner circles of these anarchist camps.

F and Mr. X were not suspected to be investigators and managed to present personae that lifted them above suspicion. The printing shop setup described in these reports, however, resembled the actual situation in Chicago preceding the Haymarket bombing in 1886. August Spies, who was put on trial for the Haymarket affair, ran three German-language anarchist newspapers in Chicago and allegedly had dynamite shipped to his newspaper office from New Jersey.[75] Because Easley perceived a "problem" with Italian as well as German immigrants, he employed slightly modified imagery to fulfill his xenophobic purpose. This is not to suggest, however, that the reports were entirely untrue. Mr. X and F described what they saw and to whom they spoke; they provided diagrams, maps, and drawings of the towns, taverns, shops, and meeting rooms they visited. But Easley, in the process of compiling these raw materials into narrative reports, took artistic license. By borrowing from contemporary popular fiction and traumatic events like the Haymarket bombing, he rendered the situation in New Jersey believable, dire, and in need of immediate action.

To further assess the situation, F and Mr. X followed leads and clues provided by the anarchists they encountered on their reconnaissance mission. On October 14, 1915, F and Mr. X visited another active anarchist cell in Passaic, New Jersey. They uncovered that Salvatore Fulfano's grocery store at 455 Main Street served as a secret "meeting place for the bomb makers." Fulfano, as it turned out, was also the alleged contact person in Passaic for "anything from arson, assault to murder." The investigators also learned that Fulfano had been arrested several times but was released each time "on account of his political pull." They discovered that he was an important and well-connected man who "control[led] the foreign vote of Northern New Jersey, who, are in the habit of 'voting early and often.'" He also served as the link between the Paterson and Passaic anarchist camps through his relationship with the Claret brothers, Abram and Esedo, both of whom were described as "members of the local lodge of anarchy." One of the Claret brothers was a lawyer, and the other was a magistrate in the Court of Special Sessions. According to the report, because the Claret brothers enjoyed "political [and] official connections," many anarchists in New Jersey were never charged or convicted. An anarchist simply had to pay "a large fee to the lawyers," and then "the magistrates will never convict."[76]

Continuing to follow clues and build on the relationships they were establishing throughout this section of New Jersey, the investigators then paid a visit to Vincenso Salerno's store in Garfield, New Jersey. Salerno had connections to the Paterson anarchist camp; he was the man "who handle[d] the gangs that [were] secreting explosives in[to] the different factories throughout Northern New Jersey." Salerno welcomed F and Mr. X warmly and introduced them to three other men, whose responsibilities included carrying "out the orders of Vincenso in his destruction engagements." All of the men present were members of the local anarchist cell, and they "talked freely of the money they are receiving from the *German-Austrian agents* for performing the destruction" in the factories throughout New Jersey.[77]

While in Salerno's store, the investigators heard a disturbance outside. According to their report, "Vincenso and the other men leapt into action, quickly grabbing four empty barrels, which they "turned . . . up side down, placed them on their heads and stooped down, so that the barrels completely covered them." Vincenso ordered F and Mr. X to "take seats on the barrels, and directed his wife to serve us with drinks."[78] As the agents sat on their barrels enjoying a beverage, three men rushed in, explaining that they were police officers "detailed to arrest three suspicious characters, wanted for the recent explosion in the Powder factory at Pompton Lake. Then they proceeded to search the house in a most thorough manner."[79] The officers never found the men they were looking for, who were cleverly concealed under the barrels. At this point, was it not incumbent upon the NCF investigators to assist the police in apprehending these criminals? Had the investigators placed their own goals—of gathering information, of protecting their disguises, of continuing their employment—above the law? Or would they be risking their own lives if they broke role?

The priority of the NCF investigators was collecting information, which Easley then sent in amended or repackaged form to the MID. F and Mr. X were not armed, and unlike investigators for the Committee of Fourteen, they lacked the legal authority to make arrests or apprehend suspected criminals. Interestingly, the MID never brought NCF investigators onto the staff during the war years, even though in New York City alone several newspaper reporters, steel workers, National Guardsmen, and others were issued identification cards whose purpose, in the language of the MID, was to "authorize [them] to make investigations for this office."[80] The MID issued identification cards to volunteers who then conducted investigations and made arrests. For example, John Ringling, "the head of the Great Circus Trust," was given an MID identification card and worked out of the New York City MID office,[81] suggesting that any clown could work for the MID. The NCF investigators, however, had no such powers. In a sense, they were vigilantes. So even if they had decided to act as patriotic Americans and leapt off those barrels to reveal Salerno and his murderous cronies stooping below, F and Mr. X could not legally have done anything, and they might have been arrested by the "real" police or killed by the anarchists. So they remained seated and took in the relevant information, returning it to Easley in the form of written narratives.

Easley and the NCF read these reports as evidence that a number of agencies of the federal government and law enforcement were broken. The Bureau of Immigration was incapable of identifying and excluding criminals at Ellis Island or other immigrant landing depots; the Bureau of Investigation and local law enforcement officials failed to apprehend anarchists and criminals once they entered the United States. The sense of alarm was enhanced by images of anarchists hiding under barrels while the inept and bumbling police officers neglected "to examine the four barrels [through which] the heads of [the men] . . . were plainly visible." The investigators learned, however, that Salerno was a "subordinate" of Fulfano and was therefore "guaranteed protection . . . by the brothers CLARET, of Paterson."[82] Immigrant criminals had taken over this section of New Jersey, as suggested by this report, and the state and federal governments had failed to act. But so had the NCF's vigilante investigators.

During the course of their investigations, F and Mr. X realized that the kingpin of anarchist activities in the region was Father Alfonzo D'Angelo. The reports described him as the *"financial agent* for the *Austrian-Hungarian* interests," but he was also "a fugitive from justice." According to the three NCF reports, D'Angelo immigrated to the United States after he was arrested and convicted for molesting a child in his parish in Italy. He arrived in the United States with letters of introduction from his anarchist camp in Italy to the anarchist camp in Paterson. After a few years, he was "placed in charge of the anarchists outside of the Paterson district." The report noted that the federal government had a file on D'Angelo, but "the record of this case is on file in the office of the Secretary of State, marked *'not found.'*"[83] This statement was designed to point to a crack in the system of screening immigrants not only for subversive political activities but also for criminal backgrounds. Immigrant landing depots and restrictive immigration laws were supposed to bar the entry of criminals, anarchists, prostitutes, and those with contagious diseases. As the reports became more hyperbolic, the embedded question emerged: Why did the government not know about this? And why was it not doing more?

Further investigation of D'Angelo revealed that he too had a hand in corrupting local law enforcement officials. NCF reports concluded that D'Angelo "handled the local police for the anarchists of Passaic and Paterson as well as the state officials in Northern New Jersey." The priest crafted a plan to keep the anarchists and police in cahoots and above public suspicion. According to the investigators, D'Angelo regularly bribed private detectives to file false reports; he then obtained lists from "anarchist bomb makers as to the identity of those purchasing explosives who are *not anarchists.*" D'Angelo passed that information on to the police, which allowed them to "make important arrests (of persons in whom they have no interest)." This system served to "cover the officers with glory" and protect the anarchists. If police officials were to arrest well-known anarchists, they first notified D'Angelo, who promptly warned the accused. Therefore, the "dangerous element who are under his protection are never discovered."[84] In these reports, D'Angelo was above the law, which suggested that only undercover investigators who were freed from the constraints of uniforms or professional codes of conduct could catch such a wily fellow.

From these positions, F and Mr. X learned of D'Angelo's plans to bomb powder plants. In fact, on December 1, 1915, the investigators were in his company the day that the Hagley Yard Powder Plant in Wilmington, Delaware (a DuPont munitions factory), exploded. According to the investigators, D'Angelo was in a jubilant mood. He described "the Wilmington affair as a *'beautiful piece of work'*—but not large enough to satisfy him." He claimed that much more could have been destroyed. He acknowledged that workers were injured, but that those responsible for the bombing had put up flyers in a number of languages in advance, warning the men that something was afoot and to quit their jobs to avoid injury or death. D'Angelo hoped that a few more similar bombings would incapacitate these plants altogether because they would not be able to "obtain men to work in the plants, and this . . . would soon stop the shipment of munitions to the Allies."[85]

In the course of this conversation, the investigators also discovered that Father D'Angelo had plans to destroy the Dover plant in New Jersey and had asked the Doctor to be prepared for that attack. D'Angelo instructed the Doctor that he should be on hand to treat the injured and simultaneously "warn them to keep still,—*say nothing!*"[86] D'Angelo told the investigators Dover was a good target because an elderly man in his parish told him that there was an old iron mine there. D'Angelo explained that iron ore production began to move out of New Jersey in the 1880s with the discovery of iron ore in the Lake Superior region. The Dover mines shut down, and the industry never returned. All of the buildings deteriorated, and the town eventually moved the train station to a more lucrative location near the Morris Canal. However, D'Angelo explained, the DuPont Company had recently purchased the old Dover site and was refurbishing all of the dilapidated facilities. He claimed that no one in the area knew or remembered that these underground mine shafts—under the works currently being built by DuPont—existed.[87]

With this information, D'Angelo orchestrated a diabolical plan in concert with several Austrian-Hungarian employees of the Hercules plant, who, over a six-month period, had stolen and stored nearly a ton of powder. With the help of an informant and an Austrian civil engineer, "*the openings to all the Mines under the Town of Dover—and the Hercules Powder Plant of the duPont Company—were reopened—and* a survey made of the several levels of each Mine."[88] They also acquired the necessary equipment for touching off the explosion in the abandoned mine shafts under the new powder plant.

D'Angelo stated that he and his colleagues intended to perform these "formidable acts" after January 1, 1916.

D'Angelo explained to F and Mr. X that one positive result of his plan would be "the complete destruction of one of the largest munitions plants in the United States." Assuming that it would take at least a year to repair and replace the machinery and buildings, D'Angelo estimated that the war would be over by that point. He also claimed that the "loss of life would be so great to the employees and their families . . . that it will be impossible for Powder companies all over the United States to secure men to operate the plants."[89]

After he detailed his plans, D'Angelo asked Mr. X, F, the Professor, and the Doctor for their opinions on the matter. The Professor expressed his dismay, pointing out to D'Angelo that the Triangle had recently given orders that "*human life must be spared at any cost.*" D'Angelo disagreed; according to the investigators' report, he believed that he could convince the Triangle that by "sacrificing a few lives this winter," he could block future shipments of explosives to the Allies "and thus make it possible for the German-Allied powers *to dictate the terms of peace.*" D'Angelo figured that ultimately his plan would save "thousands of lives of soldiers now in the trenches, which would be a greater triumph than a long, drawn-out War, with its loss of thousands upon thousands of men.[90]

D'Angelo's plans horrified the Professor, who exclaimed, "You should be over on Grand Street (N.Y.C.)—You are not an anarchist, you are a butcher—You are worse than the 'Black Hander' of Mulberry Street." For the Professor, there was a moral code or idealism associated with the tenets of anarchism, and he distinguished between anarchists' acts of violence for the sake of a "utopian" future, and the violence of the Black Hand, which was a tool for individual financial gain and personal power. The Professor informed D'Angelo, "If you attempt to put this horrible scheme over without first obtaining written permission from the *Triangle—I shall hand you over to the Police.*" D'Angelo reminded the Professor of an informer who turned up dead after snitching on a comrade. The Professor instantly backed down, telling D'Angelo that he could not support him unless he first received permission from the Triangle to proceed.[91] The investigators then witnessed D'Angelo taking out his cipher book and writing a letter in code to the Triangle, detailing his plans. F and Mr. X left shortly thereafter, with D'Angelo resolved to carry out his plot.

One week later, F, Mr. X, the Doctor, and the Professor convened to construct "a campaign in opposition to D'ANGELO's plan of DESTRUCTION, as we are a unit *against* his method as outlined by him at our interview last Sunday (5th)." At this point, the investigators were fully enmeshed in this circle of men and their plans, acting from inside this anarchist cell to prevent D'Angelo's plan of destruction. The Doctor explained to F and Mr. X that everything D'Angelo said about the Hercules Powder Company (the mines, the Austrian employees, the powder stores) was accurate. The Professor interjected that he had already intervened and contacted the secretary of the Triangle to explain "the great loss of life that would occur of a lot of poor people . . . if the plan suggested by D'Angelo were permitted to proceed, and that he *begged* the Triangle to call both D'Angelo and himself to Chicago, so that the situation could be given in detail." He hoped it would be stopped in advance.[92]

After dinner, D'Angelo joined the other men. He quickly learned that the Professor had gone behind his back to foil his plans. D'Angelo informed the group that the third member of the Triangle would be returning from Europe shortly and would be staying with him—out of the Professor's reach. He was certain that his plans would be approved. The investigators noted in the report dated January 2, 1916, that D'Angelo had met with the returning member of the Triangle in Baltimore, Maryland, and that he considered it a "satisfactory meeting." Apparently, the Professor and D'Angelo "placed in the hands of the Triangle member a written statement of each side, that they had drawn up and by which they agreed to stand." The member of the Triangle apparently "expressed no opinion" but promised to present both letters to the full Triangle as soon as he arrived in Chicago. D'Angelo expressed concern to F and Mr. X that the Professor would go over his head and "secretly communicate with the Triangle."[93]

In the report dated January 23, 1916, the investigators noted that they met with the Professor, the Doctor, and D'Angelo. They learned that, after reading the Professor's and D'Angelo's letters, the Triangle ruled that the Dover plan "could not be successfully performed—*without the loss of many lives.*" The report also noted that the Triangle would not authorize any activities that threatened the loss of lives; "on the contrary, the TRIANGLE is *obligated* to prevent such activities."[94] D'Angelo, after reading the letter, announced that they must all obey the wishes of the Triangle until the ban on destructive activities was lifted because their desire to protect innocent humans was paramount.

Despite the Triangle's "humane" ruling, the investigators reported that, on January 30, 1916, D'Angelo started working with Ferrara (the Black Hander from Grand Street in New York City) to smuggle some kind of munitions into Dover in the hopes of carrying out his plan. D'Angelo told F and Mr. X that he wanted their help in finding "the best point of conceal-ment for the gun after the shot was fired,—which would not be difficult to find on account of this isolated section of rather a wild, abandoned moun-taintop—full of dangerous mine shaft holes!"[95] From here, F and Mr. X's records taper off as to the actions of D'Angelo and his dealings in Dover.

According to a *New York Times* article from May 16, 1915, however, the secretary of the navy sent thirty marines to Lake Denmark, near Dover, New Jersey. The article claimed that this was a precautionary measure following an explosion in Carney's Point, New Jersey (near Wilmington, Delaware). Several mysterious explosions had occurred in munitions plants since the beginning of the year. In addition, according to the *Times*, federal authorities received information on May 15, 1915, about schemes to destroy govern-ment plants that manufactured and supplied ammunition and arms to the Allies.[96] Perhaps the marines were dispatched to Dover after the National Civic Federation shared F and Mr. X's information on D'Angelo's plan with the MID; it is not possible to say conclusively.[97]

Who was Father Alfonzo D'Angelo? Did he really exist, or was he merely a figment of Felix Pereira's, B. F. Garland's, and Ralph Easley's imagina-tions? Perhaps not. Dr. Walter B. Platt of the U.S. Public Health Service also encountered a wily priest while working "in connection with the influenza epidemic at the DuPont works at Carneys Point, NJ (opposite Wilming-ton)." Platt reported to Captain Brooks Shepherd of the MID that he had concerns about "the Russian priest living at the upper end of the Russian village, at which is situated the Greek church and the priest's house. (This is at Plant #1)." Platt noted that as he approached, he found the priest "pacing up and down in his garden, wearing a dark blue military cloak on which were brass buttons." He noted that the priest's "whole bearing was that of a man who had past [sic] a large part of his life in camps and barracks. From my previous experience in Germany I should think he might have come from a south eastern part of Germany bordering upon Russia. If a Russian at all he was totally unlike any of the various types of Russians I had previously seen and on the contrary he strongly resembled one type of German." Platt arrived at the conclusion that because this priest of indeterminate ethnicity was "located at our great powder works it might be advisable to look into his antecedents, friends, comings and goings, and if possible correspon-dence."[98] Captain Shepherd concurred that this was an important matter requiring further investigation.[99]

Who was this priest? Had Dr. Platt actually encountered the Italian priest Father D'Angelo and mistaken him for a Russian (or a German)? Did Easley decide, for the sake of his own agenda, that it would be more rhetorically effective to turn a Russian or German priest into an Italian priest? Or were there two crazy, intense foreign priests perched near the DuPont works? Could the MID have been as inefficient and confused as Easley and Gompers feared?

Ultimately, the true identity of the priest is inconsequential because the larger point is that Ralph Easley mobilized the figure of a destructive priest to push for a more activist federal state. Only then would policies and procedures be implemented to guarantee the America he envisioned: one with swift deportation of foreign radicals and easy surveillance of domestic radical activities, and in which wartime labor provisions were kept in place to prevent strikes and protests. The war gave the NCF an unprecedented opportunity to place itself in relation to the federal government to help in constructing this state. By producing "evidence" of domestic dissent and forwarding it to key federal agencies, the NCF guaranteed its continued necessity. The problems its reports depicted could not be solved by the People's Institute's English-language classes or supervised dances in public school buildings. The individuals portrayed in the NCF reports were beyond the influence of such activities; in fact, they suggest that immigrants who participated in supervised events such as those organized by the People's Institute were a self-selecting group, those who were perhaps already inclined toward loyalty and Americanization.

The NCF's reports clearly suggested that another policy needed to be put in place regarding immigrants and their slow pace of Americanization. They pointed to failures in the government's bureaucracies and systems: humane Ellis Island had failed; local politics were corrupt, and politicians were corruptible; and newspaper offices, those guardians of the democratic public sphere, were perverted by immigrants, who used them as blinds for selling explosives. It is no coincidence that by 1917, Ralph Easley directed the League for National Unity, with Samuel Gompers as the vice chairman, which worked closely with George Creel's Committee on Public Information. The League pushed for all immigrant aliens to become U.S. citizens; in 1918, it adopted a campaign for a Congress that was 100 percent American and proposed a loyalty oath for congressmen.

The Military Intelligence Division continued to rely on the National Civic Federation during the postwar period, resulting in increased persecution of immigrant radicals, which then extended to include African Americans. In August 1920, Charles Mowbray White, working for the National Civic Federation, began "a survey of the negro situation insofar as it affects the United States."[100] He focused on New York City, from where, he claimed, "the heads of five principal radical factions" conducted their operations. White identified the five factions as the socialist group represented by Chandler Owen and A. Philip Randolph, editors of the *Messenger*; Marcus Garvey and the Universal Negro Improvement Association; W. E. B. DuBois and the National Association for the Advancement of Colored People; the National Urban League; and the "Negro Republican group," represented by Frederick R. Moore, editor of the *New York Age*.[101] Although White divided the groups into separate categories, he considered (and portrayed) all of them as exceedingly dangerous.

White's depictions of these groups were grossly oversimplified, if not completely misguided, but they served the purpose of inspiring the MID and the Bureau of Investigation to continue and extend surveillance activities in peacetime. For example, White characterized the conservative *New York Age* as "dangerously radical," on the basis of what he termed a "series of purely Bolshevist editorials" by James Weldon Johnson. When White questioned Moore about his decision to run these editorials, Moore responded that he did "not see anything radical or Socialistic in them."[102] White determined that, because Moore disagreed with his characterization of Johnson's opinion pieces, Moore must be a socialist in disguise. White, however, had conveniently elided "socialism" and "problack/pro–civil rights" opinions. The *New York Age* remained under federal surveillance until 1920 for publishing "antiwhite" opinions. Not until Herbert S. Boulin, black informant for federal intelligence agencies, described the conservative ethos of the *Age* did his superiors halt their investigation.[103]

White also honed in on the NAACP; he characterized the *Crisis* as a "propaganda periodical" with a "venomously" antiwhite agenda. The NAACP's call for racial equality was deemed radical. In White's judgment, these sentiments "clearly put [members] in the category of extreme Socialists or Bolshevists." He recognized that they considered "themselves to be absolutely loyal Americans," but that fact failed to move him. He pointed to the NAACP's attempts to "have [southern state] legislatures pass various laws looking toward the elimination of lynching, poor schools, the Jim Crow cars, unequal justice in courts and things economic" as evidence that it was an organization full of disloyal and dangerous people.[104] The Bureau of Investigation shared White's thinking. DuBois and the NAACP were monitored by the Bureau and the MID after 1917, and in May 1918 the U.S. attorney for New York warned DuBois that the *Crisis* had violated the Espionage and Sedition acts and would continue to be monitored.[105]

White concluded his report by claiming that the white people active in organizations such as the National Urban League or the NAACP were of "a Socialist turn," and as a result they had "further agitated and embittered" their black counterparts. White resorted to the "outside agitator" thesis of black political activism. The benefit of portraying black Americans' demands for equality as socialistic or Bolshevist was that it provided legal justification for prosecuting such groups under New York State sedition or criminal anarchy statutes, which empowered the attorney general to conduct "secret investigations" into any issues "concerning the public peace, public safety and public justice."[106]

In the end, MID files provide a slightly different picture of Easley, Gompers, and the NCF's activities.[107] Easley, in his zeal to stomp out socialist activities in the United States, occasionally did some investigating himself. On March 7, 1919, he and his wife attended a banquet in New York City in honor of the famed Russian revolutionary Mme. Catherine Breshkovsky. Among the other attendees were Henry Simpson, former editor of the socialist newspaper *New York Call*, and other socialist writers, editors, and Russian politicians. Easley must have imagined that he was "passing" in this milieu, all the while keeping a watchful eye on a potentially dangerous situation. Could he have imagined that the MID also had an undercover officer there? The MID officer even had a photograph of the banquet, with numbers written on each of the attendees' faces; he identified Ralph and Gertrude Easley of "Civic Federation of N.Y. City." The MID officer then issued the caveat that all of those in attendance were "supposed to be loyal and to have supported the government during the war," but that the agencies of the federal government "must still bear in mind that they are socialists and at some time have spoken in favor of the social revolution, which they claim could be had with out bloodshed."[108] Ralph Easley, who saw himself as the defender of America, had been identified by an undercover agent of the federal government as a dangerous radical.

EPILOGUE

After the excesses of the late nineteenth and early twentieth centuries, represented by events such as Pinkerton detectives massacring striking workers at the Homestead Steel Mill in 1892 and the Lexow Committee (1895) and Mazet Commission (1900) revealing the extent of police department malfeasance in New York City, public confidence in private detective agencies and municipal police departments waned. Such developments tarnished the reputation of private detectives in the eyes of social activist organizations, which were forced to find a balance between the risks of public humiliation that professional detectives carried along with the benefits of employing persons who could work undercover. In the end, the activists rejected professional detectives and instead relied on investigators whom they could bring more directly under their control. Prized by social activist organizations for their skills and experience, residents of the immigrant and working-class neighborhoods of the Lower East Side, Little Italy, and Chinatown, as well as white-collar professionals such as social workers, newspaper reporters, and former employees of the New York State Department of Excise, all joined the stable of investigators maintained by such groups.

During the war years, this mode of investigative social activism reached its apotheosis. Private organizations and government agencies cooperated on a variety of projects, such as policing moral conditions around military encampments, assisting immigrants in their transition to their new country, and monitoring domestic political subversion. A diverse range of private organizations, like the Committee of Fourteen and the People's Institute, contributed their staff and investigators to these federal projects; they viewed these collaborations as a ratification of their particular vision for social improvement. After World War I, though, the task of defining the direction of subsequent policing and measures of social change largely slipped out of the control of the private organizations, even though, in most cases, activists had initiated the partnerships. The private organizations became handmaidens to the federal agencies, relegated to implementing governmental imperatives, rather than setting their own agendas and seeing them endorsed by the federal government. When the social activists leapt at the chance to demonstrate the investigative expertise they had developed over the previous two decades, however, they could not have predicted that they would lose their autonomy in this process.

Expanding on its efforts to administer and organize the workforce and the economy for the war, the federal government formalized and professionalized policies and procedures in other sectors as well—particularly in agencies dedicated to police work. The Military Intelligence Division, the (Federal) Bureau of Investigation, and the Bureau of Prohibition assumed surveillance work previously conducted by private organizations. Given the dramatically increased power wielded by these federal agencies, the consequences for many ordinary Americans were dire. The men (and few women) who worked for the professional, federal police forces were no less corruptible than the Committee of Fifteen's John Earl or the Committee of Fourteen's David Oppenheim; federal agents, however, had vast legal powers at their disposal to persecute and prosecute radicals, "sexual deviants," and others who threatened to rend the nation's fabric.

During this transformative period for the nation's intelligence agencies, power shifted significantly from civil society to the government. The Progressive Era organizations for social improvement that had planned and conducted their own investigations a decade earlier became subsidiary to their federal partners; these same private organizations participated in their own obsolescence and loss of influence by entering into collaborations that ultimately usurped them. Their prestige and power slipped significantly with the rise of a stronger Bureau of Investigation. The Bureau's Radical Division, which was reorganized and christened the General Intelligence Division in July 1920, and the military intelligence agencies, including those of the War Department and the Department of the Navy, publicly announced that they had watchers everywhere—not only official men with titles and badges, but also sympathetic private citizens who willingly conducted surveillance work.

For instance, in July 1917, in the midst of the war, R. H. Van Deman of the MID opened a case file on a new domestic threat—"Negro subversion" in the United States. Van Deman expressed a belief that African Americans themselves were not responsible for erupting racial tensions or disruptions in munitions plants but that, instead, outside agitators had engineered these events. Indeed, the first items in the "Negro subversion" file were reports detailing the activities (and putative successes) of the Germans and Bolsheviks among African Americans.[1]

After opening the new case file, the MID gathered reports from other agencies to expand its knowledge and understanding of the "Negro situation." One such agency was the British Military Intelligence Division, which shared a report titled "Revolutionary Movements in America." The report's author noted that "Japanese agents have been behind the colored disturbances in America. This may be due to the fact that the negroes are demanding the inclusion of the yellow races in their world-wide claims for social and political equality with the white races." The American MID official who received and processed this dispatch noted in green pencil that this was "an excellent report!"[2]

High-placed Washington officials had trouble understanding the reasons behind "Negro unrest." Had the war not opened job opportunities for black Americans? Had black Americans not served in the armed forces, albeit in segregated regiments? For federal officials, the facts of "Negro subversion" fit more easily into the existing schema, which held that undercover agents—especially those from the IWW, Germany, and the newly Bolshevik Russia—had convinced Americans (in this case, black Americans) to engage in a conspiracy to undermine the American war effort and, ultimately, the United States government.

Senator Benjamin Tillman of South Carolina provided one such explanation. Reacting to the 1917 race riot in East St. Louis, Illinois, Tillman declared, "I have undoubted evidence from my viewpoint that the riot arose because negroes from the South had been brought to East St. Louis for the purpose of taking the place of white laborers."[3] Tillman suggested that when they were taken out of the paternalistic labor environment of the South, exceptionally naïve African Americans were vulnerable to the inducements of the IWW. He asserted that the Wobblies, by exploiting unsuspecting African Americans through promises of high wages, equality, and dignity, were solely responsible for the pogrom in East St. Louis. Tillman concluded his statement by holding forth on the evils and duplicity of this labor organization. A British military intelligence report from August 1919 echoed Tillman's thinking and used the "outside agitator" thesis to explain "the recent agitation among the negro population, which has led to much rioting between whites and blacks." The British report concluded that the violence was the result of "Bolshevik propaganda among the negroes, who were urged to support the Industrial Workers of the World organization."[4]

The MID had benefited in the past from spreading the belief that politically radical organizations, like the IWW, had infiltrated American society. This time, though, it stoked the fear that the black population was at risk—at risk of being incited to overthrow the social and racial order of the United States. This interpretation, created by those in Washington, D.C., and buttressed by the reports of British military intelligence and private American organizations, permitted the MID and other federal agencies to continue domestic surveillance activities even after the war had ended, extending the reach of the state further into people's lives.

As a result, in part, of reports like the one Charles Mowbray White produced on "black subversion" for the National Civic Federation and, in part, of actual unrest among black Americans, federal authorities in the postwar period feared a cataclysmic uprising. In addition, more than twenty race riots took place during the Red Summer of 1919, with black Americans vigorously fighting back in Chicago and Washington, D.C. (in stark contrast to the pogrom that had occurred in East St. Louis).[5] As a consequence, the Bureau of Investigation and the Military Intelligence Division kept black radicals (and not-so-radicals) under constant surveillance during the post–World War I era. Chandler Owen and A. Philip Randolph, black socialists and editors of the *Messenger*, were arrested in 1918 for violating the Espionage Act. Unable to raise bail money, the two men languished in prison until the Socialist Party sent an attorney to represent them. The judge ended up releasing them because he did not believe that either of the "boys" was "intelligent enough to have written such articulate, if inflammatory, editorials." He concluded that someone else had written the pieces and signed their names to them.[6] Nonetheless, the Bureau of Investigation (and its successor, the Federal Bureau of Investigation) did not dismiss Randolph so lightly. Considering him to be the most dangerous of the black radicals to emerge during this period, the Bureau kept an active file on him until his death in 1979.

Perhaps most famously, federal agencies hounded black nationalist and Universal Negro Improvement Association founder Marcus Garvey throughout the 1920s because of his opinions, power, and influence among black Americans. For years, the government attempted unsuccessfully to prosecute Garvey for a variety of alleged infractions. Finally, in 1928, he was convicted of mail fraud and deported to Jamaica.[7] Undercover investigation continued to be a useful way for the government to identify, prosecute, and deport "dangerous radicals" in order to head off possible crimes against the United States, but it also served to maintain a repressive racial status quo.

Many factors explained black dissatisfaction, particularly after the Armistice, and few were attributable to collusion with Germans or Soviets. With peacetime reconversion of industry and the economy, many African Americans who had migrated from the South to the urban North were laid off, which increased the suffering brought on by postwar economic inflation. These issues compounded the housing and job discrimination already experienced by blacks during the war years. The conviction that the unrest among black Americans resulted from Bolshevik agitation was implausible, but it reflected the federal government's political orientation in the postwar moment. Similarly, the labor insurgency that followed the Armistice and the domestic bombings in 1919 and 1920 (including that of Attorney General A. Mitchell Palmer's home) were exploited by high-placed government officials and like-minded private citizens to create widespread fear and hysteria among Americans to justify extending surveillance plans and programs.

After the Armistice, many Progressives and activists hoped and believed that the "social possibilities" of the war could now be enacted at home. Many spoke of the postwar period as one of "reconstruction," a term selected because of its self-conscious echo of the period following the Civil War, which had also seemed ripe for social transformation.[8] The abandonment of wartime labor protections, an increase in layoffs, changes in the economy, and actual radical sentiments among sizeable sectors of the American population (women, African Americans, workers, and social activists) contributed to a significant rise in antiradical sentiment among the elite and those affiliated with the federal government. Attorney General Palmer and J. Edgar Hoover, head of the newly formed antiradical General Intelligence Division of the Bureau of Investigation, contributed to and encouraged repressive antiradicalism at the local and state government levels, which overwhelmed the Progressives' optimism.

At the end of the war, outgoing Bureau of Investigation chief A. Bruce Bielaski cut his organization back to prewar levels; he reasoned that the Espionage, Sabotage, and Sedition acts of 1917 and 1918 and the Selective Service Act of 1918 had formed the legal basis for the Bureau's internal security investigations. Therefore, when the war ended and these laws lapsed, the Bureau lost most of its caseload in addition to its official mandate. By 1921, Congress had slashed the Bureau's budget by 80 percent, reducing the staff and personnel by half. Those in the federal government who wished to continue the new projection of state power that was inherent in the

Bureau's activities justified their efforts by redefining the repression of radical political dissent as a regular police activity and not an extraordinary measure legitimated by the emergency of war. To accomplish this task, they argued that "parlor Bolsheviks" (which included academics such as the historian Charles Beard, social activists such as Jane Addams, and wealthy dilettantes who Bureau agents and their associates believed were funding the impending revolution) had incited the passions that generated the postwar wave of labor strikes, race riots, and radical activities. This rhetorical strategy was part of the Bureau's goal to communicate to ordinary Americans, radicals, and parlor Bolsheviks that although the war had ended, the Bureau would still be pursuing its antiradical agenda because there was still a threat.

Bureau agents remained out there. They busily identified the owners of cars parked outside radical meetings; indexed the names of those who signed petitions and resolutions; and conducted "routine surveillance" of speeches by famous radicals, meetings, and other gatherings. Emma Goldman, "Big Bill" Haywood, and John Reed were but three of the radicals who enjoyed permanent, personal surveillance details, courtesy of the Bureau of Investigation. In addition, during the postwar period, Bureau agents adopted ever more legally questionable techniques. For instance, they broke into offices leased by radical groups and conducted warrantless searches. They also started "bugging" radical meetings and monitoring bank accounts.[9] Despite the Bureau's loss of its legal basis for domestic surveillance activities, the marriage of Progressive Era organizations, their undercover investigators, and agencies of the federal government created a sophisticated network of political repression and surveillance that ordinary Americans came to perceive as normal by the 1920s—even if they did not explicitly approve of it.

There were, however, actual radical activities taking place, which helped to move sentiments beyond a generalized fear of radical invasion and served to mobilize government agencies and passions. In 1919, rampant inflation hit working-class Americans particularly hard, and employers, no longer bound by the provisions of the War Labor Board, began to revoke benefits, such as union recognition, that it had ensured. As a consequence, an unprecedented number of strikes occurred in 1919, involving more than 4 million workers. In the most famous—the Seattle general strike—25,000 shipyard workers and members of the Metal Trades Council walked off the job to protest wage cuts. The Seattle Central Labor Council held a vote for affiliated unions to decide whether to strike in solidarity; by early February, approximately 30,000 additional workers had gone on strike. Although the action was largely peaceful, Mayor Ole Hanson stoked fears that the Bolshevik revolution, after succeeding in Russia, had come to the streets of Seattle. He accused the striking workers of bringing the anarchy of Russia to Seattle and vowed that they would not be permitted to rule the city's affairs.[10] The Washington State legislature responded by passing an antisyndicalism law early in its 1919 session, which served as the basis for numerous raids on labor and radical meetings and the arrests of suspected radicals. The Boston police strike, which started in September 1919, and the strikes in the steel industry during 1919–20 also generated rumors that Bolshevik agitators had infiltrated the ranks of these protesting workers.[11] All in all, these and the thousands of other strikes in the immediate aftermath of the Armistice fanned the flames of antiradical opinion in the United States.

Political and labor "subversives" were not the only Americans that the Bureau of Investigation kept under surveillance during the post–World War I period. When they were unable to make other charges stick, the Bureau mobilized "morals legislation" to control subversives. The Mann (White-Slave Traffic) Act of 1910 gave federal prosecutors copious powers, which they exploited through the 1910s and beyond. Prosecutions changed significantly after *Caminetti v. United States* (1917), in which the Supreme Court ruled that the Mann Act applied not only to the traffic in women for commercial purposes, but also to noncommercial travel across state lines by romantically involved consenting adults.[12] Although this decision clearly did not reflect the original intent of the Mann Act, *Caminetti* permitted the Bureau of Investigation (particularly under J. Edgar Hoover) to use concern over morals to control the behavior of black men, Communist sympathizers, and various other radicals and "undesirables." The Mann Act became a convenient political tool because "the crime [was] complete the moment the female has been transported across the state line with the intent to entice her into debauchery." According to one federal judge, it was not necessary to prove that the man had "accomplished his illicit purpose" in order to convict.[13]

Hoover and the Bureau of Investigation zealously, yet selectively, pursued Mann Act violations. The persecution and prosecution of black boxer Jack Johnson under the Mann Act are perhaps the best known. Johnson was arrested in 1912, convicted in 1913, and fled the country the same year. He eventually surrendered to federal authorities in 1920 and was sent to prison.[14] Johnson's case is perhaps the most egregious example of the abuse of police power that was permitted under the Mann Act; he was, however, but one victim of an overzealous Bureau of Investigation that used this legislation for political ends. University of Chicago sociologist W. I. Thomas was arrested in 1918 for an alleged violation of the Mann Act, although in actuality the Bureau of Investigation was interested in his wife and her pacifist activities during World War I. Thomas was acquitted, but the University of Chicago had fired him without waiting for the jury's decision, effectively ruining his career and tarnishing his professional reputation. Jack Gebardi, also known as "Machine Gun" Jack McGurn, was convicted of Mann Act violations for traveling throughout the South with his lover in 1928. Gebardi had worked for Al Capone, perhaps as a murderer for hire, and was suspected of having planned the St. Valentine's Day Massacre. Insufficient evidence deterred authorities from prosecuting Gebardi for those murders, but he was handed a six-year jail sentence and five years' probation for traveling through several states with his girlfriend-cum-wife, whom he married during this surveillance.[15]

By the end of the 1920s, federal prosecutors had largely stopped pursuing noncommercial Mann Act cases because, as the overall moral climate grew more tolerant of sexual relations out of wedlock, juries were less likely to find defendants guilty. Ultimately, the Mann Act, much like mail or tax fraud, was what the Bureau of Investigation used when it could not obtain evidence of other violations. For ordinary Americans—those who were not gangsters, radicals, or Mann Act violators—the 1920s brought agents of the federal government and surveillance into their lives in a significant way in the shape of the Bureau of Prohibition. In many ways, Prohibition represented the consummation of the relationship that organizations for social improvement and the federal government had initiated in the Progressive Era and strengthened during World War I.

Prohibition, as enacted by the Eighteenth Amendment, is another example of how the government, in partnership with local agencies and private organizations, policed and patrolled the private behavior of Americans. Enforcement of national prohibition was ultimately a failure, though, because the simple fact that alcoholic beverages had been made illegal did not stop Americans from making and drinking them, although the legislation's authors and supporters had imagined it would be so. This belief was naïve, and the Bureau of Prohibition was overwhelmed by its enforcement duties. Initially, the Bureau of Prohibition hired only 1,500 enforcement agents for the entire country. Even though the Bureau of Prohibition employed more agents than any other nonmilitary law enforcement body in the country, including the FBI, the numbers remained inadequate to control something as widespread and commonplace as alcohol consumption and production. Congress understaffed and underfunded the Bureau of Prohibition because it assumed that local police departments would participate in the policing of drinking, and that temperance and social reform organizations would lend a hand as well.[16] Such was not the case.

What seriously hampered the Bureau of Prohibition was that its enforcement agents were political appointees, not civil servants. For instance, New York City politicians distributed these enforcement agent positions "like candy." Men from all walks of life—from restaurant workers to professional athletes to war veterans—were nominated by local politicians to serve as Bureau of Prohibition agents. Those hired were sent out with little training and less regard for the "dry agenda" to enforce the amendment. Many were lured by the benefits of a steady government job; others found the possibilities for graft and bribery to be the job's most attractive feature.[17]

The most sensational example of agent corruption was the case of Jeremiah Bohan, a former liquor dealer and longtime friend of notorious gangster Monk Eastman. In the early morning hours of December 26, 1920, after a long evening of drinking and carousing through Brooklyn and Manhattan, Bohan shot and killed Eastman during a heated argument.[18] The Bohan case brought to light many of the reasons the Bureau of Prohibition failed to eliminate drinking in New York City: its employees were associated with gangsters, and they themselves regularly broke the law they were charged with enforcing.

Ultimately, for New Yorkers, Prohibition represented a "dangerous expansion of police powers," and they feared that "strict enforcement of the law would come at the expense of their civil liberties and right to privacy."[19] Prohibition normalized the surveillance of ordinary Americans and made that surveillance visible and legal. These were not David Oppenheims skulking around dive bars chatting up possible prostitutes; these were men with guns and badges backed by the power of the U.S. government. Citizens were no longer surprised to find that undercover agents sat next to them at the bar or even bought them drinks, or that agents busted down doors and brandished pistols.

During the 1920s, the American state expanded in size and professionalized its agencies. Government agents assumed responsibilities that private, social reform organizations had held from the late nineteenth century through World War I. Federal agents pursuing Prohibition or Mann Act prosecutions occasionally struck temporary coalitions with private organizations, but the private organizations were increasingly supplanted by agencies of the federal government.[20] The postwar period, then, cemented state surveillance as a regular practice. Gone were the amateur investigators faking Greek accents or working-class roots; trained agents of the federal government replaced them. Investigations were routine and professional on the surface. As the technologies of surveillance matured beyond intercepting mail and jotting down license plate numbers to bugging hotel rooms, tapping phones, and placing agents provocateurs inside organizations, the reach of the federal government extended into places where technically it should not have been and where it was most certainly not welcome.

By the 1920s, concerns over civil liberties and revelations that partisan purposes motivated some members of the Bureau of Investigation led opponents in Congress to purge the Bureau's ranks. President Calvin Coolidge forced Attorney General Harry M. Daugherty and Bureau director William J. Burns to resign. Before coming to the Bureau of Investigation in 1921, Burns had operated his own private detective agency, the William J. Burns International Detective Agency, which had a reputation for employing corrupt agents and in 1919 nearly had its New York State license revoked.[21] Burns, as a throwback to an older style of policing, did not run a Bureau that conformed to the vision of a modern, professional, federal police force. Harlan Fiske Stone was appointed the new attorney general, and J. Edgar Hoover was promoted to acting director of the Bureau of Investigation in 1924.

Stone moved to professionalize the Bureau and save its reputation by curtailing some of its abuses, but this realignment proved to be just window dressing. The Bureau's network of private organizations continued to return reports on domestic political activities. In addition, the Military Intelligence Division, the Post Office, local authorities, and private citizens continued to funnel reports to the Bureau of Investigation.[22] By claiming a continuing risk that domestic radicals could undermine American institutions, the Bureau of Investigation justified such activities.

Ironically, by the end of the 1920s, many social activists sought to address the abuses by the Bureau of Investigation by bringing it into a closer relationship with the executive branch, which they believed was the only branch of the federal government that was "a genuine expression of the people's will." As a result, the Bureau continued to be used for political, partisan purposes. For example, Herbert Hoover relied on the Bureau of Investigation to provide intelligence on the Bonus Army March of 1932 and the Midwestern Farmers' Strike of the same year; the Bureau concluded that communists, criminals, and other dangerous radicals influenced both organizations.[23] This partnership served not only to create and maintain a chilling climate for political dissent but also to justify such continued activities by the federal government. Franklin Delano Roosevelt enjoyed a close personal relationship with J. Edgar Hoover, authorizing investigations into Nazi activities in the United States. Roosevelt also used the Bureau to maintain surveillance of his political opponent Huey Long from 1932 to 1934.

By the late 1930s, the FBI's involvement in the surveillance of domestic political subversion and radicalism was a foregone conclusion, in part because of the conscious actions of the executive branch, and in part because of the unintended consequences of Progressive social activism.

In 1939, FBI director Hoover claimed that a "presidential directive of September 1939 [provided the Bureau] with an open-ended intelligence mission unrelated to law enforcement."[24] The Bureau's most serious abuses would grow out of this open-ended mandate: the Bureau's support of the House Un-American Activities Committee (HUAC) and the Red Scare of the 1950s, the information it collected on Martin Luther King, Jr.'s extramarital sex life, its disruption of civil rights and New Left organizations through its Counter Intelligence Program (COINTELPRO), and the abuses of executive power in the post-9/11 era.

Even without a "presidential directive," the FBI still enjoyed conditions that permitted extensive surveillance of individuals and groups—conditions created through the relationships that social activist organizations and the government forged leading up to and during World War I. This process began during the mid- to late nineteenth century, when preventive societies, attuned to social issues that the government ignored or avoided (ranging from prostitution to animal welfare), engaged in the investigation and policing of violations. The official government apparatus in New York City benefited from this arrangement, because it did not have to invest its fiscal or personnel resources in these issues; law enforcement power and authority were granted to these organizations—a seemingly simple and elegant solution. This step was the first in the process of developing and extending the power of government in New York. The "state" grew to encompass not only official government agencies but also private organizations and their social activist adjuncts; the government benefited from the creation of a state comprised of social reformers, vigilantes, and other parties who willingly engaged in this expensive and difficult work.[25] These social activist organizations created a government that appeared to be a "human thing," as People's Institute director Frederic C. Howe described it—one that offered its citizens programs, resources, and protections that they could not secure for themselves or to which the government had never paid attention.[26]

Private organizations that collaborated with the government extended its "infrastructural power" and allowed the government to remain above reproach for a period.[27] The precedent set by the relationship between the preventive societies, such as the American Society for the Prevention of Cruelty to Animals and the Society for the Suppression of Vice, and the New York municipal government allowed for organizations concerned with the moral conditions of New York to deputize themselves. These organizations took on the "vice syndicates" of the Lower East Side, those corrupt arrangements among Tammany Hall politicians, police officers, gambling parlor operators, brothel keepers, unscrupulous saloon owners, and shady landlords of tenement apartment buildings that were based in financial gain and not high-minded moral visions of a well-organized, law-abiding, modern city of the future. By the time World War I erupted in Europe, organizations such as the Committee of Fourteen (influenced by the groundbreaking work of the Committee of Fifteen), the People's Institute, and the National Civic Federation enjoyed a symbiotic relationship with municipal, state, and federal government agencies. Such private bodies were an integral part of the state, broadly conceived, and extended the mechanisms of state power—in the form of surveillance, undercover investigators' reports, and limited law enforcement powers—even farther into working-class and immigrant communities.

These public-private partnerships all have antecedents, dating back to Progressive Era organizations. World War I brought these private agencies and the government into a close relationship, which produced disastrous and long-term consequences for the American populace. The architecture for this style of collaboration was erected in the late nineteenth century and perfected during World War I. The federal government, by stoking and exploiting antiradical sentiment, justified ever more intrusive investigations and actions. They continue today.

NOTES

INTRODUCTION

1. Founders of the Strand Roof Garden included Anne Morgan, daughter of J. P. Morgan; Elsie de Wolfe, actress and interior decorator; and Elisabeth Marbury, agent and theatrical producer. Natalie Sonnichsen, reports on the Strand Roof Garden, 5 and 6 May 1915, box 28, folder "The Strand Roof Garden," Committee of Fourteen records (hereafter C14), Manuscripts and Archives Division, The New York Public Library, Astor, Lenox, and Tilden Foundations.

2. Ibid. Sonnichsen refers to the young man as "B" throughout her report.

3. On Progressive Era movements and mentalities, see Paul Boyer, *Urban Masses and Moral Order in America, 1820–1920* (Cambridge: Harvard University Press, 1978); Alan Dawley, *Struggles for Justice: Social Responsibility and the Liberal State* (Cambridge: Harvard University Press, 1991); Peter Filene, "An Obituary for 'The Progressive Movement,'" *American Quarterly* 22 (Spring 1970): 20–34; Samuel P. Hays, *The Response to Industrialism, 1885–1914* (Chicago: University of Chicago Press, 1957); Richard Hofstadter, *The Age of Reform: From Bryan to FDR* (New York: Vintage, 1955); Robert D. Johnston, *The Radical Middle Class: Populist Democracy and the Question of Capitalism in Progressive Era Portland, Oregon* (Princeton: Princeton University Press, 2006); Mara L. Keire, "Vice in American Cities, 1890–1925" (Ph.D. diss., Johns Hopkins University, 2002); James T. Kloppenberg, *Uncertain Victory: Social Democracy and Progressivism in European and American Thought, 1870–1920* (New York: Oxford University Press, 1986); James T. Kloppenberg, *Virtues of Liberalism* (New York: Oxford University Press, 1998); Gabriel Kolko, *Triumph of Conservatism: A Re-Interpretation of American History, 1900–1916* (New York: Free Press of Glencoe, 1963); Robyn Muncy, *Creating a Female Dominion in American Reform, 1890–1935* (New York: Oxford University Press, 1991); William J. Novak, "The Myth of the 'Weak' American State," *American Historical Review* 113, no. 3 (2008): 752–72; John Louis Recchiuti, *Civic Engagement: Social Science and Progressive-Era Reform in New York City* (Philadelphia: University of Pennsylvania Press, 2006); Claire Marie Renzetti, "Purity vs. Politics: The Legislation of Morality in Progressive New York, 1890–1920" (Ph.D. diss., University of Delaware, 1983); Daniel T. Rodgers, *Atlantic Crossings: Social Politics in a Progressive Age* (Cambridge: Harvard University Press, 1998); Stephen Skowronek, *Building a New American State: The Expansion of National Administrative Capacities, 1877–1920* (Cambridge: Cambridge University Press, 1982); Camilla Stivers, *Bureau Men, Settlement*

Women: Constructing Public Administration in the Progressive Era (Lawrence: University Press of Kansas, 2000); Roland Richard Wagner, "Virtue against Vice: A Study of Moral Reformers and Prostitution in the Progressive Era" (Ph.D. diss., University of Wisconsin, 1971); James Weinstein, *The Corporate Ideal in the Liberal State, 1900–1918* (Boston: Beacon Press, 1968); Robert H. Wiebe, *The Search for Order, 1877–1920* (New York: Hill and Wang, 1967); and Christopher Wilson, *The Labor of Words: Literary Professionalism in the Progressive Era* (Athens: University of Georgia Press, 1985).

4. Thomas C. Mackey, *Pursuing Johns: Criminal Law Reform, Defending Character, and New York City's Committee of Fourteen, 1920–1930* (Columbus: Ohio State University Press, 2005), is a terrific exploration of the temporary coalitions struck by reform organizations.

5. Frederic C. Howe, *The Confessions of a Reformer* (1925; reprint, Kent: Kent State University Press, 1988), 55.

6. Special report, 21 Chatham Square, Chatham Inn, 3 February 1915, box 28, C14.

7. A remarkable article by Mark A. Pittenger explores the techniques and scholarship produced by the Progressive "down-and outers." See Pittenger, "A World of Difference: Constructing the 'Underclass' in Progressive America," *American Quarterly* 49, no. 1 (March 1997): 26–65. For a similar perspective, see Peter Gurney, "'Intersex' and 'Dirty Girls': Mass Observation and Working-Class Sexuality in England in the 1930s," *Journal of the History of Sexuality* 8, no. 2 (1997): 256–90; and Eric Schocket, "Undercover Explorations of the 'Other Half,' or the Writer as Class Transvestite," *Representations* 64 (Fall 1998): 109–33.

8. On narratives in history and historical writing, see Ann Fabian, *The Unvarnished Truth: Personal Narratives in Nineteenth-Century America* (Berkeley: University of California Press, 2002); and Karen Halttunen, "Cultural History and the Challenge of Narrativity," in *Beyond the Cultural Turn,* ed. Victoria E. Bonnell and Lynn Hunt, 165–81 (Berkeley: University of California Press, 1999).

9. Report, Foresters Hunters Hall, 781 Wycoff Avenue, 9 January 1916, box 30, folder 9, C14. On the Beecher-Tilton affair to which the proprietress alludes, see Richard Wightman Fox, *Trials of Intimacy: Love and Loss in the Beecher-Tilton Scandal* (Chicago: University of Chicago Press, 1999).

10. Report, 76 Seventh Avenue, 5 April 1913, box 28, C14.

11. E. F. Sanderson, "General Considerations Bearing upon the Proposed Community Clearing House," 30 January 1917, box 22, folder 11, People's Institute records (hereafter PI), Manuscripts and Archives Division, The New York Public Library, Astor, Lenox, and Tilden Foundations.

12. On the American Protective League and similar efforts, see Christopher Capozzola, *Uncle Sam Wants You: World War I and the Making of the Modern American Citizen* (New York: Oxford University Press, 2008); and David Kennedy, *Over Here: The First World War and American Society,* 25th anniversary ed. (New York: Oxford University Press, 2004).

CHAPTER ONE

1. Frank Morn, *"The Eye That Never Sleeps": A History of the Pinkerton National Detective Agency* (Bloomington Indiana University Press, 1982), viii, 30.

2. Pinkerton came to the United States in 1842, fleeing government persecution in his native Scotland for his Chartist activities. He settled in Dundee, Illinois, where he quickly became involved in the Underground Railroad, helping slaves escape to Canada. This pursuit brought him notice and notoriety, and he ran for statewide of-

fice in 1848. Within a decade, Pinkerton had moved to Chicago and become active in abolitionist circles there; he even assisted John Brown and a small group of slaves in reaching Canada in 1859.

3. Morn, *Eye That Never Sleeps*, 23.

4. On the history of the undercover technique in policing and labor control, see Frank J. Donner, *The Age of Surveillance: The Aims and Methods of America's Political Intelligence System* (New York: Knopf, 1980); Gary T. Marx, *Undercover: Police Surveillance in America* (Berkeley: University of California Press, 1988); Regin Schmidt, *Red Scare: FBI and the Origins of Anticommunism in the United States* (Copenhagen: Museum Tusculanum Press, 2000); Samuel Walker, *Popular Justice: A History of American Criminal Justice*, 2nd ed. (New York: Oxford University Press, 1998); and Robert P. Weiss, "Private Detective Agencies and Labour Discipline in the United States, 1855–1946," *Historical Journal* 29, no. 1 (March 1986): 87–107. On the Pinkertons and the Molly Maguires, see Kevin Kenny, *Making Sense of the Molly Maguires* (New York: Oxford University Press, 1998).

5. Morn, *Eye That Never Sleeps*, 36–37.

6. Ibid., 84–86.

7. Jean Marie Lutes, "Into the Madhouse with Nellie Bly: Girl Stunt Reporting in Late Nineteenth-Century America," *American Quarterly* 54, no. 2 (2002): 218.

8. Nellie Bly, *Ten Days in a Mad-House, or, Nellie Bly's Experience on Blackwell's Island* (New York: Norman L. Munro, 1887), 8.

9. After the success of "Ten Days in a Mad-House," Bly authored stories such as "The Girls Who Make Boxes: Nellie Bly Tells How It Feels to Be a White Slave," "Trying to Be a Servant: Nellie Bly's Strange Experience," "Nellie Bly as a Mesmerist," and "Around the World with Nellie Bly." Nell Nelson of the *Chicago Times* followed in Nellie Bly's footsteps, writing *The White Slave Girls of Chicago* in 1888 and other pieces on the "City Slave Girls." Popular magazines such as *Everybody's*, the *Independent*, and *McClure's* published similar tales. Inez Godman published an essay in the *Independent* in 1901 about working as a maid; Marie and Bessie Van Vorst's *The Woman Who Toils* was first serialized by *Everybody's* in 1903; Maud Younger's "The Diary of an Amateur Waitress" appeared in *McClure's* in 1907; and Rheta Childe Dorr's "Christmas from Behind the Counter," in which Dorr worked in a department store, appeared in the *Independent*. Lillian Pettengill published *Toilers of the Home: The Record of a College Woman's Experience as a Domestic Servant* in 1903, and Dorothy Richardson's *The Long Day: The Story of a New York Working Girl, as Told by Herself* was published in 1905. See Laura Hapke, *Tales of the Working Girl: Wage Earning Women in American Literature* (New York: Twayne Publishers, 1992); Brooke Kroeger, *Nellie Bly: Daredevil, Reporter, Feminist* (New York: Times Books, 1994); Lara Vapnek, "The Politics of Women's Work in the United States, 1865–1909" (Ph.D. diss., Columbia University, 2000).

10. Stephen Crane is best known for *Maggie: A Girl of the Streets* (1893), and Jack London's story of "tramping," *The Road* (1907), is considered a classic of the genre. See also Frank Tobias Higbie, *Indispensable Outcasts: Hobo Workers and Community in the Midwest, 1880–1930* (Urbana: University of Illinois, 2003); Pittenger, "World of Difference"; Schocket, "Undercover Explorations."

11. Patricia Madoo Lengermann and Jill Niebrugge-Brantley, *The Women Founders: Sociology and Social Theory, 1830–1930* (Boston: McGraw Hill, 1998), 229. See also Ellen Fitzpatrick, *Endless Crusade: Women Social Scientists and Progressive Reform* (New York: Oxford University Press, 1990).

12. See, for example, Alice Hamilton, *Exploring the Dangerous Trades: The Autobiography of Alice Hamilton, M.D.* (Boston: Little, Brown, 1943); Mary Van Kleeck, "Working Hours of Women in Factories," *Charities and the Commons* 17 (1906–7): 13–21. See also Jane Addams and the Residents of Hull House, *Hull House Maps and Papers: A Presentation of Nationalities and Wages in Congested District of Chicago, Together with Comments and Essays on Problems Growing out of the Social Conditions* (1895; reprint, Urbana: University of Illinois Press, 2007).

13. Bessie Van Vorst and Marie Van Vorst, *The Woman Who Toils: Being the Experiences of Two Gentlewomen as Factory Girls* (New York: Doubleday, Page, 1903), 5.

14. On women and the Chicago School, see Mary Jo Deegan, "The Chicago Men and the Sociology of Women," in *The Chicago School: Critical Assessments*, vol. 1: *A Chicago Canon?* ed. Ken Plummer, 198–230 (New York: Routledge, 1997); Mary Jo Deegan, "*Hull House Maps and Papers*: The Birth of Chicago Sociology," in *The Chicago School: Critical Assessments*, vol. 2: *Theory, History and Foundations*, ed. Ken Plummer, 5–19 (New York: Routledge, 1997); and Mary Jo Deegan, "Women and Sociology, 1890–1930," *Journal of the History of Sociology* 1 (Fall 1978): 11–34.

15. Lengermann and Niebrugge-Brantley, *Women Founders*, 232.

16. Ibid., 234–35. MacLean also served on the General Committee of the Brooklyn Recreation Committee in 1913, which is how she had contact (albeit probably quite limited) with Frederick Whitin of the Committee of Fourteen. Box 2, folder 17, file "Gen Corr 1913 April," C14.

17. Lengermann and Niebrugge-Brantley, *Women Founders*, 259.

18. Annie Marion MacLean, "Two Weeks in Department Stores," *American Journal of Sociology* 4, no. 6 (May 1899): 725–26.

19. Ibid., 722.

20. Annie Marion MacLean, "The Sweat-Shop in Summer," *American Journal of Sociology* 9, no. 3 (November 1903): 289–90.

21. Amy Tanner, "Glimpses at the Mind of a Waitress," *American Journal of Sociology* 13 (July 1907): 48, 49, 51.

22. Ibid., 55.

23. Nancy Cott, *The Grounding of Modern Feminism* (New Haven: Yale University Press, 1987), 34.

24. Maud Younger, "The Diary of an Amateur Waitress," pt. 1, *McClure's Magazine* 28 (March 1907): 543, 544.

25. Pittenger, "World of Difference," 36–37.

26. Moral reform in the antebellum period was largely woman's domain. As historian Mary Ryan has argued, women were greatly involved in and influenced by the religious revivals of the first decades of the nineteenth century, known as the Second Great Awakening. Women drew influence and moral authority from the importance that ministers placed on them; consequently they became responsible for bringing male members of their households back into the church. Women also used this authority to spread their moral influence throughout society. Historian Lori Ginzberg has demonstrated that women used these popular notions of their own higher morality to engage in the "work of benevolence." As a result, female moral reform societies flourished in the first decades of the nineteenth century, and their interests ranged from prostitution reform to abolitionism, suffrage, and temperance. On antebellum moral reform and women's roles, see Lori Ginzberg, *Women and the Work of Benevolence: Morality, Politics, and Class in the Nineteenth-Century United States* (New Haven: Yale University Press, 1990); Barbara Meil Hobson, *Uneasy Virtue: The*

Politics of Prostitution and the American Reform Tradition (New York: Basic Books, 1987); Mary Ryan, *Cradle of the Middle Class: The Family in Oneida County, New York, 1790–1865* (Cambridge: Cambridge University Press, 1983); Mary Ryan, *Civic Wars: Democracy and Public Life in the American City during the Nineteenth Century* (Berkeley: University of California Press, 1998); Mary Ryan, *Women in Public: Between Banners and Ballots, 1825–1880* (Baltimore: Johns Hopkins University Press, 1992); and Carroll Smith-Rosenberg, *Disorderly Conduct: Visions of Gender in Victorian America* (New York: Oxford University Press, 1986).

27. Timothy Gilfoyle, "The Moral Origins of Political Surveillance: The Preventive Society in New York City, 1867–1918," *American Quarterly* 38 (Autumn 1986): 639. The Society for the Suppression of Vice was a spin-off from the YMCA of New York City's Committee for the Suppression of Vice. See also Andrea Friedman, *Prurient Interests: Gender, Democracy, and Obscenity in New York City, 1909–1945* (New York: Columbia University Press, 2000); and Helen Lefkowitz Horowitz, *Rereading Sex: Battles over Sexual Knowledge and Suppression in Nineteenth-Century America* (New York: Knopf, 2002).

28. Gilfoyle, "Moral Origins of Political Surveillance," 640.

29. For a full discussion of this transition, see Eric H. Monkkonen, *Police in Urban American, 1860–1920* (New York: Cambridge University Press, 1981), esp. 148–61.

30. Gilfoyle, "Moral Origins of Political Surveillance," 640.

31. Ibid., 641.

32. James F. Richardson, *The New York Police: Colonial Times to 1901* (New York: Oxford University Press, 1970), 236. See also James Lardner and Thomas Repetto, *NYPD: A City and Its Police* (New York: Henry Holt, 2000), esp. chap. 5, "Down with the Police."

33. Charles W. Gardner, *The Doctor and the Devil, or Midnight Adventures of Dr. Parkhurst* (1894; reprint, New York: Vanguard Press, 1931), 17.

34. Ibid., 57.

35. Ibid., 58, 60–62.

36. Richardson, *New York Police*, 236–37.

37. Lardner and Repetto, *NYPD*, 100. See also Gardner, *Doctor and the Devil*.

38. "Memorial to Rev. Charles H. Parkhurst by the Society for the Prevention of Crime and Adopted by Its Board of Directors at a Regular Monthly Meeting of Board Held October 27, 1933," box 50, folder "Miscellaneous, 1901–1950," Society for the Prevention of Crime records (hereafter SPC), Rare Book and Manuscript Library, Columbia University.

39. Lardner and Repetto, *NYPD*, 100–101.

40. Richardson, *New York Police*, 238–39.

41. Lardner and Repetto, *NYPD*, 110. Parker was the non-Tammany Democrat.

42. Richardson, *New York Police*, 239.

43. Ibid., 240.

44. The New York Police Department's records are neither plentiful nor easily accessible. According to James F. Richardson, the department "sold many of their old records for scrap around 1914. A departmental spokesman informed me that the police did not have any records from the nineteenth century. . . . The only police records that are readily available to scholars are those connected with the mayor's office" (*New York Police*, 291).

45. Timothy J. Gilfoyle, *A Pickpocket's Tale: The Underworld of Nineteenth-Century New York* (New York: Norton, 2007), 253–54.

46. Richardson, *New York Police*, 268–69. The charge for consolidation had evolved "out of efforts by the city's merchant elite . . . to improve New York Harbor and promote the development of shipping, railroads, and utilities by substituting centralized municipal government for the existing system, which was highly fragmented because control was shared by forty local governments"; Kenneth T. Jackson, ed., *The Encyclopedia of New York City* (New Haven: Yale University Press, 1995), 277–78.
47. "Chairman Mazet's Powers," *New York Times*, 8 June 1899.
48. Richardson, *New York Police*, 275.
49. Morn, *Eye That Never Sleeps*, 112.
50. Gilfoyle, "Moral Origins of Political Surveillance," 647–48.
51. Friedman, *Prurient Interests*, 19.
52. Timothy J. Gilfoyle, *City of Eros: New York City, Prostitution, and the Commercialization of Sex, 1790–1920* (New York: Norton, 1992), 189.
53. Gardner, *Doctor and the Devil*, 111. Gardner's conviction was ultimately overturned. "Gardner to Be Set Free: Conviction of the Parkhurst Agent Reversed," *New York Times*, 18 November 1893; and "Gardner to Be Free To-Day," *New York Times*, 20 November 1893.
54. In addition, similar reform organizations in Chicago used undercover investigators. On Chicago, see Chad Heap, *Slumming: Sexual and Racial Encounters in American Nightlife, 1885–1940* (Chicago: University of Chicago Press, 2009); Joanne Meyerowitz, *Women Adrift: Independent Wage Earners in Chicago, 1880–1930* (Chicago: University of Chicago Press, 1988); Kevin J. Mumford, *Interzones: Black/White Sex Districts in Chicago and New York in the Early Twentieth Century* (New York: Columbia University Press, 1997); and Michael Willrich, *City of Courts: Socializing Justice in Progressive Era Chicago* (New York: Cambridge University Press, 2003).
55. These organizations are not considered in this book because of the paucity of their records. For example, the Society for the Prevention of Crime used private detectives extensively. Their records, however, for the years from about 1892 to 1920, the period covered in this book, are not very detailed. There are references to the detectives, but there are not the elaborate, narrative reports like those found in the records of the Committee of Fourteen, for example, or even the investigative forms, like those used by Committee of Fifteen investigators. In addition, the records of the Committee on Amusement Resources of Working Girls, founded by Belle Lindner Israels, have been lost, but many of their reports survive in the records of the Committee of Fourteen, with which they shared information and investigators. (For example, Natalie Sonnichsen went to work with the Committee of Fourteen after working for Israels. See Elisabeth I. Perry, "'The General Motherhood of the Commonwealth': Dance Hall Reform in the Progressive Era," *American Quarterly* 37, no. 5 [Winter 1985]: 723n9.) The five main organizations discussed in this study and the other few discussed in this note shared board members as well as reform techniques and the goal of a morally cleaner and more efficient New York. For example, Jacob Schiff was on the executive committee of both the Kehillah and the Committee of Fifteen. Rabbi H. Pereira Mendes served on the executive committee of both the Kehillah and the Committee of Fourteen. The Russell Sage Foundation, the People's Institute, the Committee of Fourteen, and the Committee on Amusement Resources of Working Girls all worked together on an investigation of dance halls and commercial amusements. Michael M. Davis, Jr., worked for the Russell Sage Foundation, collaborated with Whitin of the Committee of Fourteen, and went on to serve as secretary of the People's Institute; he was also one of the founders of the Committee on the Amusement Resources of Working Girls.

56. Arthur Goren, *New York Jews and the Quest for Community: The Kehillah Experiment, 1908–1922* (New York: Columbia University Press, 1970), 25.

57. "Gambling," 20 November 1913, p. 6, Kehillah (Jewish Community of New York City) records (hereafter Kehillah), Judah L. Magnes Archives, Jerusalem, Israel. Prof. Arthur Goren loaned me his microfilmed copies of the Kehillah's records for this portion of my research; I extend my deepest thanks to him.

58. In addition to its work on crime, the Kehillah was also concerned with, for example, maintaining kashruth (Jewish dietary laws) and supervising kosher butchers, in addition to opening temporary synagogues for the high holidays so that all could participate in services. The Kehillah, however, adapted to the needs of the growing and changing community by creating a Bureau of Education, an Employment Agency, and a Clearing-House for Feeble-Minded Persons. The Kehillah was also concerned with public claims that Jews were trafficking in women and that Jewish women were disproportionately found among prostitutes and female inmates. They worked closely with the Sisterhood of Shearith Israel, which provided social services to "wayward" Jewish sisters. For a more complete discussion, see Goren, *New York Jews*; and Anne M. Polland, "'The Sacredness of the Family': New York's Immigrant Jews and Their Religion, 1890–1930" (Ph.D. diss., Columbia University, 2004).

59. F. Elisabeth Crowell, "The Midwives of New York," *Charities and the Commons* 17, no. 15 (12 January 1907): 668, 676.

60. John W. Clark, "Street Crap Playing," *Charities and the Commons* 17, no. 15 (12 January 1907): 684–85.

61. The "government," in this case, refers to the agencies and departments of the official government apparatus. The "state" refers not just to the agencies, departments, and officials of the government apparatus, but also to the nonstate actors and social practices that helped bring the government into a larger field of power than it had traditionally enjoyed. Beatrice Hibou, "From Privatising the Economy to Privatising the State: An Analysis of the Continual Formation of the State," in *Privatising the State*, ed. Beatrice Hibou, trans. Jonathan Derrick (London: Hurst, 2004), 15. See also Michel Foucault, "Governmentality," in *The Foucault Effect: Studies in Governmentality*, ed. Graham Burchell, Colin Gordon, and Peter Miller (Chicago: University of Chicago Press, 1991), 87–104.

62. On investigation, ethnic impersonation, and "passing," see Laura Browder, *Slippery Characters: Ethnic Impersonators and American Identities* (Chapel Hill: University of North Carolina Press, 2000); Gurney, "'Intersex' and 'Dirty Girls'"; and Hapke, *Tales of the Working Girl*.

63. David Oppenheim and Harry Kahan worked for the Committee of Fourteen but also traveled and produced reports for the Military Intelligence Division during World War I.

64. Vern Countryman, "The History of the FBI: Democracy's Development of a Secret Police," in *Investigating the FBI*, ed. Pat Watters and Stephen Gillers (Garden City, NY: Doubleday, Inc., 1973), 36–39. See also Morn, *Eye That Never Sleeps*, viii. On the history of the FBI, see Richard Gid Powers, *G-Men: Hoover's FBI in American Popular Culture* (Carbondale: Southern Illinois University Press, 1983); Richard Gid Powers, *Not without Honor: The History of American Anticommunism* (New Haven: Yale University Press, 1995); Richard Gid Powers, *Secrecy and Power: The Life of J. Edgar Hoover* (New York: Free Press, 1987); Athan Theoharis, *Chasing Spies: How the FBI Failed in Counterintelligence but Promoted the Politics of McCarthyism in the Cold War Years* (Chicago: Ivan R. Dee, 2002); and Athan Theoharis and John Stuart Cox, *The Boss:*

J. Edgar Hoover and the Great American Inquisition (Philadelphia: Temple University Press, 1988).

65. Morn, *Eye That Never Sleeps*, 180.

66. Countryman, "History of the FBI," 36–39.

67. "Traffic in 'White Slaves,'" *New York Times*, 18 July 1909.

68. David J. Langum, *Crossing over the Line: Legislating Morality and the Mann Act* (Chicago: University of Chicago Press, 1994), 38. On "white slave" hysteria, see Brian Donovan, *White Slave Crusades: Race, Gender, and Anti-Vice Activism, 1887–1917* (Urbana: University of Illinois Press, 2006).

69. Langum, *Crossing over the Line*, 49.

70. Countryman, "History of the FBI," 36–39. Between 1932 and 1934, Congress passed a number of "criminal statutes forbidding the transportation of kidnapped persons in interstate commerce, extortion by means of threats sent through the mails of interstate commerce, theft from interstate shipments, traveling in interstate commerce to avoid state prosecution, robbery of national banks, of transportation of stolen property in interstate commerce, transportation of unregistered firearms in interstate commerce and extortion 'in any way or in any respect affecting' interstate commerce" (38–39). In 1934, Congress authorized Bureau agents to carry guns for the first time. In a 1935 appropriations bill, Congress rechristened the Bureau of Investigation the "Federal Bureau of Investigation." On the relationship between private detective agencies and the growth of the Bureau of Investigation, see Beverly Gage, *The Day Wall Street Exploded: A Story of America in Its First Age of Terrorism* (New York: Oxford University Press, 2009). On the Mann Act, see Langum, *Crossing over the Line*, chaps. 2 and 3.

CHAPTER TWO

1. "Reformers in Evening Dress Make Ten Raids," *New York Times*, 27 February 1901.

2. "Justice Jerome's Offer," *New York Times*, 27 June 1901.

3. *New York World*, 7 June 1901, as quoted in Jeremy P. Felt, "Vice Reform as a Political Technique: The Committee of Fifteen in New York, 1900–1901," *New York History* 54, no. 1 (January 1973): 42.

4. "The Fifteen Define Their Policy Anew," *New York Times*, 13 June 1901.

5. "The Fifteen Will Abandon All Raids," *New York Times*, 11 June 1901.

6. *New York World*, 17 March 1901, as quoted in Felt, "Vice Reform," 41.

7. Committee of Fifteen, *The Social Evil: With Special Reference to Conditions Existing in the City of New York* (New York: G. P. Putnam's, 1902), v.

8. "Police Blackmail Laid Bare," in *The Redemption of New York: Told by New York Newspapermen for the Press Scrap Book*, ed. Milo T. Bogard (New York: P. F. McBreen and Sons, 1902), 125–26.

9. General letter, 30 November 1900, reel 2, Committee of Fifteen records (hereafter C15), Manuscripts and Archives Division, The New York Public Library, Astor, Lenox, and Tilden Foundations. Both the original paper records and the microfilmed records of the Committee of Fifteen are available in the Manuscript and Archives Division of the New York Public Library; researchers are required to use the microfilmed records.

10. "Civic Societies Honor William H. Baldwin," *New York Times*, 6 February 1905.

11. Felt, "Vice Reform," 30. See also "Committee of Fifteen: Completed by the Appointment of Five New Members," *New York Times*, 15 December 1900.

12. Minutes of meeting, 27 February 1901, reel 2, C15. See also "Committee of Fifteen after Bigger Game," *New York Times*, 28 February 1901.

13. William Baldwin, as quoted in Felt, "Vice Reform," 37n17.

14. Committee of Fifteen, *Social Evil*, 172–73.

15. Committee of Fifteen to Jacob Schiff, 24 November 1900, reel 1, C15.

16. Fusionism became an important political strategy for those seeking to undercut the power of ethnic and machine politics. It emerged during the 1840s but came to full flower in the decades following the Civil War. Essentially, the strategy obliged those who were interested in political reform to build temporary coalitions and unite against Tammany Hall and Democratic Party candidates. Fusionists, however, ultimately "suffered from their rejection of the 'spoils system,' an inability to maintain party structures, [and] a tendency for lawyers and other professionals within their administrations to tire quickly of governance." Perhaps most damaging was the Democrats' depiction of Fusionists as pulling from among New York's elite, who tended to be seen as unsympathetic to poor and working-class New Yorkers. Ultimately, these coalitions proved more fragile and fleeting than those that worked to keep Tammany in power. Jackson, *Encyclopedia*, 446.

17. Committee of Fifteen, *Social Evil*, vi–vii. Reform groups (including members of the chamber of commerce and influential clergymen) managed to temporarily defeat Tammany in 1894 (with the Lexow investigations into police corruption), but by 1897 Tammany was back in power with the election of Robert A. Van Wyck as mayor, whose strings were pulled by Tammany boss Richard Croker. In 1901, Fusion Party candidate Seth Low became mayor largely because social reform organizations such as the Committee of Fifteen and the Citizens' Union were active in his victory. By 1903, the Democratic/Tammany candidates were again back in power, with George B. McClellan serving as mayor from 1903 to 1909, at which point William J. Gaynor, Democratic candidate, became mayor. John Purroy Mitchel, another Fusion candidate, managed to capture the mayor's office in 1913. The Democrats staged a resurgence after Mitchel and held the office until the election of Fiorello La Guardia in 1933.

18. Rev. John P. Peters, "The Story of the Fourteen," box 3, folder 7 "1914 January," C14. This article was published as "The Story of the Committee of Fourteen of New York," *Social Hygiene* 4 (July 1918).

19. Committee of Fifteen, *Social Evil*, 162–63.

20. Ibid., 73, 141, 143–44, 148.

21. On housing reform in New York City, see Robert W. DeForest and Lawrence Veiller, *The Tenement House Problem; Including the Report of the New York State Tenement House Commission of 1900* (New York: Macmillan, 1903). See also Margaret Garb, *City of American Dreams: A History of Home Ownership and Housing Reform in Chicago, 1871–1919* (Chicago: University of Chicago Press, 2005); Roy Lubove, *The Progressives and the Slums: Tenement House Reform in New York City, 1890–1917* (Pittsburgh: University of Pittsburgh Press, 1963).

22. Committee of Fifteen, *Social Evil*, 173–74.

23. Minutes of meeting, 9 and 23 January 1901, reel 2, C15.

24. Ibid. Rev. Dr. John P. Peters came to work with the Committee of Fifteen through his work with the Riverside and Morningside Heights Association. He was also pastor at St. Michael's Church and went on to found the Committee of Fourteen.

25. James Bronson Reynolds to George Wilson Morgan, 19 February 1901, reel 1, C15.

26. William Lustgarten to George Wilson Morgan, 15 September 1901, reel 1, C15.

27. Henry Moskowitz to George Wilson Morgan, 24 February 1901, reel 1, C15.

28. Lillian Wald to George Wilson Morgan, 9 January 1901, reel 1, C15.

29. Jacob Kreiswirth to the Committee of Fifteen, 2 October 1901, reel 1, C15.
30. L. L. Rosenbaum to Jacob Schiff, 22 July 1901, reel 1, C15.
31. Disorderly Tenement House in the City of New York form, C15. These forms can be found primarily in reels 3 and 4 of the microfilmed Committee of Fifteen records and are organized by police precinct and address.
32. Ibid.
33. E. C. Becherer, report on 563 Seventh Avenue, 31 July 1901, reel 4, C15.
34. Edward C. Becherer, affidavit, 563 Seventh Avenue, reel 4, C15.
35. Ibid.
36. Ibid.
37. Ibid.
38. Max Moskowitz, report on 8 James Street, 5 June 1901, reel 3, C15.
39. Ibid.
40. A. E. Wilson, report on 8 James Street, 5 June 1901, reel 3, C15.
41. Jacob Kreiswirth, report on 8 James Street, 5 June 1901, reel 3, C15.
42. L. L. Rosenbaum, report on 90 James Street, 25 September 1901, reel 3, C15.
43. Max Moskowitz, report on 55 Oliver Street, 25 September 1901, reel 3, C15.
44. Charles S. Copeland, report on 563 Seventh Avenue, 22 August 1901, reel 4, C15.
45. Albert Conklin, report on 55 Oliver Street, 23 August 1901, reel 3, C15.
46. John W. Earl, report on 331 E. 122nd Street, 22 July 1901, reel 4, C15.
47. Young Men's Chinese Christian Association to the Committee of Fifteen, reel 3, C15.
48. Peter Kwong, *Chinatown, N.Y.: Labor and Politics, 1930–1950*, rev. ed. (New York: New Press, 2001), 106; Gilfoyle, *Pickpocket's Tale*, 91–92.
49. On Quan Yick Nam, see Louis Beck, *New York's Chinatown: An Historical Presentation of Its People and Places* (New York: Bohemia Publishing, 1898), 284.
50. See, for instance, Quan Yick Nam to George W. Morgan, 27 May 1901, reel 3, C15.
51. Frank Moss, *The American Metropolis: From Knickerbocker Days to the Present Time: New York City Life in All Its Various Phases* (New York: Peter Fenelon Collier, 1897), 2:404–5.
52. The original act was put into place for ten years; in 1892, when it was set to expire, Congress renewed the act for another ten years. It became permanent in 1902 and was finally repealed in 1943. In 1892, Congress issued a report titled *The Chinese Menace*, which outlined the rationale for extending the Chinese Exclusion Act for another ten years. The report argued that the Chinese in America had "no attachment to our country, its laws or institutions, nor are they interested in its prosperity. They never assimilate with our people, our manners, tastes, religion, or ideas. With us they have nothing in common. . . . They are a distinct race." U.S. Congress, House of Representatives, *The Chinese Menace*, congressional report on immigration, report no. 255, 10 February 1892. This is not to suggest, however, that the Chinese in the United States stood by and allowed the laws to act upon them. Recent historiography reinscribes the Chinese as actors in this process—particularly as plaintiffs in court cases testing the constitutionality of the Geary Act (which aimed to strengthen Chinese exclusion). See L. Eve Armentrout Ma, "Chinatown Organizations and the Anti-Chinese Movement, 1882–1914," in *Entry Denied: Exclusion and the Chinese Community in America, 1882–1943*, ed. Sucheng Chan (Philadelphia: Temple University Press, 1991), 147–69. See also Charles J. McClain and Laurene Wu McClain, "The Chinese Contribution to the Development of American Law"; Christian G. Fritz, "Due Process, Treaty Rights, and Chinese Exclusion, 1882–1891"; and Lucy E.

Salyer, "'Laws Harsh as Tigers': Enforcement of the Chinese Exclusion Laws, 1891–1924"; all in Chan, *Entry Denied*, 3–93; and K. Scott Wong, "Cultural Defenders and Brokers: Chinese Responses to the Anti-Chinese Movement"; Qingsong Zhang, "The Origins of the Chinese Americanization Movement: Wong Chin Foo and the Chinese Equal Rights League"; Renqiu Yu, "'Exercise Your Sacred Rights': The Experience of New York's Chinese Laundrymen in Practicing Democracy"; and Sue Fawn Chung, "Fighting for Their American Rights: A History of the Chinese American Citizens Alliance"; all in *Claiming America: Constructing Chinese American Identities during the Exclusion Era*, ed. K. Scott Wong and Sucheng Chan (Philadelphia: Temple University Press, 1998).

53. Ma, "Chinatown Organizations," 148–49. See also Jeffrey Scott McIlwain, *Organizing Crime in Chinatown: Race and Racketeering in New York City, 1890–1910* (Jefferson, NC: McFarland, 2004), 92; Kwong, *Chinatown*, 42. These Triad societies were founded in seventeenth-century China, where their aim was to overthrow the Qing dynasty and reinstate the Ming. Although the Triads had become less political in nature by the mid-nineteenth century, they remained secretive and ganglike. The earliest tongs in the United States were those established in San Francisco in the 1850s; by the 1890s, two had been organized in New York City.

54. Ma, "Chinatown Organizations," 155; McIlwain, *Organizing Crime in Chinatown*, 35, 74.

55. Kwong, *Chinatown*, 43.

56. There is some dispute among scholars as to the nature of the tongs. McIlwain contends that tongs were not "inherently criminal organizations" but instead were "a natural means of obtaining and using individual and associational *guanxi* (symbiotic relationships of power and obligation) for both criminal and non-criminal purposes" (*Organizing Crime in Chinatown*, 33).

57. Ivan Light, "From Vice District to Tourist Attraction: The Moral Career of American Chinatowns, 1880–1940," *Pacific Historical Review* 43 (1974): 385, 389. Light explains that the Chinese Peace Society, a group of Chinatown merchants, "mediate[d] quarrels among criminal factions. The merchants had always been opposed to tong warfare, but until 1913 they had been too weak to compel tongs to arbitrate their differences. The formation of the Peace Society was, therefore, a manifestation of the merchants' augmented influence in Chinatowns" (389). The tong wars continued to rage intermittently until 1933. See also Arthur Bonner, *Alas! What Brought Thee Hither? The Chinese in New York, 1850–1950* (Madison, NJ: Fairleigh Dickinson University Press, 1997), 149–59.

58. Beck, *New York's Chinatown*, 101.

59. *Pak kop piu* was a lottery game in which eighty characters were printed on each ticket, and twenty were drawn every night. It cost one dollar to play ten numbers, and "the lottery company paid prizes to those who purchased a certain number of characters drawn." McIlwain, *Organizing Crime in Chinatown*, 68–69.

60. *Lobbygow* seems to be a bastardization of the Chinese term *low gui gow*, which roughly translates as "servant" or "attendant." See Beck, *New York's Chinatown*, 118.

61. Tyler Anbinder, *Five Points: The Nineteenth-Century New York City Neighborhood That Invented Tap Dance, Stole Elections, and Became the World's Most Notorious Slum* (New York: Plume Books, 2001), 32–34. See also Bonner, *Alas*, 96–97, 107–12.

62. Light, "Vice District to Tourist Attraction," 389, 390.

63. For example, George Washington "Chuck" Connors, New York City's first documented tour guide, worked as a *lobbygow* in Chinatown through the 1890s. Luc

Sante, *Low Life: Lures and Snares of Old New York* (New York: Farrar, Straus and Giroux, 1991), 128–29. Similarly, James Weldon Johnson describes "slumming parties" to African American establishments in the Tenderloin; see Johnson, *Autobiography of an Ex-Coloured Man* (1912; reprint, New York: Vintage, 1989).

64. Arthur E. Wilson, report on Chinatown, undated, reel 3, C15.

65. Ibid.

66. McIlwain, *Organizing Crime in Chinatown*, 100.

67. Bonner, *Alas*, 45; Anbinder, *Five Points*, 412. On Lee's political clout, see McIlwain, *Organizing Crime in Chinatown*, chaps. 7 and 8; and Gilfoyle, *Pickpocket's Tale*, 90–94.

68. Anbinder, *Five Points*, 412. See also Herbert Asbury, *The Gangs of New York* (1927; reprint, New York: Thunder's Mouth Press, 1998), 280–81.

69. "Chinese Benevolence," *New York Times*, 28 April 1880.

70. Beck, *New York's Chinatown*, 135.

71. Ibid., 95–101; Anbinder, *Five Points*, 408.

72. "From Police to Tammany," *New York Times*, 28 June 1894.

73. Ibid.

74. Bonner, *Alas*, 143. See also "There's a New Tong in Chinatown Now," *New York Times*, 13 February 1906; "Avenging On Leongs Descend on Hip Sings: Factional Spies Pilot Police in Big Chinatown Raid," *New York Times*, 31 May 1905; "Tong Dinner Peaceful; On Leongs Stay Away," *New York Times*, 2 February 1906; "Chinatown's Warriors Agree to Real Peace," *New York Times*, 31 January 1906; "Capt. Waldo Calls on Warring Tongs: Sees Mock Duck, Who Tells of Those Wicked On Leongs. Tom Lee's Version Differs," *New York Times*, 27 January 1906.

75. Bonner, *Alas*, 143–44.

CHAPTER THREE

1. A. I. Eilperin, report on 577 Broadway, Brooklyn, 1 November 1916, box 30, folder "1916," C14.

2. T. W. Veness, report on Harlem River Casino, 5 October 1912, box 28, folder 3, C14.

3. Natalie Sonnichsen, report of Harlem River Casino, 19 October 1912, box 28, folder 3, C14.

4. As historian Michael A. Lerner explains, "saloons reflected the life and rhythm of the neighborhood as few other institutions could, from dawn into the late evening." Lerner also argues that saloons were an important way to foster and preserve ethnic identity: "They served as bridges between the old world and the new, places where newly arrived immigrants could learn from their predecessors and begin the often painful process of adapting to a new homeland." Lerner, *Dry Manhattan: Prohibition in New York City* (Cambridge: Harvard University Press, 2007), 102–4. See also Madelon Powers, *Faces along the Bar: Lore and Order in the Workingman's Saloon, 1870–1920* (Chicago: University of Chicago Press, 1998); and Roy Rosenzweig, *Eight Hours for What We Will: Workers and Leisure in an Industrial City, 1870–1920* (Cambridge: Cambridge University Press, 1983).

5. On the topic of working-class women's leisure culture, the now classic text is Kathy Peiss, *Cheap Amusements: Working Women and Leisure in Turn-of-the-Century New York* (Philadelphia: Temple University Press, 1986). See also Elizabeth Alice Clement, *Love for Sale: Courting, Treating, and Prostitution in New York City, 1900–1945* (Chapel Hill: University of North Carolina Press, 2006); Nan Enstad, *Ladies of Labor, Girls of*

Adventure: Working Women, Popular Culture, and Labor Politics at the Turn of the Twenti-eth Century (New York: Columbia University Press, 1999); and Kathy Peiss, "'Charity Girls' and City Pleasures: Historical Notes on Working-Class Sexuality, 1880–1920," in *Passion and Power: Sexuality in History*, ed. Kathy Peiss and Christina Simmons with Robert A. Padgug, 57–69 (Philadelphia: Temple University Press, 1989).

6. Peters, "Story of the Fourteen."

7. Baldwin and Haynes founded the Committee on Urban Conditions among Negroes in 1910; in 1911, the National League for the Protection of Colored Women, the Committee on Urban Conditions among Negroes, and the Committee for the Improvement of Industrial Conditions among Negroes (founded in New York City in 1906) came together to create the National League on Urban Conditions among Negroes (which shortened its name to the National Urban League in 1920).

8. "Honor F. H. Whitin as Vice Crusader," *New York Times*, 20 January 1927.

9. Peters, "Story of the Fourteen."

10. "Committee of Fourteen Report of the Secretaries Made at the Annual Meeting October 30th 1913," bulletin book, box 86 "Minutes and Reports, 1905–1932," C14.

11. Peters, "Story of the Fourteen."

12. Ibid.

13. John Peters to Frederick Whitin, 17 November 1906, box 1, folder 2, C14.

14. Keire, "Vice in American Cities," 43.

15. Eilperin, report on 879 Broadway, Brooklyn, 1 November 1916.

16. Research Committee of the Committee of Fourteen, *The Social Evil in New York City: A Study in Law Enforcement* (New York: Andrew H. Kellogg Co., 1910), xxv.

17. Ibid., 22.

18. *Police Practice and Procedure Manual* (New York: Cornelius F. Cahalane, 1914), 179.

19. Committee of Fourteen to Dodge's Detective Agency, 110 East 125th Street, 11 November 1905, box 1, folder 2, C14.

20. Judges were quick to dismiss the evidence in so-called observation cases. Frederick Whitin wrote to Arthur P. Kellogg, Esq.: "You will remember that Mayor Gaynor publicly announced that under his administration the police officers must not accompany women to hotel rooms and be subjected to temptation to sexual immorality in order that evidence might be gotten. He said that it was sufficient if women known to be immoral should be seen entering and leaving suspected places with various men at late hours of the night. Such cases have been designated 'observation cases' and we have been waiting some six months to get these tried. You see the Court disposed of them in short order, it not being considered that the People had even made out a prima facie case" (Whitin to Kellogg, 22 October 1912, box 2, folder 9 "Gen Corr 1912 October 21–31," C14).

21. Whitin also had some concern about Dodge's price ($5 plus expenses per night) and stated that he preferred to use "men over whom [he] had full control . . . at $2.50 a night." Frederick Whitin to William Bennet, 8 November 1907, box 1, folder 5 "General Correspondence, October 1907–February 1908," C14. Dodge tendered his resignation on 14 November 1907. His letter stated that "since my appointment as Chief Inspector of the Committee of Fourteen the character of the work done has changed. This change, not calling for the kind of work for which I was appointed, there is no call for activity on my part" (Dodge to John Peters, 14 November 1907, box 1, folder 5, "General Correspondence, October 1907–February 1908," C14). It is unclear what led up to this divorce, but after Whitin took over, there were allusions to Dodge's expenses and general unreliability. Or perhaps Dodge, who had registered his desire to serve as

the executive secretary of the Committee, felt betrayed when Frederick H. Whitin was appointed executive secretary, and thus terminated his relationship with the Committee. William Dodge to John Peters, 17 November 1906, box 1, folder 2, C14.

22. Whitin to Bennet, 8 November 1907.

23. Frederick Whitin to John Peters, 17 November 1906, box 1, folder 2, C14. Whitin wrote: "A question also arises in my mind as to whether work of this kind had not better be done by a married man; what you told me of your own feelings after the necessary study of certain reports caused this to occur to me. Not being married myself, it seems to me that the investigator of such an evil would be under a physical strain or come to hold a perverted view of the sexual relation according to his own temperament."

24. Frederick Whitin to Duncan McMillan, 8 February 1917, box 10, folder "Committee of Twelve," C14.

25. From 1905 to 1917, the Committee did not employ investigators full time; in 1917, however, it began to cooperate with the War Department's Commission on Training Camp Activities, which is discussed in chapter 6.

26. Frederick Whitin to Washington Railway and Electric Company, in reference to B. J. Cunningham, former investigator for the Committee of Fourteen, 6 May 1918, box 13, folder "References," C14.

27. Frederick Whitin to Hugh Doyle, 9 August 1915, box 3, folder 18 "Correspondence, 1915," C14.

28. Frederick Whitin to Faith Habberton, 14 October 1913, box 3, folder 2 "Gen. Corr. 1913 October," C14.

29. Clarence J. Primm, report on 7th Avenue, 20 February 1915, box 28, folder "1914–15," C14.

30. Edna Arbing, report, box 30, folder "1916," C14; and Maud Robinson Tombs, report, box 30, folder "1916," C14.

31. Frederick Whitin, recommendation letter for W. K. Van Meter, 7 December 1923, box 13, folder "References," C14.

32. Frederick Whitin, recommendation letter for Abram I. Eilperin, undated, box 13, folder "References," C14.

33. Samuel Auerbach, report on Greek restaurant, undated, box 28, folder "1914–15," C14.

34. David Oppenheim was in the garment business. A few of his business cards are in the Committee of Fourteen's boxes. They read: "Oppenheim's Clothes Shop / 402 Sixth Avenue between 24th and 25th streets / David Oppenheim / High grade sample garments from leading houses."

35. David Oppenheim, report on Point Pleasant Hotel, 24 June 1916, box 30, untitled folder, C14.

36. David Oppenheim, report on DeFaust's, 24 November 1915, box 30, folder 3, C14.

37. David Oppenheim, report on Martin Busch's, 13 September 1916, box 30, folder 2, C14. The dash in "c—s" is in the original report.

38. Ibid.

39. Ibid.

40. Ibid.

41. Ibid.

42. Ibid.

43. Nicholas Santella to "The Honorable Committee of Fourteen," box 28, folder "1914–15," C14.

44. Oppenheim, report on Martin Busch's, 13 September 1916.

45. This investigator identifies himself as "L" in his reports. Henry is the name L used to address the bartender.

46. L, report on Avenel Hotel, 8 July 1913, box 28, folder "1913," C14.

47. Ibid.

48. Clason Point was located in the Bronx at the confluence of the East and Bronx rivers, which encouraged the development of resorts in the early twentieth century, including dance halls and restaurants.

49. L to Walter Hooke, memo on Clason Point, 26 May 1913, box 28, folder "1913 June–July," C14.

50. L, report on Avenel Hotel, 26 June 1913, box 28, folder "1913," C14.

51. L, report on Avenel Hotel, 8 July 1913.

52. Whitin first contacted Mrs. Sonnichsen by letter, dated 29 April 1912, box 14, folder "Sn–Sp," C14; "Natalie De Bogory," 7 September 1939, *New York Times*. For more on the Committee on Amusement Resources of Working Girls, see Perry, "General Motherhood of the Commonwealth," 719–33.

53. Frederick Whitin to Sigrid Wynbladh, 27 September 1913, box 16, folder "Gen. Corr. Wi–Z," C14.

54. "Supplementary Report to November 19, 1913," box 39, folder V "DSI Investigator's Reports (raw and edited): Sonnichsen," C14.

55. Peiss, *Cheap Amusements*, 54. Historian Kathy Peiss has argued that women's low wages precluded them from participating in the emerging leisure culture. They therefore began to trade sexual favors for "treats": food, clothing, theater tickets. Peiss contends that this "widely accepted practice" allowed a woman to "accept [these goods] without compromising her reputation." Peiss argues that sexual barter was a double bind: although it freed young women from older moral and sexual constraints, it also taught them that they occupied a lower socioeconomic category, one in which their bodies were commodities. Historian Elizabeth Alice Clement (*Love for Sale*, 2–12) follows up on Peiss's analysis of treating, claiming that treating occupied a new moral space between prostitution and chastity. Clement optimistically views the treating exchange, seeing this shift in working-class sexual mores as liberating for young women. I see this device as a pyrrhic victory, however. Treating (and prostitution, for that matter) was one of a few choices for women in a constrained labor market that was determined and demarcated by gender, and during a time when women—working-class and immigrant in particular—were occasionally forced by circumstances to sell their bodies. There is little that is liberating about "choosing" to sell one's body in order to feed children, pay rent, or get a new pair of shoes. See also Karen Dubinsky, *Improper Advances: Rape and Heterosexual Conflict in Ontario, 1880–1929* (Chicago: University of Chicago Press, 1993); Jennifer Fronc, "Narratives of Sexual Conquest: A Historical Perspective on Date Rape," in *Why We Write: The Politics and Practice of Writing for Social Change*, ed. Jim Downs, 61–69 (New York: Routledge, 2005); and Stephen Robertson, *Crimes against Children: Sexual Violence and Legal Culture in New York City, 1880–1960* (Chapel Hill: University of North Carolina Press, 2005).

56. David Oppenheim, report on John Herbst's, 26 April 1916, box 30, folder 11, C14.

57. David Oppenheim, report, 1 September 1916, box 30, folder 4, C14.

58. The *Police Practice and Procedure Manual* defines a rapist as "a person who perpetrates an act of sexual intercourse with a female not his wife, against her will or without her consent; or when through imbecility or other unsoundness of mind she is incapable of giving consent; or when her resistance is forcibly overcome; or when her resistance

is prevented by fear of immediate bodily harm; or when her resistance is prevented by stupor produced by an intoxicating or narcotic agent; or when she is at the time unconscious of the nature of the act and this is known to the defendant; or when she is in the custody of the law or of any officer thereof; or when the female not his wife is under the age of 18 years, with or without her consent, is guilty of rape. In the crime of rape, it is very difficult to obtain witnesses, and a conviction cannot be had upon the uncorroborated statement of the person raped. It is very necessary and important for the officer whose attention is called to such a crime to establish corroboration. If the crime has been committed in a building, try to find some person who saw the male and female going in or out of the building or some person who heard the girl protesting or resisting, or evidence of a struggle in the premises, such as furniture in disorder or any part of the female's clothing in the room, or her clothing torn or soiled. If a woman complains to you that she has been raped, it is your duty to immediately arrest the man she accuses, if possible. Question the prisoner regarding his movements at the time of the alleged commission of the crime. Examine his clothing for evidence, noting if it is soiled or torn as a result of a struggle" (113).

59. Ibid.
60. Natalie Sonnichsen, report on Martin's Saloon, 1 August 1912, box 29, folder 2, C14.
61. Frederick Whitin to Frances Kellor, 22 July 1912, box 2, folder "General Correspondence July 1912," C14. Whitin went to great lengths to secure such investigators, relying on his allies in the city's reform community. For example, he contacted Frances Kellor, social activist and director of the New York State Bureau of Industries and Immigration, about possible investigators. She offered a Polish interpreter/investigator named Sigmund Dattner, who had been working for her in the bureau. Frances Kellor to Frederick Whitin, 20 July 1912, box 2, folder "General Correspondence July 1912," C14. Whitin replied that he knew of Dattner but that he was really in need of an "Italian inspector who might be valuable for our use in the Italian districts of Manhattan, Brooklyn, and Coney Island."
62. Frederick Whitin to Eula Harris, 29 September 1915, box 3, folder "Correspondence 1915," C14.
63. Reports by Edna Arbing and Maud Robinson Tombs.
64. Sonnichsen, report on Martin's Saloon, 1 August 1912.
65. Ibid.
66. Natalie Sonnichsen, report on Martin's Saloon, 8 August 1912, box 29, folder 2, C14.
67. Ibid.
68. Natalie Sonnichsen, report on Martin's Saloon, 9 October 1913, box 29, folder "Bklyn—Inv. Reports and Related Material 1913," C14.
69. Ibid.
70. Oppenheim, report on Martin Busch's, 13 September 1916.
71. Ibid. For ease of reading, I have added punctuation to this report.

CHAPTER FOUR

1. James Weldon Johnson, *Black Manhattan* (1930; reprint, New York: DaCapo Press, 1991), 118–19; David Levering Lewis, *When Harlem Was in Vogue* (New York: Penguin Books, 1979), 28–29. James Marshall even took out an advertisement for his establishment in the first issue of the *Crisis*, the publication of the NAACP. David Levering Lewis, *W. E .B. DuBois: Biography of a Race, 1868–1919*, new ed. (New York: Owl Books, 1994), 411.

2. D. Slattery to Frederick Whitin, 28 September 1908, box 1, folder 7, C14.

3. William S. Bennet to Walter Hook (*sic*), 24 December 1910, box 1, folder 1, C14. I have rearranged the order of this quote for clarity, but the logic remains the same.

4. D. Slattery to Frederick Whitin, 28 September 1908.

5. In *Black Manhattan*, James Weldon Johnson distinguishes between gambling clubs, honky-tonks, and professional clubs. He defines professional clubs as establishments that "nourished . . . artistic effort." He notes that these places were "the rendezvous of the professionals, their satellites and admirers. Several of these clubs were famous in their day and were frequented not only by blacks, but also by whites" (74–75). He lists the Criterion Café and Barron Wilkins, among others. See also Lerner, *Dry Manhattan*, esp. chap. 8.

6. Frederick Whitin to Ruth Baldwin, 15 November 1912, box 2, folder 10 "General Correspondence 1912 November 1–15," C14.

7. Advertisements in *New York Age*, 1913. See also Gilbert Osofsky, *Harlem: The Making of a Ghetto*, 2nd ed. (Chicago: Elephant Paperbacks, 1996).

8. William F. Pogue, report on Marshall's, 6 April 1911, box 28, folder "1910–1912," C14.

9. Ibid.

10. George Francis O'Neill, report on Marshall's, 28 September 1912, box 28, folder "Invest. Reports 1912," C14.

11. Ibid.

12. Ibid.

13. Ibid.

14. Pogue, report on Marshall's, 6 April 1911.

15. Unnamed investigator, report on the Green Cup Café, n.d., box 28, C14.

16. David Oppenheim, report on Mollie Druckerman's, 30 December 1915, box 30, folder 13 "Investigators' Reports, 1916," C14; David Oppenheim, report on the Sunshine, 2 December 1915, box 30, folder 13 "Investigators' Reports, 1916," C14.

17. Frederick Whitin to Ruth Baldwin, 31 August 1909, box 1, folder 12 "Gen. Corr. 1908–1911," C14.

18. Mary Ting Yi Lui provides a fascinating discussion of similar miscegenation fears about Chinese men and white women in New York City in *The Chinatown Trunk Mystery: Murder, Miscegenation, and Other Dangerous Encounters in Turn-of-the-Century New York City* (Princeton: Princeton University Press, 2005), chaps. 2 and 3.

19. Edwin G. Burrows and Mike Wallace, *Gotham: A History of New York City to 1898* (New York: Oxford University Press, 1999), 1034–35.

20. *New York State Laws of 1905*, sec. 1, chap. 1042, as reprinted in an editorial, *New York Age*, 21 January 1909. See also Pauli Murray, ed., *States' Laws on Race and Color* (1951; reprint, Athens: University of Georgia Press, 1997), 301–28.

21. *New York State Consolidated Laws, Civil Rights Laws of 1909*, chap. 6, article 40, secs. 40–45; http://caselaw.lp.findlaw.com/nycodes/c17/a6.html. (accessed 27 January 2004). See also "Plans to Prevent Discrimination in Public Places in New York State," *New York Age*, 30 January 1913. See also David Gellman and David Quigley, *Jim Crow New York: A Documentary History of Race and Citizenship, 1777–1877* (New York: New York University Press, 2003); and David Quigley, *Second Founding: New York City, Reconstruction, and the Making of American Democracy* (New York: Hill and Wang, 2003).

22. "Civil Rights Bill Passes Assembly," *New York Times*, 11 March 1913. "Discrimination Bill Is Signed—Can't Draw Color Line," *New York Age*, 17 April 1913.

23. "Fight For Civil Rights in New York," *New York Age*, 13 February 1913, editorial page.
24. David Oppenheim, report on Anstel Hotel, 7 August 1916, box 30, folder 3, C14.
25. Ibid.
26. Ibid.
27. Ibid.
28. As historian Kathy Peiss explains, "young women looked to men for financial assistance and gifts.... Treating was a widely accepted practice, especially if the woman had a fiancé, or 'steady,' from whom she could accept food, clothing, and recreation [in exchange for sex] without compromising her reputation" (*Cheap Amusements*, 54).
29. Oppenheim, report on Anstel Hotel, 7 August 1916.
30. Ibid.
31. William Banks to Frederick Whitin, 24 August 1908, box 1, folder "General Correspondence: 1908, July–December," C14.
32. David Oppenheim, report on 293 Remsen Avenue, 10 August 1918, folder "Coney Is., Queens, Staten Island Inv. Reports 1917–18," box 32, C14. Oppenheim wrote: "Later Max asked me what I was doing here, I told him I came out to Rockaway to see some friends and I dropped in here. We started to speak Yiddish and he told me he dasnt let any one in the back room, said this place had a very bad name and when he got the place he had to promise that he wouldn't let any white men in there. Said if the police come in and find white men in there with the colored women it makes trouble. I told him I used to go to the colored places up in Harlem, said there was places up there where they wouldn't let a white man in, still they let me in, I said if a cop would come around and they were asked why they let me in, they would say that I am a Cuban. He said theres a lot of them that come around here too and play that trick on him."
33. David Oppenheim, report on Rickey's, 23 October 1915, box 30, folder 9, C14. This place was called Rickey's, although Oppenheim referred to it, and the proprietor, as Richey throughout.
34. Ibid.
35. David Oppenheim, report on Chadwick's Novelty Café, 21 November 1915, box 30, folder 9, C14.
36. Ibid.
37. David Oppenheim, report on the Al Reeves Beauty Show at the Casino Theatre, 96 Flatbush Avenue, box 32, folder "Coney Is., Queens, Staten Island, Inv. Reports 1917–18," C14.
38. Whitin to Baldwin, 31 August 1909.
39. Ibid.
40. Ibid.
41. Booker T. Washington, "The Atlanta Exposition Address," in *Up from Slavery: An Autobiography* (1901; reprint, New York: Modern Library, 1999), 145.
42. Baldwin did not immediately deliver that Washingtonian helpmate to Whitin. One year later, Whitin again contacted Baldwin on the "race issue." In a letter dated 10 August 1910, he gently reminded her that "a year ago I had special difficulty in the matter of blacklisting the colored places. Among these places was one that was especially notorious as being a resort not merely for colored people, but also for whites." Whitin also noted that the National Negro Business League will be "held in this city next week. Dr. Washington, as its president, will be in town. . . . I would like very much to see Dr. Washington on the subject." Frederick Whitin to Ruth Baldwin, 10 August 1910, box 10, folder "Baldwin, Mrs. Wm. H.," C14.

43. Booker T. Washington to Ruth Baldwin, 14 August 1910, box 10, folder "Baldwin, Mrs. William H.," C14.

44. Dr. William Lewis Bulkley was born in slavery in 1861 in South Carolina. In the 1890s he earned a Ph.D. at Syracuse University and moved to New York City, where he worked as a teacher in the New York City public schools and eventually became a school principal. Bulkley was "a pragmatist" and tried to address "conditions in the city as he saw them and tried to improve them immediately as best he could." He was acquainted with Ruth Baldwin through the National League for the Protection of Colored Women (Osofsky, *Harlem*, 50, 64).

45. Ibid., 54.

46. See, for example, Allan H. Spear, *Black Chicago: The Making of a Negro Ghetto, 1890–1920* (Chicago: University of Chicago Press, 1967), chaps. 5 and 6.

47. Osofsky, *Harlem*, 241n13.

48. Guichard Parris and Lester Brooks, *Blacks in the City: A History of the National Urban League* (Boston: Little Brown, 1971), 9–10, 33, 62.

49. Henry Louis Gates, Jr., introduction to Johnson, *Autobiography of an Ex-Coloured Man*, viii. See also Charles Flint Kellogg, *NAACP: A History of the National Association for the Advancement of Colored People*, vol. 1: *1909–1920* (Baltimore: Johns Hopkins University Press, 1967), 23, 133–34.

50. Kevin Gaines, *Uplifting the Race: Black Leadership, Politics, and Culture in the Twentieth Century* (Chapel Hill: University of North Carolina Press, 1996), 2.

51. There is a very rich historiography on reform in African American communities. On the "politics of respectability," see Evelyn Brooks Higginbotham, *Righteous Discontent: The Women's Movement in the Black Baptist Church, 1880–1920* (Cambridge: Harvard University Press, 1993). See also Michele Mitchell, *Righteous Propagation: African Americans and the Politics of Racial Destiny after Reconstruction* (Chapel Hill: University of North Carolina Press, 2004); Christina Simmons, "African Americans and Sexual Victorianism in the Social Hygiene Movement, 1910–40," *Journal of the History of Sexuality* 4, no. 1 (1993): 51–75; and Deborah Gray White, *Too Heavy a Load: Black Women in Defense of Themselves, 1894–1994* (New York: Norton, 1999).

52. "Conduct on the Corners," *New York Age*, 27 May 1909, editorial page.

53. "A Fulfilled Need?" *New York Age*, 13 January 1910, editorial page.

54. Frederick Whitin to William Bulkley, 2 September 1911, box 1, folder 18 "General Correspondence, September 1911," C14.

55. Ibid.

56. Walter Hooke to Fred R. Moore, 15 September 1911, box 1, folder 18 "General Correspondence, September 1911," C14.

57. Ibid.

58. Ibid.

59. Fred R. Moore letter, forwarded to Walter Hooke, 2 July 1913, box 2, folder 20 "General Correspondence 1913 July," C14.

60. "About Committee of Fourteen," *New York Age*, 2 November 1911, 1. In the original article, all of the *w*'s were printed as *y*'s. I have made the appropriate changes for ease of reading.

61. "Saloonkeepers Organize," *New York Age*, 8 June 1911, front page.

62. Ibid. For Wilkins's promissory note dated 23 September 1909 for his saloon at 253 W. 35th Street, see David E. Tobias to Walker (*sic*) G. Hooke, 12 September 1910, box 15, folder "Tobias, David Elliott," C14.

63. See, for example, unnamed investigator's report on 331 W. 37th Street, Walter Herbert's Criterion Club Café, box 28, folder "1910–1912," C14; and William Pogue, "report of Investigations April 5th (1911)," section on Young's Café, box 28, folder "1910–1912," C14.

64. Present were Fred R. Moore, Dr. E. P. Roberts, Counselor James L. Curtis, and Dr. P. A. Johnson for the Committee of Fourteen, and the saloon men were represented by Barron Wilkins, G. L. Young, J. W. Connor, William Banks, and J. H. Press.

65. "To Raise the Moral Tone of Local Saloons," *New York Age*, 14 December 1911.

66. W. E. B. DuBois to William Bennet, 23 September 1911, box 11, folder "W. E. B. DuBois Correspondence," C14. There is no reply to this letter in the Committee's records.

67. W. E. B. DuBois to Frederick Whitin, 10 October 1912, box 11, folder "W. E. B. DuBois Correspondence," C14.

68. Frederick Whitin to W. E. B. DuBois, 11 October 1912, box 11, folder "W. E. B. DuBois Correspondence," C14.

69. W. E. B. DuBois to Frederick Whitin, 14 October 1912, box 11, folder "W. E. B. DuBois Correspondence," C14.

70. Whitin wrote a letter about his exchange with DuBois to Committee member Ruth Standish Baldwin in which he said that he needed "to confer with you upon the perennial problem of the proper treatment of the colored race." Whitin to Baldwin, 15 November 1912.

71. Frederick Whitin to W. E. B. DuBois, 15 October 1912, box 11, folder "W. E. B. DuBois Correspondence," C14.

72. W. E. B. DuBois to Frederick Whitin, 18 October 1912, box 2, folder "General Correspondence 1912 October 1–20," C14.

73. Whitin to DuBois, 15 October 1912.

74. DuBois to Whitin, 18 October 1912.

75. Frederick Whitin to W. E. B. DuBois, October 1912, box 2, folder "General Correspondence 1912 October 21–31," C14.

76. W. E. B. DuBois to Frederick Whitin, 29 October 1912, box 2, folder "General Correspondence 1912 October 21–31," C14.

77. Ibid.

78. Frederick Whitin to W. E. B. DuBois, 30 October 1912, box 2, folder "General Correspondence 1912 October 21–31," C14.

79. James Marshall to Walter Hooke and Frederick Whitin, 11 October 1912, box 2, folder 8 "General Correspondence 1912 October 1–20," C14.

80. "Too Many Saloons in Harlem," *New York Age*, 1 October 1914.

81. Committee of Fourteen, *Annual Report for 1913* (New York, 1914), 41–42.

82. Gilchrist Stewart to Frederick Whitin, 28 September 1912, box 14, folder St–Sz, C14.

83. Ibid.

84. Moore letter, forwarded to Hooke, 2 July 1913.

85. Ibid.

CHAPTER FIVE

1. Edward Barrows to V. Everit Macy, n.d., box 11, folder 13 "Community Center Work, Committee on Recreation, Correspondence, 1913–1917," People's Institute records (hereafter PI), Manuscripts and Archives Division, The New York Public Library, Astor, Lenox, and Tilden Foundations.

2. In 1859, Peter Cooper founded the Cooper Union for the Advancement of Art and Science. The People's Institute, during its entire history, 1897 to 1934, was housed at the Cooper Union, even though it had intended to procure its own dedicated space. In 1934, when the People's Institute folded, the Cooper Union established a Department of Social Philosophy, which absorbed sections of the People's Institute. Dr. Everett Dean Martin, the last director of the People's Institute, was appointed head of this new department. For an institutional history of the People's Institute, including its relationship with the Cooper Union, see Robert B. Fisher, "The People's Institute of New York City, 1897–1934: Culture, Progressive Democracy, and the People" (Ph. D. diss., New York University, 1974).

3. For instance, People's Institute founder and director Charles Sprague Smith became interested in what he saw as the failings of American educational system and subsequently founded the Comparative Literature Society in 1895. Forerunner to the People's Institute, the Comparative Literature Society aimed to facilitate the integration of immigrants into American culture and society. As Smith saw it, his organization's purpose was to "win the control over the progressive movement for intelligent and consecrated elements of the community, not to allow it to pass into the hands of the unintelligent and revolutionary. . . . We propose to study fundamental social problems." Smith to Senator William Armstrong, 21 May 1908, box 3, folder "Smith. General Correspondence, Agar–Astor," PI. The People's Institute's supporters and founders were well positioned to take up this work. Smith noted that "leaders in all the important social and ethical movements; every church, save the Catholic, the synagogues, the Ethical Society, the settlements, the philanthropists, organized labor, the international socialists, single taxers, the professions, leading educators, including the presidents of various universities and theological seminaries, the leading professors of sociology" were represented on the general committee. Smith added, however, that "this committee is not as yet complete . . . [but when] completed, there will not be a profession or pursuit that is not represented by its strongest men [and women]" (People's Institute finding aid, Manuscripts and Archives Division, The New York Public Library, 1).

4. For example, the People's Institute was the guiding force behind having polling places moved out of neighborhood saloons and into municipal buildings such as schools.

5. Howe, *Confessions of a Reformer*, 59.

6. Many of the Institute's other plans and programs, such as public ownership of utilities, local governmental control of New York City, and censorship of motion pictures, were progressive goals intended to assist and uplift all of the people of New York City. As the constitution of the People's Institute proclaimed, the "purpose of the Institute is first, to furnish to the people continuous and ordered education in Social Science, History, Literature and such other subjects as time and the demand shall determine. Second, to afford opportunities for the interchange of thought upon topics of general interest between people of different occupations in order thereby to assist in the solution of present problems" ("Constitution of the People's Institute," vol. 1A, PI). The Institute also developed neighborhood social centers in public schools and hosted concerts, lectures, a community chorus, and the Wage Earner's Theatre League. The National Board of Review, the first organization to develop a system for rating motion pictures, was organized by members of the People's Institute in 1909.

7. Timothy J. Gilfoyle, "Street-Rats and Gutter-Snipes: Child Pickpockets and Street Culture in New York City, 1850–1900," *Journal of Social History* 37, no. 4 (2004): 854.

Gilfoyle provides a compelling explanation of the emergence of street kids and child criminals—changes in apprenticeship systems and increased immigration, among other factors. See also Ruth M. Alexander, *The "Girl Problem": Female Sexual Delinquency in New York, 1900–1930* (Ithaca: Cornell University Press, 1995); Gilfoyle, *Pickpocket's Tale*; Linda Gordon, *The Great Arizona Orphan Abduction* (Cambridge: Harvard University Press, 2001); Linda Gordon, *Heroes of Their Own Lives: The Politics and History of Family Violence* (New York: Viking, 1988); Linda Gordon, "Putting Children First: Women, Maternalism, and Welfare in the Early Twentieth Century," in *U.S. History as Women's History: New Feminist Essays*, ed. Linda K. Kerber, Alice Kessler-Harris, and Kathryn Kish Sklar (Chapel Hill: University of North Carolina Press, 1995); Laura Hapke, *Girls Who Went Wrong: Prostitutes in American Fiction, 1885–1917* (Bowling Green, OH: Bowling Green State University Popular Press, 1989); David Nasaw, *Children of the City: At Work and at Play* (New York: Oxford University Press, 1985); Mary E. Odem, *Delinquent Daughters: Protecting and Policing Adolescent Female Sexuality in the United States, 1885–1920* (Chapel Hill: University of North Carolina Press, 1995); Robertson, *Crimes against Children*; and David B. Wolcott, *Cops and Kids: Policing Juvenile Delinquency in Urban America, 1890–1940* (Columbus: Ohio State University Press, 2005).

8. Gilfoyle notes that the prosecutions of pickpockets tripled between 1869 and 1876, and by 1876, 79 percent of all child pickpocket cases "resulted in conviction" ("Street-Rats," 870).

9. A notable absence in the People's Institute's plans was discussion of the plight of girls. Girls' criminality was often defined as sexual in nature, and their issues were discussed in terms of low wages, prostitution, treating, and dance hall problems. For example, in a People's Institute fund-raising pamphlet, Jane Addams is cited: "We see thousands of girls walking up and down the streets on a pleasant evening, with no chance to catch the sight of pleasure even through a lighted window save as these lurid places provide it. Apparently the modern city sees in these girls only two possibilities, both of them commercial: first a chance to utilize by day their new and tender labor power in its factories and shops and then another chance in the evening to extract from them their petty wages by pandering to their love of pleasure." Christmas fund-raising pamphlet, box 27, folder 2 "People's Institute Brochures 1898–1909, ND," PI.

10. For a discussion of this dynamic, see Gordon, *Arizona Orphan Abduction*. She argues that part of the conflict was an underlying power struggle between Presbyterians and Irish Catholics in New York City.

11. John Collier and Edward M. Barrows, *The City Where Crime Is Play: A Report by the People's Institute* (New York: People's Institute, 1914), 28.

12. Nasaw, *Children of the City*, 17.

13. Ibid., 20. Nasaw describes a boy who was lured into the hallway of a tenement building by an older man who tried to molest him. "The boy's shout for help brought assistance at once" from people on the streets, other children, and mothers.

14. Jacob Riis, *The Battle with the Slum* (1902; reprint, Mineola, NY: Dover Publications, 1998), 296, 299. See also Boyer, *Urban Masses and Moral Order*, esp. 239–45; and Nasaw, *Children of the City*, chap. 10.

15. *Report of the Assistant Director of the People's Institute to the Chairman of the Board of Trustees of the People's Institute: Covering the Activities of the Institute from October 1, 1914 to June 1, 1915 Inclusive* (New York: People's Institute, 1915), 15 (from box 26, folder "Reports of the Assistant Director," PI).

16. Clark, "Street Crap Playing," 685.
17. Gaylord S. White, "How to Combat Crap Shooting," *Charities and the Commons* 17, no. 23 (9 March 1907): 1046.
18. John Collier, "The Place of Recreation in a Religious Program," reprint from *The Association Seminar*, May 1914, 3 (from box 27, folder 13, PI).
19. "Report of Field Secretary, Dept of Recreations, April 28th, 1913—Edward M. Barrows," box 11, folder 14 "Community Center Work, Committee on Leisure, Reports nd," PI.
20. Collier and Barrows, *City Where Crime Is Play*, 12.
21. Collier, "Place of Recreation in a Religious Program," 2.
22. Collier and Barrows, *City Where Crime Is Play*, 13.
23. Gilfoyle, *Pickpocket's Tale*, 60–61.
24. Collier and Barrows, *City Where Crime Is Play*, 13.
25. Ibid., 11.
26. *Police Practice and Procedure Manual*, 55.
27. See Christopher Thale, "The Informal World of Police Patrol: New York City in the Early Twentieth Century," *Journal of Urban History* 33, no. 2 (2007): 183–216; Wolcott, *Cops and Kids*.
28. Collier and Barrows, *City Where Crime Is Play*, 14, 11.
29. Ibid., 17, 12, 16.
30. Ibid., 18, 12.
31. Ibid., 18.
32. Ibid., 19. On the economy of gangs, see Gilfoyle, "Street-Rats," 864–66.
33. Collier and Barrows, *City Where Crime Is Play*, 12. In the early twentieth century, public playgrounds were open during certain hours, with adult supervisors at the playgrounds. The supervisors were paid on a per diem basis, and the People's Institute was engaged in a campaign to get these people paid in the same fashion as school teachers: that is, to pay them an annual salary, which would encourage them to take their work more seriously. The board of education employed and supervised the playground staff.
34. Ibid., 12, 25.
35. Ibid., 28, 27. Natalie Sonnichsen, investigator for the Committee of Fourteen, was one of the volunteers who participated in the flashlight survey. New York City uses a similar method today to quantify the number of homeless people. On 7 March 2005, the city conducted its first survey of homelessness in all five boroughs. Volunteers were sent out to count the people sleeping in parks, on benches, in subway and train stations, and in the streets. This survey was used to secure more government funding for the city's homeless outreach efforts.
36. Ibid., 28.
37. Helen Ruth Richter, "Why Play Streets?" box 11, folder 14 "Community Center Work, Committee on Leisure, Reports nd," PI.
38. Ibid.
39. Ibid.
40. "People's Institute Seventeenth Annual Report, 1913–1914," p. 11, box 26, folder 6 "Annual Reports," PI.
41. People's Institute, *19th Yearbook* (New York: People's Institute, 1917), 60.
42. "People's Institute Sixteenth Annual Report for Year Ending September 30, 1913," p. 7, box 26, folder 6 "PI 1911–1913, Annual Reports," PI. The People's Institute "was the pioneering New York agency in advocating and organizing the wider use of

school buildings on a democratic and self-supporting basis." The first of these social centers was established at Public School 63, on East Fourth Street between First Avenue and Avenue A. The second one was founded at Public School 17, in the Hell's Kitchen neighborhood on the Middle West Side. Collier and Barrows, *City Where Crime Is Play*, inside back cover.

43. People's Institute, *20th Yearbook* (New York: People's Institute, 1918), 56.

44. "People's Institute Sixteenth Annual Report," 9. Some of the individuals who assisted in the opening of P.S. 63's community center were Belle Lindner Israels (Moskowitz) and Henry Moskowitz, as well as John Collier, V. Everit Macy, and Frederic C. Howe.

45. For the social centers, dancing was the most successful and lucrative activity; in fact, P.S. 101 in Manhattan and P.S. 4 in the Bronx also began to hold dances, which led to the founding of social centers there as well. "People's Institute Seventeenth Annual Report," 12–13.

46. Clinton Childs, *A Year's Experiment in Social Center Organization* (New York: Social Center Committee, 1912), 7. The club paid the expenses "of the Center for four nights each week, raising money through the dancing and by weekly contributions from the clubs which use the building." The municipal government provided the lights and heat, and the center paid for janitorial services, as well as any other expenses incurred in running the center.

47. Collier and Barrows, *City Where Crime Is Play*, 28.

48. Barrows to Macy, n.d.

49. "People's Institute Sixteenth Annual Report," 15.

50. Ibid. Mayor John Purroy Mitchel was a strong advocate of the parks and playground movement. Settlement house worker Mary Kingsbury Simkhovitch also served on this committee.

51. "First Things in New York City Recreation Work Through the Committee on Recreation," box 11, folder 13 "Community Center Work, Committee on Recreation, Correspondence 1913–1917," PI.

52. Ibid.

53. People's Institute, *19th Yearbook*, 29.

54. People's Institute, *20th Yearbook*, 20–21.

55. Ibid., 21, 26–27. Both Mary Simkhovitch and Frederick Whitin of the Committee of Fourteen served as lecturers in the Training School for Community Workers. See "Plans for Training Centre Heads," *New York Times*, 11 August 1915.

56. People's Institute, *20th Yearbook*, 26–27.

57. "People's Institute Eighteenth Annual Report, 1914–15," and "People's Institute Twenty-fourth Annual Report, 1920–21," p. 20, both in box 26, folder 7, PI.

58. People's Institute, *19th Yearbook*, 27–28.

59. Ibid.

60. Ibid.

CHAPTER SIX

1. Paul Avrich, *Sacco and Vanzetti: The Anarchist Background* (Princeton: Princeton University Press, 1991), 55, 99–100. Avrich explains that Campbell "was just about to ascend the bench when the device was noticed and disarmed."

2. "Many Explosions since War Began—List Covering Two Years Shows Accidents in This Country and Abroad—Tells of Enormous Loss—The du Pont Company Has Been a Heavy Sufferer in the United States," *New York Times*, 31 July 1916.

3. "Explosions Said to Have Been Set by Spies on Ships and in Powder Plants Making Munitions," *New York Times*, 25 October 1915.

4. Untitled document, p. 4, reel 405, National Civic Federation records (hereafter NCF), Manuscripts and Archives Division, the New York Public Library, Astor, Lenox, and Tilden Foundations. Most of the collection has been microfilmed, and researchers are required to use the microfilmed version.

5. Ibid., 4, 5.

6. "Seized as Suspect in Black Tom Case," *New York Times*, 6 July 1921.

7. Christopher J. Cyphers, *The National Civic Federation and the Making of a New Liberalism, 1900–1915* (Westport, CT: Praeger, 2002), 3.

8. Prospectus of the National Civic Federation, as quoted in Morris Hillquit, "Socialism and the National Civic Federation" (New York, 1911), 5, on microform, Butler Library, Columbia University. The business arm of the National Civic Federation was made up of prominent men like Andrew Carnegie and banker and transit mogul August Belmont. American Federation of Labor president Samuel Gompers represented labor's interests. Social scientists such as economists E. R. A. Seligman (also of the Committee of Fifteen), Richard T. Ely, Jeremiah W. Jenks, and John R. Commons served in the industrial economics department. Men of progressive credentials like James Bronson Reynolds of the Citizens' Union and the University Settlement Society and Seth Low, president of Columbia University and mayor of New York, were also represented in the NCF's roll call.

9. Ibid., 6.

10. David Montgomery, *The Fall of the House of Labor: The Workplace, the State, and American Labor Activism, 1865–1925* (Cambridge: Cambridge University Press, 1987), 263. Cyphers, *National Civic Federation*, 8.

11. See Boyer, *Urban Masses and Moral Order*, 164; Cyphers, *National Civic Federation*, 20–21. See also Marguerite Green, *The National Civic Federation and the American Labor Movement, 1900–1925* (1956; reprint, Westport, CT: Greenwood Press, 1973); and James Weinstein, "Big Business and the Origins of Workmen's Compensation," *Labor History* 8 (Spring 1967): 156–74. The organization was initially attuned to a wide variety of municipal reforms, such as tax reform, state regulation of savings banks, and unemployment relief (prospectus, as quoted in Hillquit, "Socialism and the National Civic Federation," 7–8). Ralph Montgomery Easley was the secretary of the Civic Federation of Chicago, and largely through his work, the scope of the group's reform efforts was national. Easley was the guiding force behind the National Civic Federation's agenda and activities until his death in 1939. His wife, fellow activist Gertrude Beeks Easley, took the helm and continued to lead the NCF until her death in 1950 (Cyphers, *National Civic Federation*, 19–21).

12. Army Bill H.R. 3545, document 19961, box 39, entry 393, RG 165, National Archives and Records Administration records (hereafter NARA), College Park, MD. See also Allan M. Brandt, *No Magic Bullet: A Social History of Venereal Disease in the United States since 1880* (New York: Oxford University Press, 1987), 52–95; Nancy K. Bristow, *Making Men Moral: Social Engineering during the Great War* (New York: New York University Press, 1996); Clement, *Love for Sale*, chaps. 4 and 5.

13. Bristow, *Making Men Moral*, 5.

14. Raymond B. Fosdick, "The Commission on Training Camp Activities," in "Economic Conditions of Winning the War," special issue, *Proceedings of the Academy of Political Science in the City of New York* 7, no. 4 (1918): 169, 170, 164–65.

15. Ibid., 170.

16. Ibid., 166, emphasis added.

17. David Oppenheim, untitled report, box 30, folder 2, C14.

18. David Oppenheim, report on John Herbst's, 26 April 1916, box 30, folder 11 "1916," C14.

19. Eula Harris to Frederick Whitin, box 30, folder 15 "1916," C14.

20. David Oppenheim, report, 3 May 1916, box 30, C14.

21. David Oppenheim, report, "Street conditions and General stuff, L.I. Depot, Bklyn," 20 March 1919, box 32, folder "Coney Is., Queens, Staten Island Inv. Reports 1917–18," C14.

22. Brandt, *No Magic Bullet*, 83–84.

23. "By March 1918, thirty-two states had passed laws requiring compulsory examinations of prostitutes for venereal diseases." Ibid., 85.

24. David Oppenheim, report, "Wmsburgh Bridge Plaza and Vicinity, Bklyn," 28 February 1919, box 32, folder "Coney Is., Queens, Staten Island Inv. Reports 1917–18," C14.

25. Harry Kahan, report on Rockaway Beach, 21 July 1918, box 32, folder "Coney Is., Queens, Staten Island Inv. Reports 1917–18," C14.

26. Ibid.

27. Oppenheim, report on John Herbst's, 26 April 1916.

28. These cloak-and-dagger schemes culminated in an embarrassing incident in the 1930s, when one of Easley's undercover investigators, Gaston Means, sold him trunk loads of evidence of alleged "communist subversion." All of these documents turned out to be forgeries. Gaston Means eventually ended up on the wrong side of the Lindberg baby kidnapping case. See Edwin P. Hoyt, *Spectacular Rogue: Gaston B. Means* (New York: Bobbs-Merrill, 1963).

29. Ralph Easley, confidential memorandum, reel 407, NCF.

30. The National Civic Federation "formed a special secret service bureau which at first confined its activities to the investigation of industrial disturbances on the docks and in munition and ordnance centers. . . . Gompers was particularly active in bringing to the attention of the governmental authorities any efforts to discredit and disrupt the labor movement, since this would constitute interference with neutral rights in the manufacture of war supplies." Green, *National Civic Federation and the Labor Movement*, 366.

31. Cyphers, *National Civic Federation*, 9.

32. Ralph Easley, as quoted in Hillquit, "Socialism and the National Civic Federation," 4. The historiography on the NCF has focused on its quintessentially progressive characteristics. David Montgomery discusses the mediation work of the National Civic Federation, arguing that it "provided trade-union executives with an agency that enjoyed sufficient standing in the business community to escort employers and unionists to the bargaining table. . . . In its heyday, the NCF offered a means of settling disputes that was less hazardous than reliance on sympathy strikes and boycotts, and it also imported into industrial controversies the businessmen's style of dealing with one another" (*Fall of the House of Labor*, 279). Alan Dawley explains that the National Civic Federation aimed "to combat class ideologies by bringing together the likes of J. P. Morgan and Samuel Gompers through the mediation of social engineers such as Ralph Easley in a tripartite structure of capital, labor, and the public that would bargain as corporate entities to resolve their differences peaceably within the overarching solidarity of the nation" (*Struggles for Justice*, 114). Historians have discussed the mediation work of the National Civic Federation—such as its fo-

cus on welfare capitalism and its creation of industrywide labor agreements. Behind the scenes, however, the National Civic Federation was engaged in unseemly activities—activities kept hidden from most of its board members and donors.

33. Green, *National Civic Federation and the Labor Movement*, 371.
34. "Socialists Lose Battle against Civic Federation," *Atlanta Constitution*, 22 November 1911, in *Progress and Reaction in the Age of Reform, 1909–1913*, vol. 8 of *The Samuel Gompers Papers*, ed. Peter J. Albert and Grace Palladino (Urbana: University of Illinois Press, 2001), 286, 287. On Gompers, the federal government, and labor during World War I, see Kennedy, *Over Here*, 71–72, and chap. 5.
35. Samuel Gompers to Orion Thomas, 30 October 1911, in Albert and Palladino, *Samuel Gompers Papers*, 8:282, 280–81.
36. Albert and Palladino, *Samuel Gompers Papers*, 8:xii.
37. Green, *National Civic Federation and the Labor Movement*, 362.
38. Ibid., 373–74n28.
39. Untitled, undated memo, reel 406, NCF.
40. "A Secret Service Squad to Hunt the Black Hand," *New York Times*, 20 December 1906. The Black Hand, a secret society comprised of Italian criminals, seemed only to target and terrorize fellow Italians. Their activities included blackmailing prosperous Italian merchants, bombing Italian businesses, and kidnapping Italian children. Their calling card was the symbol of a black hand. There were a few different Black Hand societies.
41. "Petrosini, Detective and Sociologist," *New York Times*, 30 December 1906. Interestingly, the NYPD sent Petrosini to Palermo, Sicily, in the early 1920s to carry out a coordinated attack with Sicilian officials on the Honored Society, or Mafia. During this project, he was murdered by Carlo Gambino, the future godfather of New York City's Mafia. John H. Davis, *Mafia Dynasty: The Rise and Fall of the Gambino Crime Family* (New York: Harper Paperbacks, 1993), 23.
42. Marx, *Undercover*, 25.
43. Untitled report, reel 405, NCF. This report comes from series X in the NCF records, which contains the folders labeled "Subversive Activities Files, c. 1907–1942."
44. Untitled document, first page, reel 405, NCF. As Gary T. Marx argues, the founding of the Italian squad and other similar special squads "ironically . . . introduced a degree of equal opportunity into local departments because, in order to infiltrate Italian, Black, Jewish, or Chinese groups, one had to use an undercover agent from that group" (*Undercover*, 25).
45. Untitled document, p. 11, reel 405, NCF.
46. Countryman, "History of the FBI," 40.
47. Kennedy, *Over Here*, 81.
48. Theodore Kornweibel, Jr., *"Investigate Everything": Federal Efforts to Compel Black Loyalty during World War I* (Bloomington: Indiana University Press, 2002), 12.
49. John Higham, *Strangers in the Land: Patterns of American Nativism, 1860–1925*, 2nd ed. (New York: Atheneum, 1969), 211–12.
50. Kennedy, *Over Here*, 82–83.
51. Ralph Easley to George Sylvester Viereck, 16 May 1934, reel 389, NCF.
52. According to the "Name Index to Correspondence of the Military Intelligence Division of the War Dept. General Staff, 1917–1941" (on microfilm at the National Archives and Records Administration II in College Park, MD), the Military Intelligence Division (MID) received the National Civic Federation's reports on anarchist activities in Paterson, New Jersey, and reports on anarchist conventions in New York

City; the MID recorded these as received on 15 April 1917. A search of the appropriate boxes, however, revealed that these files were "missing or transferred with no record." Records of the War Department General Staff, Military Intelligence Division Correspondence, 1917–41, RG 165, file "9948-25" and file "10110-1393," box 2535, NARA.

53. Ralph Easley, confidential memorandum, reel 407, NCF.
54. Ralph Easley to Theodore Bingham, as quoted in Green, *National Civic Federation and the Labor Movement*, 373.
55. The FBI has a file titled "Garland, B." in the its files at the National Archives and Records Administration. Unfortunately, the folder is empty. See Old German Files, document 89862, reel 462, FBI RG 65, M1085, NARA.
56. "Anarchists," reel 390, NCF.
57. Ralph Easley, confidential memorandum, reel 407, NCF.
58. "Anarchists," reel 390, NCF.
59. Mr. X, "Important Notes. The Haymarket Riot," reel 405, NCF.
60. On anarchists in the New York metropolitan area, see Tom Goyens, *Beer and Revolution: The German Anarchist Movement in New York City, 1880–1914* (Urbana: University of Illinois Press, 2007).
61. Avrich, *Sacco and Vanzetti*, 45–46.
62. "History of Anarchists," pp. 2, 3, reel 405, NCF. A search of EllisIslandRecords.org yielded several male immigrants named Alfonso D'Angelo who fit the general profile of the priest. The most likely match was an Alfonso D'Angelo who arrived at Ellis Island on 19 August 1901 on the *Lombardia* from Naples. He was thirty-two and single when he arrived. His information is on line 19 of the ship's manifest. http://www.ellisisland.org/search/passRecord.asp?MID=04147219090227093376&pID=604828010163&fromEI=1 (accessed 2 August 2008). In addition, the U.S. Census of 1920 shows a Reverend Alphonso D'Angelo born around 1870 who was living in Bergen, New Jersey.
63. Untitled document, p. 4, reel 405, NCF; and "History of Anarchists," 3.
64. "History of Anarchists," 3. Von Papen was instrumental in propelling Hitler to power in Germany and was one of the main players in the Nuremberg trials.
65. "Anarchists," reel 390, NCF.
66. Arthur Barkey, "Report in re Workers' International Industrial Union," 24 August 1917, MID, RG 165, NARA.
67. Ibid.
68. "Chronology," 21 and 22 August 1915, reel 405, NCF. "Chronology" contains redacted versions of reports on anarchist activities in New York and New Jersey by the undercover investigators F and Mr. X.
69. Goyens, *Beer and Revolution*, 2.
70. This first quote comes "Chronology," 21 and 22 August 1915; the second comes from "Chronology," 26 August 1915, p. 2, reel 405, NCF.
71. "Chronology," 21 and 22 August 1915.
72. "Chronology," 21 September 1915, p. 3, reel 405, NCF. The MID maintained extensive files on Berkman and his publication the *Blast*, in particular. In 1976, however, the FBI pulled all of the information out of the MID files as "restricted information." Records of the War Department General Staff, Military Intelligence Division Correspondence, 1917–41, RG 165, box 2767, folder "10110-362 (end) to 10110-395," NARA.
73. "Chronology," 21 September 1915, p. 3, emphasis in the original. The report identified Bresci as Angelo Brescia and King Umberto as Humbert.

74. Ibid., 17.
75. Caleb Crain, "The Terror Last Time," *New Yorker*, 13 March 2006, 82–89. See also Paul Avrich, *Haymarket Tragedy* (Princeton: Princeton University Press, 1984); James Green, *Death in the Haymarket* (New York: Pantheon, 2006); and Bryan D. Palmer, "CSI Labor History: Haymarket and the Forensics of Forgetting," *Labor: Studies in Working-Class History of the Americas* 3, no. 1 (Spring 2006): 25–36.
76. "Chronology," 14 October 1915, p. 8, NCF.
77. Ibid., 10, 8, emphasis in the original.
78. Ibid., 8.
79. Ibid. The Pompton Lakes explosion occurred on 4 April 1915. See "Explosions Said to Have Been Set by Spies on Ships and in Powder Plants Making Munitions," *New York Times*, 25 October 1915.
80. Nicholas Biddle to Colonel A. B. Coxe, 20 April 1918, Records of the War Department General Staff, Military Intelligence Division Correspondence, 1917–41, RG 165, box 2877, folder "10153-146 to 10153-208," NARA.
81. Nicholas Biddle to Colonel A. B. Coxe, 15 June 1918, Records of the War Department General Staff, Military Intelligence Division Correspondence, 1917–41, RG 165, box 2877, folder "10153-146 to 10153-208," NARA.
82. "Chronology," 15 October 1915, p. 12, NCF, emphasis in the original.
83. Ibid., emphasis in the original. An ongoing theme in "Chronology" is the suggestion that there was an affinity between the Catholic Church and the Italian anarchists in the United States. The only likely commonality between the Catholics and anarchists was that, by and large, they were all Italian immigrants. Father D'Angelo, though, presented a frightening picture of the possible variants of criminality among Italians. For example, the Catholic Church allegedly helped Father D'Angelo "to escape" to the United States.
84. Ibid., 13, emphasis in the original.
85. "Chronology," 1 December 1915, p. 43, NCF. According to the *New York Times*, explosions occurred at this plant a number of times during 1915. "Carney's Point, N.J.—DuPont Powder Company, one killed and sixteen injured. November. New fires break out at this plant, December." "Many Explosions Since War Began," *New York Times*, 31 July 1916.
86. "Chronology," 1 December 1915, p. 43, NCF, emphasis in the original.
87. "Chronology," 5 December 1915, p. 47, NCF.
88. Ibid., 47, 48, emphasis in the original.
89. Ibid., 52.
90. Ibid., emphasis in the original.
91. Ibid., 53, 61, emphasis in the original.
92. "Chronology," 12 December 1915, p. 63, NCF, emphasis in the original.
93. "Chronology," 2 January 1916, pp. 90, 91, NCF, emphasis in the original.
94. "Chronology," 23 January 1916, p. 128, NCF, emphasis in the original.
95. "Chronology," 30 January 1916, p. 138, NCF, emphasis in the original.
96. "Daniels Rushes Marines," *New York Times*, 16 May 1915.
97. "Gompers Book Tells Plot to Kill Wilson," newspaper clipping, reel 404, NCF. Gompers also claimed that B. F. Garland discovered a German plot to assassinate President Woodrow Wilson, which he passed on to the appropriate authorities to thwart the attack. Garland himself, however, was not so lucky. Gompers reported that while Garland was attempting to infiltrate this German spy network in the United States, he vanished. Gompers explained that "the last time I saw Mr. Garland he was engaged

in a highly dangerous venture to obtain information of the inside circles of German propaganda. During the period in which I knew him he never failed to make a report to Mr. Easley and, through him, to me. It is our opinion that Garland lost his life in the last venture, for since that time we have neither heard from [him] either directly or indirectly, nor has his family." Gompers felt certain that German spies had killed Garland when they discovered he was a double agent.

98. Walter B. Platt to Captain Brooks Shepherd, 13 October 1918, MID, RG 165, box 2535, folder "10104-1200 to 10104-1219," NARA.

99. Captain Brooks Shepherd to Walter B. Platt, 14 October 1918, MID, RG 165, box 2535, folder "10104-1200 to 10104-1219," NARA.

100. Charles Mowbray White, "Black," p. 1, reel 376, NCF.

101. Ibid., 2–3.

102. Ibid., 2.

103. Theodore Kornweibel, Jr., *"Seeing Red": Federal Campaigns against Black Militancy, 1919–1925* (Bloomington: Indiana University Press, 1998), 50.

104. White, "Black," 3.

105. Mark Ellis, "'Closing Ranks' and 'Seeking Honors': W. E. B. Du Bois in World War I," *Journal of American History* 79, no. 1 (June 1992): 99.

106. "Chapter 595 of the Laws of the State of New York of 1917," as quoted in Archibald Stevenson to Nicholas Biddle, 23 November 1918, reel 11, NCF.

107. The NCF regularly shared information with the MID, where receipt was recorded, but the reports were either lost or thrown away by someone in the MID offices. What still exists in the MID files on the NCF, though, is revealing.

108. Inspector C. L. Converse to Captain W. L. Moffatt, Jr., 6 November 1919, "Report on Photograph of persons attending a banquet in honor of Mme. C. Breshkovsky, March 7th 1919," MID, RG 165, box 2256, folder "10058-291 to 10058-312," NARA.

EPILOGUE

1. R.H. Van Deman, as quoted in Kornweibel, *Investigate Everything*, 226.

2. "Subject: Revolutionary Movements in America," 16 September 1919, document 10110-1241, MID, RG 165, box 2801, NARA.

3. "Tillman Warns of Race Clashes," *New York Times*, 17 July 1917. On the East St. Louis race riot, see Charles Lumpkins, *American Pogrom: The East St. Louis Race Riot and Black Politics* (Columbus: Ohio State University Press, 2008).

4. "Subject: British Report covering the Progress of the Revolutionary Movements in American during the Past Month," 16 August 1919, document 10110-1241, MID, RG 165, box 2801, NARA.

5. On the Chicago riot, see William M. Tuttle, Jr., *Race Riot: Chicago in the Red Summer of 1919* (Urbana: University of Illinois Press, 1996).

6. Kornweibel, *Investigate Everything*, 183.

7. Kornweibel, *Seeing Red*, chap. 6: "'An Undesirable, and Indeed a Very Dangerous, Alien': The Federal Campaign against Marcus Garvey." See also John Henrik Clark, *Marcus Garvey and the Vision of Africa* (New York: Vintage Press, 1974).

8. John Dewey, as quoted in Kennedy, *Over Here*, 246.

9. Schmidt, *Red Scare*, 167–68.

10. On Seattle, see Dana Frank, *Purchasing Power: Consumer Organizing, Gender, and the Seattle Labor Movement, 1919–1929* (New York: Cambridge University Press, 1994).

11. On the Boston police strike, see Francis Russell, *A City in Terror: Calvin Coolidge and the 1919 Boston Police Strike* (Boston: Beacon Press, 2005). On the steel strike, see

David Brody, *Labor in Crisis: The Steel Strike of 1919* (Urbana: University of Illinois Press, 1987).

12. Langum, *Crossing over the Line*, 89; on the *Caminetti* decision, see chaps. 5 and 6.

13. Ibid., 65.

14. On Jack Johnson, see Gail Bederman, *Manliness and Civilization: A Cultural History of Gender and Race in the United States, 1880–1917* (Chicago: University of Chicago Press, 1995), esp. chap. 1, "Remaking Manhood through Race and 'Civilization.'"

15. Langum, *Crossing over the Line*, 177.

16. Lerner, *Dry Manhattan*, 64–65.

17. Ibid., 65–66.

18. Ibid., 63.

19. Ibid., 44.

20. The Committee of Fourteen, for instance, continued to investigate and attempt to rout out prostitution in New York City because the police department proved unable to curtail it in the context of Prohibition, which had increased the number of people going to speakeasies, where they would then encounter prostitutes and other forms of sexual immorality. The Committee folded in 1932, however, largely because its donors could no longer afford to sustain the organization during (and as a result of) the Great Depression.

21. "William J. Burns on Stand; Detective Testifies at Inquiry into His Agency," *New York Times*, 6 August 1919. See also Gage, *Day Wall Street Exploded*.

22. Schmidt, *Red Scare*, 327.

23. Ibid., 331, 336–40.

24. Donner, *Age of Surveillance*, 7. Donner and other scholars have pointed out that this directive may never have actually been issued, as no evidence of it exists other than Hoover's claim.

25. Hibou, "Privatising the Economy to Privatising the State."

26. Howe, *Confessions of a Reformer*, 59.

27. Novak, "Myth of the 'Weak' American State," 763.

BIBLIOGRAPHY

PRIMARY SOURCES
Manuscript Collections

Manuscripts and Archives Division, The New York Public Library

Committee of Fifteen records (C15)
Committee of Fourteen records (C14)
National Civic Federation records (NCF)
People's Institute records (PI)

Rare Book and Manuscripts Library, Columbia University, New York

Society for the Prevention of Crime papers (SPC)

National Archives and Records Administration II, College Park, Maryland (NARA)

Record group 65. Records of the Federal Bureau of Investigation.
Record group 165. Records of the War Department General and Special Staffs, Military
   Intelligence Division.

Judah L. Magnes Archives, Jerusalem, Israel

Kehillah (Jewish Community of New York City) records

Serials, Journals, and Newspapers

The Call	*The Nation*
Charities and the Commons	*New York Age*
Collier's	*New York Times*
The Crisis	*New York World*
Current Opinion	*Scribner's*
Everybody's Magazine	*The Survey*
McClure's	*Vigilance*

Published Primary Sources

Albert, Peter J., and Grace Palladino, eds. *The Samuel Gompers Papers*. Vol. 8: *Progress and Reaction in the Age of Reform, 1909–1913*. Urbana: University of Illinois Press, 2001.

———, eds. *The Samuel Gompers Papers*. Vol. 9: *The American Federation of Labor at the Height of Progressivism, 1913–16*. Urbana: University of Illinois Press, 2001.

Addams, Jane. *A New Conscience and an Ancient Evil*. New York, 1912.

———. *The Spirit of Youth and the City Streets*. 1909. Reprint. Urbana: University of Illinois Press, 1972.

Addams, Jane, and the Residents of Hull House. *Hull House Maps and Papers: A Presentation of Nationalities and Wages in Congested District of Chicago, Together with Comments and Essays on Problems Growing out of the Social Conditions*. 1895. Reprint. Urbana: University of Illinois Press, 2007.

Beck, Louis. *New York's Chinatown: An Historical Presentation of Its People and Places*. New York: Bohemia Publishing, 1898.

Bly, Nellie. *Ten Days in a Mad-House, or, Nellie Bly's Experience on Blackwell's Island*. New York: N. L. Munro, 1887. Microfilm. Washington, DC: Library of Congress, 1969.

Bogard, Milo T., ed. *The Redemption of New York: Told by New York Newspapermen for the Press Scrap Book*. New York: P. F. McBreen and Sons, 1902.

Childs, Clinton. *A Year's Experiment in Social Center Organization*. New York: Social Center Committee, 1912.

Clark, John W. "Street Crap Playing." *Charities and the Commons* 17, no. 15 (12 January 1907): 684–85.

Collier, John. "Leisure Time: The Last Problem of Conservation." Reprint from *The Playground*. New York: Playground and Recreation Association of America, 1912.

Collier, John, and Edward M. Barrows. *The City Where Crime Is Play: A Report by the People's Institute*. New York: People's Institute, 1914.

Committee of Fifteen. *The Social Evil: With Special Reference to Conditions Existing in the City of New York*. New York: G. P. Putnam's, 1902.

Committee of Fourteen in New York City. *Annual Report for 1913*. New York, 1914.

———. *Annual Report for 1914*. New York, 1915.

Conrad, Joseph. *The Secret Agent: A Simple Tale*. 1907. Reprint. Ed. Martin Seymour Smith. New York: Penguin Books, 1990.

Crowell, Elizabeth F. "The Midwives of New York." *Charities and the Commons* 17, no. 15 (12 January 1907): 667–77.

DeForest, Robert W., and Lawrence Veiller. *The Tenement House Problem; Including the Report of the New York State Tenement House Commission of 1900*. New York: Macmillan, 1903.

Donovan, Frances. *The Woman Who Waits*. Boston, 1920.

DuBois, W. E. B. *The Black North in 1901: A Social Study*. 1901. Reprint. New York: Arno Press, 1969.

———. *The Philadelphia Negro: A Social Study*. 1899. Reprint. New York: Arno Press, 1967.

Fosdick, Raymond B. "The Commission on Training Camp Activities." In "Economic Conditions of Winning the War." Special issue of *Proceedings of the Academy of Political Science in the City of New York* 7, no. 4 (1918).

Gardner, Charles W. *The Doctor and the Devil, or Midnight Adventures of Dr. Parkhurst*. 1894. Reprint. New York: Vanguard Press, 1931.

Hillquit, Morris. "Socialism and the National Civic Federation." New York, 1911.

Howe, Frederic C. *The City: The Hope of Democracy*. New York: Charles Scribner's Sons, 1913.

———. *The Confessions of a Reformer*. 1925. Reprint. Kent: Kent State University Press, 1988.

James, Henry. *The Princess Casamassima*. In *Novels, 1886–1890*, ed. Daniel Mark Fogel. New York: Library of America, 1989.

Johnson, James Weldon. *The Autobiography of an Ex-Coloured Man*. 1912. Reprint. New York: Vintage, 1989.

———. *Black Manhattan*. 1930. Reprint. New York: DaCapo Press, 1991.

Kellor, Frances A. "Americanization: A Conservation Policy for Industry." Reprint from the *Annals of the American Academy of Political and Social Science* (May 1916).

———. *Out of Work: A Study of Employment Agencies, Their Treatment of the Unemployed, and Their Influence upon Home and Business*. 1904. Reprint. New York: Arno Press and the New York Times, 1971.

Kneeland, George J. *Commercialized Prostitution in New York City*. New York: Century Company, 1913.

MacLean, Annie Marion. "The Sweat-Shop in Summer." *American Journal of Sociology* 9, no. 3 (November 1903): 289–309.

———. "Two Weeks in Department Stores." *American Journal of Sociology* 4, no. 6 (May 1899): 721–41.

———. *Wage-Earning Women*. New York, 1910.

———. *Women Workers and Society*. Chicago: A. C. McClurg and Company, 1916.

McAdoo, William. *Guarding a Great City*. New York: Harper and Brother Publishing, 1906.

Miner, Maude E. *Slavery of Prostitution: A Plea for Emancipation*. New York, 1916.

Moss, Frank. *The American Metropolis: From Knickerbocker Days to the Present Time: New York City Life in All Its Various Phases*. Vol. 2. New York: Peter Fenelon Collier, 1897.

Nelson, Nell [pseud.]. *The White Slave Girls of Chicago. Nell Nelson's Startling Disclosures of the Cruelties and Iniquities Practiced in the Workshops and Factories of a Great City*. Chicago: Barkley Publishing, 1888. Microfilm. New Haven: Research Publications, 1976.

Park, Robert E., and Ernest W. Burgess. *The City: Suggestions for Investigation of Human Behavior in the Urban Environment*. 1925. Reprint. Chicago: University of Chicago Press, 1967.

Parkhurst, Charles H. *Our Fight with Tammany*. New York, 1895.

People's Institute. *19th Yearbook*. New York: People's Institute, 1917.

———. *20th Yearbook*. New York: People's Institute, 1918.

Peters, Rev. John P. "The Story of the Committee of Fourteen of New York." *Social Hygiene* 4 (1918).

———. "Suppression of the 'Raines Law Hotels.'" *Annals of the American Academy of Political and Social Science* 32 (November 1908): 556–66.

Pettengill, Lillian. *Toilers of the Home: The Record of a College Woman's Experience as a Domestic Servant*. New York, 1903.

Police Practice and Procedure Manual. New York: Cornelius F. Cahalane, 1914.

Research Committee of the Committee of Fourteen. *The Social Evil in New York City: A Study in Law Enforcement*. New York: Andrew H. Kellogg Co., 1910.

Richardson, Dorothy. *The Long Day: The Story of a New York Working Girl, as Told by Herself*. New York: Century Company, 1906.

Riis, Jacob. *The Battle with the Slum*. 1902. Reprint. Mineola, NY: Dover Publications, 1998.

———. *How the Other Half Lives: Studies among the Tenements of New York*. 1890. Reprint. Mineola, NY: Dover Publications, 1971.

Seligman, Edwin R. A., ed. *The Social Evil: With Special Reference to Conditions Existing in the City of New York. A Report Prepared [in 1902] under the Direction of the Committee of Fifteen*. 2nd ed. New York: G. P. Putnam's Sons, 1912.

Tanner, Amy. "Glimpses at the Mind of a Waitress." *American Journal of Sociology* 13 (July 1907): 48–55.

U.S. Congress. House of Representatives. *The Chinese Menace*. Report no. 255. 10 February 1892.

Van Kleeck, Mary. "Working Hours of Women in Factories." *Charities and the Commons* 17 (1906–7): 13–21.

Van Vorst, Bessie, and Marie Van Vorst. *The Woman Who Toils: Being the Experiences of Two Gentlewomen as Factory Girls*. New York: Doubleday, Page, 1903.

Washington, Booker T. *Up from Slavery: An Autobiography*. 1901. Reprint. New York: Modern Library, 1999.

White, Gaylord S. "How Combat Crap Shooting." *Charities and the Commons* 17, no. 23 (9 March 1907): 1046.

Younger, Maud. "The Diary of an Amateur Waitress." Pts. 1 and 2. *McClure's Magazine* 28 (March 1907): 543–52; (April 1907): 665–77.

SECONDARY SOURCES
Published Secondary Sources

Addams, Jane. *Twenty Years at Hull House*. New York: Macmillan, 1945.

Alexander, Ruth M. *The "Girl Problem": Female Sexual Delinquency in New York, 1900–1930*. Ithaca: Cornell University Press, 1995.

Allen, Robert C. *Horrible Prettiness: Burlesque and American Culture*. Chapel Hill: University of North Carolina Press, 1991.

Anbinder, Tyler. *Five Points: The Nineteenth-Century New York City Neighborhood That Invented Tap Dance, Stole Elections, and Became the World's Most Notorious Slum*. New York: Plume Books, 2001.

Asbury, Herbert. *The Gangs of New York*. 1927. Reprint. New York: Thunder's Mouth Press, 1998.

Astor, Gerald. *The New York Cops: An Informal History*. New York: Charles Scribner's Sons, 1971.

Avrich, Paul. *Anarchist Portraits*. Princeton: Princeton University Press, 1988.

———. *Haymarket Tragedy*. Princeton: Princeton University Press, 1984.

———. *Sacco and Vanzetti: The Anarchist Background*. Princeton: Princeton University Press, 1991.

Bailey, Beth. *From Front Porch to Back Seat: Courtship in Twentieth-Century America*. Baltimore: Johns Hopkins University Press, 1988.

Bederman, Gail. *Manliness and Civilization: A Cultural History of Gender and Race in the United States, 1880–1917*. Chicago: University of Chicago Press, 1995.

Bendersky, Joseph W. *The "Jewish Threat": Anti-Semitic Politics of the U.S. Army*. New York: Basic Books, 2000.

Benson, Susan Porter. *Counter Cultures: Saleswomen, Managers, and Customers in American Department Stores, 1890–1940*. Urbana: University of Illinois Press, 1988.

Blackmar, Elizabeth. *Manhattan for Rent, 1785–1850*. Ithaca: Cornell University Press, 1991.

Block, Alan. *East Side–West Side: Organizing Crime in New York, 1930–1950*. Swansea, Wales: University College Cardiff Press, 1980.

Blumin, Stuart. *The Emergence of the Middle Class: Social Experience in the American City, 1760–1900*. New York: Cambridge University Press, 1989.

Bodnar, John. *The Transplanted: A History of Immigrants in Urban America.* Bloomington: Indiana University Press, 1985.

Bonner, Arthur. *Alas! What Brought Thee Hither? The Chinese in New York, 1850–1950.* Madison, NJ: Fairleigh Dickinson University Press, 1997.

Bourdieu, Pierre. *The Logic of Practice.* Trans. Richard Nice. Stanford: Stanford University Press, 1990.

Boyer, Paul. *Urban Masses and Moral Order in America, 1820–1920.* Cambridge: Harvard University Press, 1978.

Brandt, Allan M. *No Magic Bullet: A Social History of Venereal Disease in the United States since 1880, with a New Chapter on AIDS.* New York: Oxford University Press, 1987.

Bristow, Edward J. *Prostitution and Prejudice: The Jewish Fight against White Slavery, 1870–1939.* Oxford: Clarendon Press, 1982.

Bristow, Nancy K. *Making Men Moral: Social Engineering during the Great War.* New York: New York University Press, 1996.

Brody, David. *Labor in Crisis: The Steel Strike of 1919.* Urbana: University of Illinois Press, 1987.

Browder, Laura. *Slippery Characters: Ethnic Impersonators and American Identities.* Chapel Hill: University of North Carolina Press, 2000.

Bulmer, Martin. *The Chicago School of Sociology: Institutionalization, Diversity, and the Rise of Sociological Research.* Chicago: University of Chicago Press, 1984.

Burchell, Graham, Colin Gordon, and Peter Miller, eds. *The Foucault Effect: Studies in Governmentality.* Chicago: University of Chicago Press, 1991.

Burrows, Edwin G., and Mike Wallace. *Gotham: A History of New York City to 1898.* New York: Oxford University Press, 1999.

Burnham, John. "The Progressive Era Revolution in American Attitudes toward Sex." *Journal of American History* 59 (March 1973): 885–908.

Byard, Eliza. "Inverts, Perverts, and National Peril: Federal Responses to Homosexuality, 1890–1956." Ph.D. diss., Columbia University, 2002.

Chan, Sucheng, ed. *Entry Denied: Exclusion and the Chinese Community in America, 1882–1943.* Philadelphia: Temple University Press, 1991.

Capozzola, Christopher. *Uncle Sam Wants You: World War I and the Making of the Modern American Citizen.* New York: Oxford University Press, 2008.

Chauncey, George. *Gay New York: Gender, Urban Culture, and the Making of the Gay Male World, 1890–1940.* New York: Basic Books, 1994.

Clark, John Henrik. *Marcus Garvey and the Vision of Africa.* New York: Vintage Press, 1974.

Clement, Elizabeth Alice. *Love for Sale: Courting, Treating, and Prostitution in New York City, 1900–1945.* Chapel Hill: University of North Carolina Press, 2006.

Cobble, Dorothy Sue. *Dishing it Out: Waitresses and Their Unions in the Twentieth Century.* Urbana: University of Illinois Press, 1991.

Connelly, Mark Thomas. *The Response to Prostitution in the Progressive Era.* Chapel Hill: University of North Carolina Press, 1980.

Cott, Nancy. *The Grounding of Modern Feminism.* New Haven: Yale University Press, 1987.

Countryman, Vern. "The History of the FBI: Democracy's Development of a Secret Police." In *Investigating the FBI,* ed. Pat Watters and Stephen Gillers. Garden City, NY: Doubleday, 1973.

Crain, Caleb. "The Terror Last Time." *New Yorker,* 13 March 2006, 82–89.

Cyphers, Christopher J. *The National Civic Federation and the Making of a New Liberalism, 1900–1915.* Westport, CT: Praeger, 2002.

Davis, John H. *Mafia Dynasty: The Rise and Fall of the Gambino Crime Family*. New York: Harper Paperbacks, 1993.

Dawley, Alan. *Struggles for Justice: Social Responsibility and the Liberal State*. Cambridge: Harvard University Press, 1991.

Deegan, Mary Jo. "The Chicago Men and the Sociology of Women." In *The Chicago School: Critical Assessments*, vol. 1: *A Chicago Canon?* ed. Ken Plummer, 198–230. New York: Routledge, 1997.

———. "*Hull House Maps and Papers*: The Birth of Chicago Sociology." In *The Chicago School: Critical Assessments*, vol. 2: *Theory, History, and Foundations*, ed. Ken Plummer, 5–19. New York: Routledge, 1997.

———. "Women and Sociology, 1890–1930." *Journal of the History of Sociology* 1 (Fall 1978): 11–34.

D'Emilio, John, and Estelle B. Freedman. *Intimate Matters: A History of Sexuality in America*. New York: Harper and Row, 1988.

Denning, Michael. *Cover Stories: Narrative and Ideology in the British Spy Thriller*. New York: Routledge, 1987.

Deutsch, Sarah. *Women and the City: Gender, Space, and Power in Boston, 1870–1940*. New York: Oxford University Press, 2002.

Donner, Frank J. *The Age of Surveillance: The Aims and Methods of America's Political Intelligence System*. New York: Knopf, 1980.

Donovan, Brian. *White Slave Crusades: Race, Gender, and Anti-Vice Activism, 1887–1917*. Urbana: University of Illinois Press, 2006.

Dubinsky, Karen. *Improper Advances: Rape and Heterosexual Conflict in Ontario, 1880–1929*. Chicago: University of Chicago Press, 1993.

Ehrenreich, Barbara. *Nickel and Dimed: On (Not) Getting By in America*. New York: Henry Holt, 2001.

Ellis, Mark. "'Closing Ranks' and 'Seeking Honors': W. E. B. Du Bois in World War I." *Journal of American History* 79, no. 1 (June 1992): 96–124.

Enstad, Nan. *Ladies of Labor, Girls of Adventure: Working Women, Popular Culture, and Labor Politics at the Turn of the Twentieth Century*. New York: Columbia University Press, 1999.

Fabian, Ann. *Card Sharps and Bucket Shops: Gambling in Nineteenth-Century Urban America*. New York: Routledge, 1999.

———. *The Unvarnished Truth: Personal Narratives in Nineteenth-Century America*. Berkeley: University of California Press, 2000.

Faris, Robert E. L. *Chicago Sociology: 1920–1932*. Chicago: University of Chicago Press, 1967.

Fass, Paula. *The Damned and the Beautiful: American Youth in the 1920s*. New York: Oxford University Press, 1977.

Feldman, Egal. "Prostitution, the Alien Woman and the Progressive Imagination, 1910–1915." *American Quarterly* 19 (Summer 1967): 192–206.

Felt, Jeremy P. "Vice Reform as a Political Technique: The Committee of Fifteen in New York, 1900–1901." *New York History* 54, no. 1 (January 1973): 24–51.

Filene, Peter. "An Obituary for 'The Progressive Movement.'" *American Quarterly* 22 (Spring 1970): 20–34.

Finch, Minnie. *The NAACP: Its Fight for Justice*. Metuchen, NJ: Scarecrow Press, 1981.

Fisher, Robert Bruce. "The People's Institute of New York City, 1897–1934: Culture, Progressive Democracy, and the People." Ph.D. diss., New York University, 1974.

Fitzpatrick, Ellen. *Endless Crusade: Women Social Scientists and Progressive Reform*. New York: Oxford University Press, 1990.

Foucault, Michel. *The Care of the Self*. Vol. 3 of *The History of Sexuality*. Trans. Robert Hurley. New York: Vintage Books, 1986.

————. "Governmentality." In *The Foucault Effect: Studies in Governmentality*, ed. Graham Burchell, Colin Gordon, and Peter Miller, 87–104. Chicago: University of Chicago Press, 1991.

————. *The History of Sexuality: An Introduction*. Vol. 1 of *The History of Sexuality*. Trans. Robert Hurley. New York: Vintage Books, 1978.

————. *Power/Knowledge: Selected Interviews and Other Writings, 1972–1977*. Ed. Colin Gordon. Trans. Colin Gordon, Leo Marshall, John Mepham, and Kate Soper. New York: Pantheon Books, 1980.

————. *The Use of Pleasure*. Vol. 2 of *The History of Sexuality*. Trans. Robert Hurley. New York: Vintage Books, 1985.

Fox, Richard Wightman. *Trials of Intimacy: Love and Loss in the Beecher-Tilton Scandal*. Chicago: University of Chicago Press, 1999.

Frank, Dana. *Purchasing Power: Consumer Organizing, Gender, and the Seattle Labor Movement, 1919–1929*. New York: Cambridge University Press, 1994.

Friedman, Andrea. *Prurient Interests: Gender, Democracy, and Obscenity in New York City, 1909–1945*. New York: Columbia University Press, 2000.

Fronc, Jennifer. "Narratives of Sexual Conquest: A Historical Perspective on Date Rape." In *Why We Write: The Politics and Practice of Writing for Social Change*, ed. Jim Downs, 61–69. New York: Routledge, 2005.

Furner, Mary O. *Advocacy and Objectivity: A Crisis in the Professionalization of American Social Science, 1865–1905*. Lexington: University Press of Kentucky, 1975.

Gaines, Kevin K. *Uplifting the Race: Black Leadership, Politics, and Culture in the Twentieth Century*. Chapel Hill: University of North Carolina Press, 1996.

Gage, Beverly. *The Day Wall Street Exploded: A Story of America in Its First Age of Terrorism*. New York: Oxford University Press, 2009.

Garb, Margaret. *City of American Dreams: A History of Home Ownership and Housing Reform in Chicago, 1871–1919*. Chicago: University of Chicago Press, 2005.

Gellman, David, and David Quigley. *Jim Crow New York: A Documentary History of Race and Citizenship, 1777–1877*. New York: New York University Press, 2003.

Gilfoyle, Timothy. *City of Eros: New York City, Prostitution, and the Commercialization of Sex, 1790–1920*. New York: Norton, 1992.

————. "The Moral Origins of Political Surveillance: The Preventive Society in New York City, 1867–1918." *American Quarterly* 38 (Autumn 1986): 637–52.

————. *A Pickpocket's Tale: The Underworld of Nineteenth-Century New York*. New York: Norton, 2007.

————. "Street-Rats and Gutter-Snipes: Child Pickpockets and Street Culture in New York City, 1850–1900." *Journal of Social History* 37, no. 4 (2004): 853–75.

Ginzberg, Lori. *Women and the Work of Benevolence: Morality, Politics, and Class in the Nineteenth-Century United States*. New Haven: Yale University Press, 1990.

Glenn, Susan. *Daughters of the Shtetl: Life and Labor in the Immigrant Generation*. Ithaca: Cornell University Press, 1990.

Goffman, Erving. *The Presentation of Self in Everyday Life*. New York: Anchor Books, 1959.

Gordon, Linda. *The Great Arizona Orphan Abduction*. Cambridge: Harvard University Press, 2001.

————. *Heroes of Their Own Lives: The Politics and History of Family Violence*. New York: Viking, 1988.

———. "Putting Children First: Women, Maternalism, and Welfare in the Early Twentieth Century." In *U.S. History as Women's History: New Feminist Essays*, ed. Linda K. Kerber, Alice Kessler-Harris, and Kathryn Kish Sklar. Chapel Hill: University of North Carolina Press, 1995.

———. "Social Insurance and Public Assistance: The Influence of Gender in Welfare Thought in the United States, 1890–1935." *American Historical Review* (February 1992): 19–54.

Goren, Arthur A. *New York Jews and the Quest for Community: The Kehillah Experiment, 1908–1922*. New York: Columbia University Press, 1970.

Goyens, Tom. *Beer and Revolution: The German Anarchist Movement in New York City, 1880–1914*. Urbana: University of Illinois Press, 2007.

Green, James. *Death in the Haymarket*. New York: Pantheon, 2006.

Green, Marguerite. *The National Civic Federation and the American Labor Movement, 1900–1925*. 1956. Reprint. Westport, CT: Greenwood Press, 1973.

Gurney, Peter. "'Intersex' and 'Dirty Girls': Mass Observation and Working-Class Sexuality in England in the 1930s." *Journal of the History of Sexuality* 8, no. 2 (1997): 256–90.

Haag, Pamela S. "In Search of 'The Real Thing': Ideologies of Love, Modern Romance, and Women's Sexual Subjectivity in the United States, 1920–1940." *Journal of the History of Sexuality* 8, no. 2 (1992): 547–77.

Halttunen, Karen. "Cultural History and the Challenge of Narrativity." In *Beyond the Cultural Turn*, ed. Victoria E. Bonnell and Lynn Hunt, 165–81. Berkeley: University of California Press, 1999.

Hamilton, Alice. *Exploring the Dangerous Trades: The Autobiography of Alice Hamilton, M.D.* Boston: Little, Brown, 1943.

Hapke, Laura. *Girls Who Went Wrong: Prostitutes in American Fiction, 1885–1917*. Bowling Green, OH: Bowling Green State University Popular Press, 1989.

———. *Labor's Text: The Worker in American Fiction*. New Brunswick, NJ: Rutgers University Press, 2001.

———. *Sweatshop: The History of an American Idea*. New Brunswick, NJ: Rutgers University Press, 2004.

———. *Tales of the Working Girl: Wage Earning Women in American Literature, 1890–1925*. New York: Twayne Publishers, 1992.

Hays, Samuel P. *The Response to Industrialism, 1885–1914*. Chicago: University of Chicago Press, 1957.

Heap, Chad. *Slumming: Sexual and Racial Encounters in American Nightlife, 1885–1940*. Chicago: University of Chicago Press, 2009.

Hibou, Beatrice. "From Privatising the Economy to Privatising the State: An Analysis of the Continual Formation of the State." In *Privatising the State*, ed. B. Hibou, trans. Jonathan Derrick. London: Hurst, 2004.

———, ed. *Privatising the State*. Trans. Jonathan Derrick. London: Hurst, 2004.

Higbie, Frank Tobias. *Indispensable Outcasts: Hobo Workers and Community in the Midwest, 1880–1930*. Urbana: University of Illinois, 2003.

Higginbotham, Evelyn Brooks. *Righteous Discontent: The Women's Movement in the Black Baptist Church, 1880–1920*. Cambridge: Harvard University Press, 1993.

Higham, John. *Strangers in the Land: Patterns of American Nativism, 1860–1925*. 2nd ed. New York: Atheneum, 1969.

Hobson, Barbara Meil. *Uneasy Virtue: The Politics of Prostitution and the American Reform Tradition*. New York: Basic Books, 1987.

Hofstadter, Richard. *The Age of Reform: From Bryan to FDR*. New York: Vintage Books, 1955.

Horowitz, Helen Lefkowitz. *Rereading Sex: Battles over Sexual Knowledge and Suppression in Nineteenth-Century America*. New York: Knopf, 2002.

Hoyt, Edwin P. *Spectacular Rogue: Gaston B. Means*. New York: Bobbs-Merrill, 1963.

Hunter, Tera. *To "Joy My Freedom": Southern Black Women's Lives and Labors after the Civil War*. Cambridge: Harvard University Press, 1997.

Jackson, Kenneth T., ed. *The Encyclopedia of New York City*. New Haven: Yale University Press, 1995.

Johnston, Robert D. *The Radical Middle Class: Populist Democracy and the Question of Capitalism in Progressive Era Portland, Oregon*. Princeton: Princeton University Press, 2006.

Joselit, Jenna Weissman. *Our Gang: Jewish Crime and the New York Jewish Community, 1900–1940*. Bloomington: Indiana University Press, 1983.

Keire, Mara. "Vice in American Cities, 1890–1925." Ph.D. diss., Johns Hopkins University, 2002.

Kellogg, Charles Flint. *NAACP: A History of the National Association for the Advancement of Colored People*. Vol. 1: *1909–1920*. Baltimore: Johns Hopkins University Press, 1967.

Kennedy, David. *Over Here: The First World War and American Society*. 25th anniversary ed. New York: Oxford University Press, 2004.

Kenny, Kevin. *Making Sense of the Molly Maguires*. New York: Oxford University Press, 1998.

Kloppenberg, James T. *Uncertain Victory: Social Democracy and Progressivism in European and American Thought, 1870–1920*. New York: Oxford University Press, 1986.

———. *Virtues of Liberalism*. New York: Oxford University Press, 1998.

Kolko, Gabriel. *Triumph of Conservatism: A Re-Interpretation of American History, 1900–1916*. New York: Free Press of Glencoe, 1963.

Kornweibel, Theodore, Jr. *"Investigate Everything": Federal Efforts to Compel Black Loyalty during World War I*. Bloomington: Indiana University Press, 2002.

———. *"Seeing Red": Federal Campaigns against Black Militancy, 1919–1925*. Bloomington: Indiana University Press, 1998.

Koven, Seth. *Slumming: Sexual and Social Politics in Victorian London*. Princeton: Princeton University Press, 2004.

Kroeger, Brooke. *Nellie Bly: Daredevil, Reporter, Feminist*. New York: Times Books, 1994.

Kwong, Peter. *Chinatown, N.Y.: Labor and Politics, 1930–1950*. Rev. ed. New York: New Press, 2001.

Langum, David J. *Crossing over the Line: Legislating Morality and the Mann Act*. Chicago: University of Chicago Press, 1994.

Lardner, James, and Thomas Repetto. *NYPD: A City and Its Police*. New York: Henry Holt, 2000.

Leach, William. *True Love and Perfect Union: The Feminist Reform of Sex and Society*. New York: Basic Books, 1980.

Lee, Erika. *At America's Gates: Chinese Immigration during the Exclusion Era, 1882–1943*. Chapel Hill: University of North Carolina Press, 2003.

Lengermann, Patricia Madoo, and Jill Niebrugge-Brantley. *The Women Founders: Sociology and Social Theory, 1830–1930*. Boston: McGraw Hill, 1998.

Lerner, Michael. *Dry Manhattan: Prohibition in New York City*. Cambridge: Harvard University Press, 2007.

Leuchtenburg, William. *The Perils of Prosperity, 1914–1932*. Chicago: University of Chicago Press, 1958.

Lewis, David Levering. *W. E .B. DuBois: Biography of a Race, 1868–1919.* New ed. New York: Owl Books, 1994.

———. *When Harlem Was in Vogue.* New York: Penguin Books, 1979.

Light, Ivan. "From Vice District to Tourist Attraction: The Moral Career of American Chinatowns, 1880–1940." *Pacific Historical Review* 43 (1974): 367–94.

Lindstrom, J. A. "Almost Worse Than the Restrictive Measures": Chicago Reformers and the Nickelodeons." *Cinema Journal* 39, no. 1 (1999): 90–112.

Lubove, Roy. "The Progressives and the Prostitute." *Historian* 24 (May 1962): 308–30.

———. *The Progressives and the Slums: Tenement House Reform in New York City, 1890–1917.* Pittsburgh: University of Pittsburgh Press, 1963.

Lui, Mary Ting Yi. *The Chinatown Trunk Mystery: Murder, Miscegenation, and Other Dangerous Encounters in Turn-of-the-Century New York City.* Princeton: Princeton University Press, 2005.

Lumpkins, Charles. *American Pogrom: The East St. Louis Race Riot and Black Politics.* Columbus: Ohio State University Press, 2008.

Lutes, Jean Marie. "Into the Madhouse with Nellie Bly: Girl Stunt Reporting in Late Nineteenth-Century America." *American Quarterly* 54, no. 2 (2002): 217–53.

Lyman, Stanford M. *Chinese Americans.* New York: Random House, 1974.

Ma, L. Eve Armentrout. "Chinatown Organizations and the Anti-Chinese Movement, 1882–1914." In *Entry Denied: Exclusion and the Chinese Community in America, 1882–1943,* ed. Sucheng Chan, 147–69. Philadelphia: Temple University Press, 1991.

Mackey, Thomas C. *Pursuing Johns: Criminal Law Reform, Defending Character, and New York City's Committee of Fourteen, 1920–1930.* Columbus: Ohio State University Press, 2005.

Marx, Gary T. *Undercover: Police Surveillance in America.* Berkeley: University of California Press, 1988.

Matthews, Fred H. *Quest for an American Sociology: Robert E. Park and the Chicago School.* Montreal: McGill-Queen's University Press, 1977.

McIlwain, Jeffrey Scott. *Organizing Crime in Chinatown: Race and Racketeering in New York City, 1890–1910.* Jefferson, NC: McFarland, 2004.

Meyerowitz, Joanne. *Women Adrift: Independent Wage Earners in Chicago, 1880–1930.* Chicago: University of Chicago Press, 1988.

Mitchell, Michele. *Righteous Propagation: African Americans and the Politics of Racial Destiny after Reconstruction.* Chapel Hill: University of North Carolina Press, 2004.

Monkkonen, Eric H. *Murder in New York City.* Berkeley: University of California Press, 2001.

———. *Police in Urban America, 1860–1920.* New York: Cambridge University Press, 1981.

Montgomery, David. *The Fall of the House of Labor: The Workplace, the State, and American Labor Activism, 1865–1925.* Cambridge: Cambridge University Press, 1987.

Morn, Frank. *"The Eye That Never Sleeps": A History of the Pinkerton National Detective Agency.* Bloomington: Indiana University Press, 1982.

Mumford, Kevin J. *Interzones: Black/White Sex Districts in Chicago and New York in the Early Twentieth Century.* New York: Columbia University Press, 1997.

Muncy, Robyn. *Creating a Female Dominion in American Reform, 1890–1935.* New York: Oxford University Press, 1991.

Murray, Pauli, ed. *States' Laws on Race and Color.* 1951. Reprint. Athens: University of Georgia Press, 1997.

Nasaw, David. *Children of the City: At Work and at Play.* New York: Oxford University Press, 1985.

———. *Going Out: The Rise and Fall of Public Amusements.* Cambridge: Harvard University Press, 1993.

Ngai, Mae M. *Impossible Subjects: Illegal Aliens and the Making of Modern America.* Princeton: Princeton University Press, 2005.

Novak, William J. "The Myth of the 'Weak' American State." *American Historical Review* 113, no. 3 (2008): 752–72.

Odem, Mary E. *Delinquent Daughters: Protecting and Policing Adolescent Female Sexuality in the United States, 1885–1920.* Chapel Hill: University of North Carolina Press, 1995.

Osofsky, Gilbert. *Harlem: The Making of a Ghetto.* 2nd ed. Chicago: Elephant Paperbacks, 1996.

Palmer, Bryan D. "CSI Labor History: Haymarket and the Forensics of Forgetting." *Labor: Studies in Working-Class History of the Americas* 3, no. 1 (Spring 2006): 25–36.

Parris, Guichard, and Lester Brooks. *Blacks in the City: A History of the National Urban League.* Boston: Little, Brown, 1971.

Peiss, Kathy. "'Charity Girls' and City Pleasures: Historical Notes on Working-Class Sexuality, 1880–1920." In *Passion and Power: Sexuality in History,* ed. Kathy Peiss and Christina Simmons with Robert A. Padgug, 57–69. Philadelphia: Temple University Press, 1989.

———. *Cheap Amusements: Working Women and Leisure in Turn-of-the-Century New York.* Philadelphia: Temple University Press, 1986.

Perry, Elisabeth I. "'The General Motherhood of the Commonwealth': Dance Hall Reform in the Progressive Era." *American Quarterly* 37, no. 5 (Winter 1985): 719–33.

Pittenger, Mark. "A World of Difference: Constructing the 'Underclass' in Progressive America." *American Quarterly* 49, no. 1 (March 1997): 26–65.

Pivar, David J. *Purity Crusade: Sexual Morality and Social Control, 1868–1900.* Westport, CT: Greenwood Press, 1973.

Plummer, Ken, ed. *The Chicago School: Critical Assessments.* Vol. 1: *A Chicago Canon?* New York: Routledge, 1997.

———. *The Chicago School: Critical Assessments.* Vol. 2: *Theory, History, and Foundations.* New York: Routledge, 1997.

———. *The Chicago School: Critical Assessments.* Vol. 3: *Substantive Concerns—Race, Crime and the City.* New York: Routledge, 1997.

———. *The Chicago School: Critical Assessments.* Vol. 4: *Methodology and Experience.* New York: Routledge, 1997.

Polland, Anne M. "'The Sacredness of the Family': New York's Immigrant Jews and Their Religion, 1890–1930." Ph.D. diss., Columbia University, 2004.

Powers, Madelon. *Faces along the Bar: Lore and Order in the Workingman's Saloon, 1870–1920.* Chicago: University of Chicago Press, 1998.

Powers, Richard Gid. *G-Men: Hoover's FBI in American Popular Culture.* Carbondale: Southern Illinois University Press, 1983.

———. *Not without Honor: The History of American Anticommunism.* New Haven: Yale University Press, 1995.

———. *Secrecy and Power: The Life of J. Edgar Hoover.* New York: Free Press, 1987.

Quigley, David. *Second Founding: New York City, Reconstruction, and the Making of American Democracy.* New York: Hill and Wang, 2003.

Raat, W. Dirk. "U.S. Intelligence Operations and Covert Action in Mexico, 1900–47." *Journal of Contemporary History* 22, no. 4 (October 1987): 615–38.

Recchiuti, John Louis. *Civic Engagement: Social Science and Progressive-Era Reform in New York City*. Philadelphia: University of Pennsylvania Press, 2006.

Renzetti, Claire Marie. "Purity vs. Politics: The Legislation of Morality in Progressive New York, 1890–1920." Ph.D. diss., University of Delaware, 1983.

Richardson, James F. *The New York Police: Colonial Times to 1901*. New York: Oxford University Press, 1970.

Robertson, Stephen. *Crimes against Children: Sexual Violence and Legal Culture in New York City, 1880–1960*. Chapel Hill: University of North Carolina Press, 2005.

Rodgers, Daniel T. *Atlantic Crossings: Social Politics in a Progressive Age*. Cambridge: Harvard University Press, 1998.

Rosen, Ruth. *The Lost Sisterhood: Prostitution in America, 1910–1918*. Baltimore: Johns Hopkins University Press, 1982.

Rosenzweig, Roy. *Eight Hours for What We Will: Workers and Leisure in an Industrial City, 1870–1920*. Cambridge: Cambridge University Press, 1983.

Ross, Dorothy. *The Origins of the American Social Sciences*. New York: Cambridge University Press, 1991.

Rubin, Gayle S. "Thinking Sex: Notes for a Radical Theory of the Politics of Sexuality." In *Pleasure and Danger: Exploring Female Sexuality*, ed. Carole S. Vance. Boston: Routledge and Kegan Paul, 1984.

Russell, Francis. *A City in Terror: Calvin Coolidge and the 1919 Boston Police Strike*. Boston: Beacon Press, 2005.

Ryan, Mary. *Civic Wars: Democracy and Public Life in the American City during the Nineteenth Century*. Berkeley: University of California Press, 1998.

———. *Cradle of the Middle Class: The Family in Oneida County, New York, 1790–1865*. Cambridge: Cambridge University Press, 1983.

———. *Women in Public: Between Banners and Ballots, 1825–1880*. Baltimore: Johns Hopkins University Press, 1992.

Sandage, Scott A. *Born Losers: A History of Failure in America*. Cambridge: Harvard University Press, 2006.

Sante, Luc. *Low Life: Lures and Snares of Old New York*. New York: Farrar, Straus and Giroux, 1991.

Schmidt, Regin. *Red Scare: FBI and the Origins of Anticommunism in the United States*. Copenhagen: Museum Tusculanum Press, 2000.

Schocket, Eric. "Undercover Explorations of the 'Other Half,' or the Writer as Class Transvestite." *Representations* 64 (Fall 1998): 109–33.

Silverberg, Helene, ed. *Gender and American Social Science: The Formative Years*. Princeton: Princeton University Press, 1998.

Simmel, Georg. *On Individuality and Social Forms*. Ed. Donald N. Levine. Chicago: University of Chicago Press, 1971.

Simmons, Christina. "African Americans and Sexual Victorianism in the Social Hygiene Movement, 1910–40." *Journal of the History of Sexuality* 4, no. 1 (1993): 51–75.

Skowronek, Stephen. *Building a New American State: The Expansion of National Administrative Capacities, 1877–1920*. Cambridge: Cambridge University Press, 1982.

Smith-Rosenberg, Carroll. *Disorderly Conduct: Visions of Gender in Victorian America*. New York: Oxford University Press, 1986.

Spear, Allan H. *Black Chicago: The Making of a Negro Ghetto, 1890–1920*. Chicago: University of Chicago Press, 1967.

Spivak, Gayatri Chakravorty. "Can the Subaltern Speak?" In *Marxism and the Interpretation of Culture,* ed. Lawrence Grossberg and Cary Nelson, 271–308. Urbana: University of Illinois Press, 1992.

Stallybrass, Peter, and Allon White. *The Politics and Poetics of Transgression.* Ithaca: Cornell University Press, 1986.

Stansell, Christine. *American Moderns: Bohemian New York and the Creation of a New Century.* New York: Metropolitan Books, 2000.

———. *City of Women: Sex and Class in New York, 1789–1860.* Urbana: University of Illinois Press, 1987.

Stivers, Camilla. *Bureau Men, Settlement Women: Constructing Public Administration in the Progressive Era.* Lawrence: University Press of Kansas, 2000.

Summers, Martin. *Manliness and Its Discontents: The Black Middle Class and the Transformation of Masculinity, 1900–1930.* Chapel Hill: University of North Carolina Press, 2004.

Thale, Christopher. "Assigned to Patrol: Neighborhoods, Police, and Changing Deployment Practices in New York City before 1930." *Journal of Social History* 37, no. 4 (2004): 1037–64.

———. "The Informal World of Police Patrol: New York City in the Early Twentieth Century." *Journal of Urban History* 33, no. 2 (2007): 183–216.

Theoharis, Athan. *Chasing Spies: How the FBI Failed in Counterintelligence but Promoted the Politics of McCarthyism in the Cold War Years.* Chicago: Ivan R. Dee, 2002.

Theoharis, Athan, and John Stuart Cox. *The Boss: J. Edgar Hoover and the Great American Inquisition.* Philadelphia: Temple University Press, 1988.

Tsai, Shih-Shan Henry. *The Chinese Experience in America.* Bloomington: Indiana University Press, 1986.

Tuttle, William M., Jr. *Race Riot: Chicago in the Red Summer of 1919.* Urbana: University of Illinois Press, 1996.

Vapnek, Lara. "The Politics of Women's Work in the United States, 1865–1909." Ph.D. diss., Columbia University, 2000.

Wagner, Roland Richard. "Virtue against Vice: A Study of Moral Reformers and Prostitution in the Progressive Era." Ph.D. diss., University of Wisconsin, 1971.

Walker, Samuel. *Popular Justice: A History of American Criminal Justice.* 2nd ed. New York: Oxford University Press, 1998.

Walkowitz, Judith R. *City of Dreadful Delight: Narratives of Sexual Danger in Late-Victorian London.* Chicago: University of Chicago Press, 1992.

———. *Prostitution and Victorian Society: Women, Class, and the State.* Cambridge: Cambridge University Press, 1980.

Watters, Pat, and Stephen Gillers, eds. *Investigating the FBI.* Garden City, NY: Doubleday, 1973.

Weinstein, James. "Big Business and the Origins of Workmen's Compensation." *Labor History* 8 (Spring 1967): 156–74.

———. *The Corporate Ideal in the Liberal State, 1900–1918.* Boston: Beacon Press, 1968.

Weiss, Robert P. "Private Detective Agencies and Labour Discipline in the United States, 1855–1946." *Historical Journal* 29, no. 1 (March 1986): 87–107.

White, Deborah Gray. *Too Heavy a Load: Black Women in Defense of Themselves, 1894–1994.* New York: Norton, 1999.

Wiebe, Robert H. *The Search for Order, 1877–1920.* New York: Hill and Wang, 1967.

Willrich, Michael. *City of Courts: Socializing Justice in Progressive Era Chicago.* New York: Cambridge University Press, 2003.

Wilson, Christopher. *The Labor of Words: Literary Professionalism in the Progressive Era*. Athens: University of Georgia Press, 1985.

Wolcott, David B. *Cops and Kids: Policing Juvenile Delinquency in Urban America, 1890–1940*. Columbus: Ohio State University Press, 2005.

Wong, K. Scott, and Sucheng Chan, eds. *Claiming America: Constructing Chinese American Identities during the Exclusion Era*. Philadelphia: Temple University Press, 1998.

Wood, Sharon E. *The Freedom of the Streets: Work, Citizenship, and Sexuality in a Gilded Age City*. Chapel Hill: University of North Carolina Press, 2005.

HISTORICAL STUDIES OF URBAN AMERICA
Edited by Timothy J. Gilfoyle, James R. Grossman, and Becky M. Nicolaides